An Outline Itinerary Of King Henry The First

William Farrer

Printing Statement:

Due to the very old age and scarcity of this book,
many of the pages may be hard to read due to the
blurring of the original text, possible missing pages,
missing text, dark backgrounds and other issues
beyond our control.

Because this is such an important and rare work, we
believe it is best to reproduce this book regardless of
its original condition.

Thank you for your understanding.

AN OUTLINE ITINERARY

OF

KING HENRY THE FIRST

BY

WILLIAM FARRER, Litt.D.

Reprinted, by permission of Messrs. Longmans, Green & Co.,
from English Historical Review, Vol. XXXIV
July and October, 1919

PRINTED AT OXFORD, ENGLAND
BY FREDERICK HALL, PRINTER TO THE UNIVERSITY

An Outline Itinerary of King Henry the First

An itinerary of Henry I will never be more than an imperfect outline of the movements of his court, for the reason that the materials at our disposal are limited to intermittent references in the chronicles to the courts held on the three great festivals of the year, or on special occasions, to certain important events, and to an inconsiderable number of dated charters. The great bulk of Henry's writs and charters can never be dated with any degree of certainty ; in the majority of instances not even the precise year can be ascertained. To make use of the bulk of the material at our disposal it is necessary to import into the scheme a variety of matter not immediately relevant to an itinerary, such as the notices of the nomination, election, and consecration of ecclesiastics to episcopal sees and to the rule of monastic houses, notices of deaths, certain events recorded in the rise and growth of monasteries, which sometimes led to the issue of a royal confirmation, political events at home and abroad, judicial proceedings, and special enactments. The duration of the term of office held by officials of the king's household and court, by ecclesiastics and sheriffs of counties, when approximately ascertained, throws light on the period to which a charter or writ addressed to, or attested by, such individuals, belongs. For convenience of comparison, writs and charters issued at a given place within a definite period of years have been brought together ; but this must not be interpreted as a suggestion that they were all issued simultaneously. To all documents of uncertain date the period within which they were issued has been added within square brackets after the place of issue. Those of ascertained date have no other indication than the marginal date there, or immediately before, cited.

With the exception of the late Mr. Eyton's manuscript notes on the dates of such charters as were known in his days,[1] no

Add. MS. 31943.

attempt had been made to compile an itinerary of Henry I until Professor Haskins prepared his *Norman Institutions* (published by the Harvard University Press in 1918) from materials collected during the period 1902–17 from the French archives. In that work he gives the Norman itinerary of Henry I during the years 1106–7, 1108–9, 1111–13, 1114–15, 1116–20, 1123–6, 1127–9, 1130–1, and 1133–5, whilst Henry was beyond seas. From that source a number of documents, until then unpublished, have been incorporated in the present essay ; an earlier arrangement of the documents here used has in some instances been modified as a result of the additional evidence afforded by that erudite work. Unfortunately the continuation of Mr. H. W. C. Davis's important *Regesta Regum Anglo-Normannorum* is still deferred in consequence of the editor's engagement during the last four years in the service of the government.

Henry's diplomas consist mainly of three classes : (1) Precepts or mandates addressed to officials, directing that some specific act shall, or shall not, be done ; (2) Notifications, addressed to the county court, a baron's court, or the king's court, of a royal grant, or the confirmation of a grant by a subject ; (3) Diplomas of confirmation drawn up on the Anglo-Saxon model and engrossed, sometimes in the chancery, but often apparently in the scriptorium of a monastery. The first class is usually attested by an official of the chancery, treasury, or household, frequently by the chancellor, at some place where the court was then established. Sometimes a writ is said to have been ' issued ' by one of the king's chaplains, or officials of the household. The second class is attested by a varying number of members of the king's court or household at some place where the court was established ; occasionally, when a council was held, by the king or queen, or by both, and by a large number of ecclesiastics, barons, and officials of the court and household. The third class bears a cross (*signum*) placed against the name of the king, and others against those of the great ecclesiastics, barons, king's chaplains, officials of the household and others ; this stands opposite, or sometimes in the middle of, the name or description of the witness. In these diplomas the place of issue is seldom recorded, possibly because the signatories did not all attest their marks at the same time or place. In some instances a date is recorded, namely the regnal or dominical year, sometimes both, and occasionally the feast day also. Instances are found where a scribe has at a later time added a date, not always a correct one. Many writs belonging to the first class have not been utilized in this itinerary owing to the evidence of date being quite indefinite. Some documents of the second and third classes have been omitted because they appear to be spurious or corrupt, and consequently untrustworthy or even misleading, as evidences of Henry's movements. A caveat must, however, be made against the condemnation of a document solely on the ground of an irregular or variable arrangement of the names of the witnesses or signatories in the existing texts, seeing that the original arrangement or continuity of the names in two, three, or more columns may have been destroyed by the carelessness or ignorance of later transcribers.

The subject-matter of the documents used in the itinerary has usually been condensed, so as to serve merely for the purpose of identification. For historical or critical purposes the full document should be consulted at the references given. This essay is nothing more than a provisional synopsis of certain of the diplomas issued by Henry. A full chartulary, giving the best and most complete text of these instruments, is much to be desired.

Certain axioms which influence the dating of some of Henry's diplomas may be stated. A bishop was so addressed officially, not as a rule from the date of his consecration, but in some instances [1] from the day on which he was invested in the temporalities of his see, which was presumably the day of his nomination. Prior to his consecration he was not always addressed or described as 'elect'. The chancellor, upon his nomination to an episcopal see, delivered up his office and seal immediately upon such nomination. An archbishop or a bishop ceased to be addressed in Henry's writs to the county court when deprived of the temporalities of his see, and similarly an earl or a baron ceased to be addressed in such missives after the forfeiture of his earldom or fief. But it would be unsafe to assume that official recognition was superseded during absence beyond seas on missions or expeditions, or during a journey to Rome or the Holy Land.

1100.

2 Aug. William II, whilst hunting in the New Forest during the afternoon of 2 August, 1100, accompanied by his brother Henry, Robert Fitz-Hamon, William of Breteuil, Walter Tirel of Poix (Somme), and others, is accidentally slain.[2]

Henry immediately rides to Winchester to secure the treasure. Hard upon his heels follows William of Breteuil, the keeper of the treasure.[3]

3 Aug. Henry is elected king by such of the Witan as are near at hand.[4] The opposing party is silenced by the efforts of Henry, earl of Warwick.[5]

Henry gives the vacant bishopric of Winchester to William Giffard, the chancellor of the late king.[6]

---

[1] See no. 115. [2] A.-S. Chron. *s. a.*; Orderic (ed. Le Prevost), iv. 87.
[3] *Ibid.* [4] Chron. [5] W. Malm., *G. R.* ii. 470.
[6] Chron. Though nominated by the king at this time, Giffard was not invested until Easter, 1101.

4 Aug. Henry goes to London.[1]

5 Aug. Before the altar at Westminster he promises that he will put down the injustices which existed in his brother's time.[2] He is consecrated by Maurice, bishop of London; the crown is placed upon the new king's head by Thomas, archbishop of York.[3]

1. The king issues a charter of liberties. It is attested by the bishops, Maurice of London, William elect of Winchester, and Gerard of Hereford, Earl Henry (of Warwick), Earl Simon (of Northampton and Huntingdon), Earl Walter Giffard, Robert de Montfort, Roger Bigot, Eudes the sewer, and Henry de Port; 'apud Westmonasterium quando coronatus fui.'[4]

2. Immediately after the coronation a charter of confirmation is issued in favour of St. Peter's, Westminster. It is addressed generally and is attested by the bishops, Maurice of London, William elect of Winchester, and G(erard) of Hereford; Earl Henry (of Warwick), Earl Simon (of Northampton), and Earl Walter Giffard.[5]

3. Writ addressed to Eudes the sewer and Herbert the chamberlain directing that the convents of Westminster, Winchester, and Gloucester shall, at all festivals at which the king shall be crowned in those churches, have full livery from the king, and their precentors shall have an ounce of gold. as by the testimony of Maurice, bishop of London, they had in the time of the king's predecessors. It is attested by William (Giffard, bishop) elect of Winchester; at Westminster.[6]

Henry gives to Robert, son of Earl Hugh (of Chester), a monk of St. Evroul, the abbey of St. Edmund (Bury St. Edmunds), namely ' nonas Augusti, die dominico, in die videlicet consecrationis ipsius regis '.[7] He restores to Abbot Odo the abbey of Chertsey.[8]

3A. Early Aug. Henry addresses a letter to Anselm announcing his election as king, and his consecration in the primate's absence. He urges his speedy return. Witnesses: Bishop Gerard, William bishop elect of Winchester, William de Warelwast, Earl Henry, Robert Fitz-Hamon, Hugh the sewer and other bishops and barons.[9]

15 Aug. Anselm, being at Chaise Dieu, near Lyons, receives the news of the late king's death, which was brought by a monk of Bec, and, simultaneously, by a monk of Canterbury.[10]

On the same day, being 18 kalends of September, Henry, by the advice of his court, causes Ranulf, bishop of Durham, to be committed to the Tower.[11] Before Michaelmas he recalls Anselm.[12]

---

[1] Chron.   [2] Eadmer, p. 119.   [3] *Flores Histor.* ii. 34.

[4] Thorpe, *Ancient Laws and Institutes*, p. 215 ; Liebermann, *Die Gesetze der Angelsachsen*, i. 521 ff. ; Matth. Paris, *Chron. Mai.* ii. 115–17 ; Hearne, *Textus Roffensis*, ch. 34, p. 51. At the fourth reference this clause is added at the end : ' Factae sunt tot cartae quot sunt comitatus in Anglia et, rege iubente, positae in abbatiis singulorum comitatuum ad monimentum.'

[5] Cotton ch. vii, 8. No place of issue is named.

[6] Chartul. of St. Peter's, Westminster, Faust. A. iii, fo. 78 *d* ; *sub tit.*: ' Liberationes in coronatione regis.' See Round, *The King's Serjeants*, pp. 321–2 ; Robinson, *Gilbert Crispin*, p. 141.

[7] *Mon. Anglic.* iii. 155 *b*.   [8] *Annals of Winchester.*

[9] Anselm, *Epistolae*, iii. 41 ; Gabriel Gerberon, *Opera S. Anselmi Cantuar. Archiep.* (Paris, 1721), p .382.

[10] Eadmer, p. 118.   [11] Sym. of Durham, i. 138 ; Chron.   [12] Chron.

Aug. Hugh, earl of Chester, and Robert of Bellême are in Normandy when they hear of the late king's death. Hastening to England they come to Henry's court, and doing homage and fealty, they receive from him their respective fees and dignities.[1]

4. 14 Sept. On the feast of the Exaltation of the Holy Cross, A. D. 1100, the king grants to St. Peter's, Bath, and Bishop John 5 hides of land in Weston. The signatories are : the king, Archbishop Thomas, Robert bishop of Chester, Bishop Gerard, Bishop William Giffard, William count of Mortain, Walter Giffard, Earl Hugh, Earl Simon, Robert Fitz-Hamon, Earl Henry, Roger de (*sic*) Bigot, Engenoulf de Ferr(ers), Winebald de Baalon, Hameline, William de Warelwast the chaplain; at Westminster.[2]

23 Sept. Anselm lands at Dover. A few days later he comes to the king, who is at Salisbury (' Serberia ').[3]

5. 29 Sept. Writ addressed to W(alter) Hosate and his ministers notifying them of the grant to Godfrey, abbot of Malmesbury, of a 5 days' fair at Malmesbury. It is attested by William (Giffard) the chancellor ; at Salisbury, in the council.[4]

6. *c.* Oct. The king confirms to the church of St. Mary, Tewkesbury, certain gifts made by Robert Fitz-Hamon, Robert de la Hai, Winebald de Balaon, and Robert Fitz-Hugh. The signatories are : King Henry, Earl Hugh, Robert of Bellême, William of Mortain, Roger le Poitevin, Henry of ' Werwik ', William the chancellor, Evrard, William de Wreowast, Eudes (' Eodorunus ') the sewer, Robert Fitz-Hamon and Hamon his brother, William de Aubigny, Miles Crispin, Hugh de ' Belcamp ', Roger de Nunant, Nigel de Monevile, Roger le Bigod, Robert Malet, Hugh Maminot ; ' apud Marlebergam in anno ab incarnatione Domini millesimo et centesimo.'[5]

7. Confirmation issued in favour of the monastery of Lewes at the prayer of William, earl of Surrey. It is addressed generally. The signatories are : (1) King Henry, Bishop Gerard, William count of Mortain, Walter Giffard ' minister ' (?), and William the chancellor ; (2) Hugh earl of Chester, Earl Henry de Beaumont, Roger Bigod, and William de Aubigny.[6] [23 Sept.–25 Dec., 1100.]

8. 1 Nov. The king, ' per manum episcopi Lincoliensis Rotberti ', sends Faricius, a monk of Malmesbury, to Abingdon to become abbot there. This shows that Bishop Robert is with the king at this time.[7]

11 Nov. Henry weds Matilda, ' daughter of King Malcolm of Scotland

---

[1] Orderic, iv. 94.

[2] ' Anno ab incarnatione domini nostri M°. C°., indictione viii, epacta xviii, concurrente vii, xviii kalend. Octobris, luna vi,' &c. ; *Two Bath Chartularies* (Somerset Rec. Soc.), i, n. 42.

[3] Eadmer, p. 119.

[4] ' apud Sarum in consilio ' : *Regist. of Malmesbury*, i. 333 ; Lansd. MS. 417, f. 31 *d*.

[5] *Mon. Anglic.* ii. 65 *b* ; *Dep. Keeper's Rep.* xxx, app. 6, p. 202 ; from Charter Roll, 28 Edw. I, m. 3.

[6] Orig. ch., Vesp. iii, n. 2. The signatories' names are in two lines. No place of issue is mentioned.

[7] *Chron. of Abingdon*, ii. 44. The chronicler is very careful in recording the date; it was in the fourth month of the reign.

and the good Queen Margaret, King Edward's kinswoman, of the right royal race of England ', the ceremony being performed at Westminster by Archbishop Anselm, who ' afterwards hallowed her to queen '.[1]

9. Two writs, addressed generally, are issued in favour of the monastery of Abingdon. Both are attested by Eudes the sewer and are issued apud Westmonasterium in nuptiis meis '.[2]

10. Confirmation issued in favour of the monks of St. Martin of Troarn, who have obtained *inter alia* property in cos. Somerset and Dorset from Robert de Rumilly. The signatories are : (1) King Henry, Queen Matilda, Robert Fitz-Hamon, the bishops, Maurice of London, John of Bath, and Ralph of Chichester ; (2) Archbishop Anselm, Gundulf bishop of Rochester, Eudes Fitz-Hubert, Hamon the sewer, Evrard son of Earl Roger, Henry earl of Warwick ; (3) the bishops, Herbert of Norwich (' Tetfordensis '), and Robert of Chester ; Walter Gifart and William the chancellor.[3] [11 Nov. 1100–3 Sept. 1101.]

11. The king by writ notifies Robert bishop of Lincoln, the sheriffs, &c., of England of his grant to Richard (de Aubigny), abbot of St. Albans, of the said abbey, to hold as beneficially as Abbot Paul held it. It is attested by Gerard bishop (of Hereford), John bishop (of Bath), Henry earl of Warwick, Roger Bigot, and William de Aubigny ; at Westminster.[4] [5 Aug.–25 Dec. 1100.]

18 Nov. On 14 kalends of December, at Ripon, dies Thomas of Bayeux, archbishop of York.[5]

12. 2 Dec. Writ addressed to Gerard bishop (of Hereford), Hugh de Laci, and the barons of Herefordshire notifying them of the king's grant to Hugh L'Asne of licence to give the manor of Ocle to the monastery of Lire (dioc. of Evreux). It is attested by Osbern Fitz-Richard, Richard Fitz-Ponce, and Roger de L'Isle ; at Newnham-on-Severn (' Neweham '), ' in primo die adventus '.[6]

13. Writ addressed to the foresters, huntsmen, and bowmen who are of this side (*ex ista parte*) of Severn and of Dean, notifying them of the king's gift to St. Peter's, Gloucester, of the tithe of his venison taken in the forests of the same province. It is attested by Robert Fitz-Hamon (and is issued) by Reginald de Berchelay ; at Newnham-on-Severn (' Niweham ').[7] [1100–7.]

25 Dec. At Christmas the king holds his court at Westminster.[8] Louis, son of Philip, king elect of France, is a visitor at Henry's court.[9] Gerard bishop of Hereford is nominated to the see of York.[10]

---

[1] Chron. Upon her marriage Matilda relinquished her baptismal name of ' Eadgyth '. Cf. Orderic, iii. 399–400 ; iv. 95–6.

[2] *Chron. of Abingdon*, ii. 88–9.

[3] *Cal. of Chart. Rolls*, iv. 282 ; Round, *Cal. of Documents, France*, n. 470.

[4] Transcr. of Royal Charters, Harl. MS. 66, fo. 6.

[5] *Histor. of the Church of York*, ii. 364.

[6] Round, *Cal. of Documents, France*, n. 402.

[7] *Chartul. of St. Peter's, Gloucester*, ii. 301.

[8] Chron. ' Coronatus est ad Natale apud Londoniam ' : *Annals of Winchester*, and Sym. of Durham, ii. 232.   [9] *Annals of Winchester*.

[10] Sym. of Durham, ii. 232. Cf. *Histor. of the Church of York*, ii. 366 ; where Gerard's death is recorded as occurring on 22 May 1108, after he had held the see ' annis vii et mensibus fere vi '.

14. Writ addressed to G(erard) archbishop of York, O(sbert) the sheriff, the barons and lieges of Yorkshire notifying them of the king's confirmation to the monks of St. Cuthbert, Durham, of land in Hundsley, co. York, given by Robert de Stutevill, and of 1 carucate in Drewton. It is attested by William (Giffard) the chancellor ; at Westminster, at Christmas.[1]

15. Writ addressed to R(ichard, son of Gotse ?) the sheriff, the barons and lieges of Nottinghamshire notifying them of a confirmation to the monks of St. Cuthbert of lands and mills in Nottinghamshire with soc and sac, &c., and a mandate to William Peverel to see that they lose nothing which they possessed at the death of William, the king's brother. It is attested by William the chancellor; [at Westminster ?], at Christmas.[2]

16. Writ addressed to O(sbert) the sheriff and the lieges of Lincoln notifying them of the king's confirmation to the monks of St. Cuthbert of the house and land of Ulfget (of Lincoln), to hold as William bishop of Durham held it at his death. It is attested by W(illiam) Peverel ; at ' Westmuster ', at Christmas.[3] [1100-3, 1105, 1107, or 1109-10.]

1101.

17. Writ addressed to Hugh de Bocheland directing him to go to Abingdon and put the monastery there in possession of the lands which Modbert (the provost of Abingdon [4]) had given, mortgaged, acquired, or alienated, being then in the possession of Herbert the chamberlain, Warin ' calvus ', and others. It is attested by William the chancellor and Roger the chaplain ; at London.[5] [4 Aug. 1100-3 Sept. 1101.]

18. The king notifies all his sheriffs and ministers that he acquits of toll and transit dues the substance required by the monks of St. Peter's, Gloucester. It is attested by William the chancellor ; at Westminster.[6] [4 Aug. 1100-3 Sept. 1101.]

19. Confirmation to the monks of St. Nicholas, Spalding, of their possessions in England and Normandy, as confirmed by the king's father and brother. It is attested by Robert bishop of Lincoln, William bishop of Durham (*sic*), Robert Fitz-Hamon, William the chancellor, Eudes the sewer, Roger Bigot, and ' many others of the king's court '.[7] [4 Aug. 1100-3 Sept. 1101.]

3 Feb. Ranulf Flambard, bishop of Durham, escapes from the Tower, evades his pursuers, and later reaches Normandy.[8]

20. 10 Mar. Henry meets Robert count of Flanders at Dover on 6 ides of March. The terms of an alliance between them are ratified by a deed. On the part of Henry there are present : Archbishop Gerard, the

---

[1] Orig. in Durham Treasury, 2da, 1^{ae}, Regalium, R. i, n. 17 ; *Journ. of the Brit. Arch. Assoc.* xxix. 239.

[2] Durham Treasury, 3^{ia}, 1^{ae}, Regalium, F. i, n. 6 ; *Journ. of the Brit. Arch. Assoc.* xxix. 237.

[3] Durham Treasury, 2da, 1^{ae}, Regalium, O. i, n. 14 ; *Journ. of the Brit. Arch. Assoc.* xxix. 237.

[4] *Chron. of Abingdon*, ii. 141. [5] *Ibid.* p. 86 ; cf. pp. 129-34.

[6] *Chartul. of St. Peter's, Gloucester*, ii. 132.

[7] Cole's transcript of the Spalding Chartul., Add. MS. 5844, p. 146.

[8] Sym. of Durham, i. 138 ; W. Malm., *G. R.* ii. 471.

bishops, Robert of Lincoln and Robert of Chester; William Giffard [1] the chancellor, Robert count of Meulan, Robert Fitz-Hamon; the sewers Eudes and Hamon; and William de Aubigny the butler. On behalf of Count Robert: Reiner his chaplain, Robert de Betun, Adelard Fitz-Conan, Baldric de Colhem, Fromund de L'Isle, and others. Henry names as pledges for his part of the agreement: Robert Fitz-Hamon, Stephen count of Brittany, Gilbert Fitz-Richard, Roger de Nonant, Hugh Maminot, Manasser Arsic, Hamon the sewer, William de Curci, Miles Crispin, Ernulf de Montgomery, and Hugh de Beauchamp; each being bound in the sum of 100 marks, save Robert Fitz-Hamon, who is bound in double that amount.[2]

21. 12 Mar. The king notifies Archbishop Anselm, Hamon the sewer, and the barons of Kent of his confirmation to Bishop Gundulf and the monks of St. Andrew's, Rochester, of certain churches in Kent. It is attested by Robert bishop of Lincoln, William Giffard the chancellor, the sewers Eudes and Hamon; William de Aubigny and William Pevrel of Dover; at Rochester, on the feast of St. Gregory.[3]

22. A charter, similarly addressed and in favour of the same monastery, with the clause 'pro anima . . . uxoris mee', is attested by the sewers Eudes and Hamon; at Rochester.[4]

23. The king notifies Archbishop Anselm, Hamon the sheriff, the men of Kent, and the barons of England of his grant to Bishop Gundulf and the monks of St. Andrew's of a fair at Rochester. It is attested by William de Werlewast; the sewers Eudes and Hamon; William Peverel and Hamon Peverel.[5] [4 Aug. 1100–Easter 1103.]

21 Apr. At Easter Henry holds his court at Winchester,[6] where he is again crowned.[7]

With the consent of Anselm, (William) Giffard assumes the bishopric of Winchester.[8]

9 June. At Whitsuntide the king wears his crown at St. Albans.[9]

At this time (i. e. Whitsuntide) reports reach the king of the projected invasion of the realm by Duke Robert.[10] Henry takes steps to secure the allegiance of the barons, men of each county and men of the royal demesnes.[11]

Among the duke's supporters are Robert of Bellême and his brothers, Count Roger the Poitevin and Arnulf (de Montgomery), William de Warenne, earl of Surrey, Walter Giffard, Ives de Grentemesnil, and Robert son of Ilbert (de Lascy).[12]

Henry's chief supporters are: Archbishop Anselm and his vassals,[13] Robert Fitz-Hamon, Richard de Redvers, Roger Bigod, Robert count of Meulan, and his brother Henry (earl of Warwick).[14]

24. June (?). Writ addressed to Robert bishop of Lincoln, Ranulf

[1] 'Gerard'; Hearne.

[2] Hearne, *Liber Niger*, i. 7; *Foedera* (Rec. Com.), i. 7.

[3] *Mon. Anglic.* i. 164, n. 14; Hearne, *Textus Roffensis*, p. 170.

[4] *Mon. Anglic.* i. 164, n. 13; *Dep. Keeper's Rep.* xxx, app. 6, p. 199.

[5] *Cal. of Chart. Rolls*, ii. 195; *Mon. Anglic.* i. 164, n. 16.

[6] Chron.   [7] *Annals of Winchester*.   [8] *Ibid.*

[9] *Mon. Anglic.* i. 242, n. 12.   [10] Eadmer, p. 126.   [11] See no. 24.

[12] Orderic, iv. 103.   [13] Eadmer, p. 127.   [14] W. Malm., *G. R.* ii. 471.

Meschin, Osbert the sheriff, Picot son of Colsuen, and the men of Lincoln-shire, confirming the laws, rights, and customs granted to them when the king first received the crown, and desiring them to take oath to defend the realm against his brother, Robert count of Normandy, until Christmas, and commanding them to receive this security from the men of his demesnes, both French and English ; his barons are to cause their men to make the same security to them (i. e. the shire-moot). It is attested by Archbishop Anselm, Robert count of Meulan, Robert Fitz-Hamon, and Eudes the sewer ; at . . . .[1]

24 June. Henry leads a powerful army, which consists largely of Englishmen and the vassals of the bishops,[2] towards Hastings, expecting Duke Robert to land there,[3] and encamps at Pevensey.[4]

20 July. Duke Robert lands at Portsmouth twelve nights before Lammas.[5] He moves towards Winchester, but, out of chivalrous regard for Queen Matilda, who was then in residence there and expecting the birth of her first child,[6] he passes by the city and takes the London road by Alresford.[7]

The opposing forces meet near Alton.[8]

Henry and Duke Robert make a treaty at Alton, after negotiations which lasted several days.[9] Twelve of the highest rank on each side ratify the agreement by oath.[10] Ranulf Flambard recovers his bishopric.[11]

27 July. Hugh earl of Chester, having taken the habit of a monk in his newly founded abbey (of St. Werburg) at Chester, dies there on 6 kalends of August.[12]

31 July. [See nos. 100 and 101.]

In the second year of the reign the queen gives birth to a daughter, who is named, after her mother, Matilda.[13]

Sept. Henry summons Anselm to court [14] and, by the advice of Duke Robert and his friends, bids Anselm become his man and consecrate those whom the king has invested, or quit the realm.[15]

25. 3 Sept. The ordination of the monks in the cathedral church of the Holy Trinity at Norwich by Bishop Herbert, and the establishment of the property of the see, are confirmed by Henry and his queen. The signatories are : [16]

    (1) the king and queen ; the archbishops, Anselm and Gerard ; the bishops, Gundulf of Rochester, Maurice of London, Robert of Lincoln, Sampson of Worcester, John of Bath, Osbern of Exeter,

---

[1] W. H. Stevenson, *ante*, xxi. 505-9 ; facsimile, *ibid*. xxvi. 488.

[2] Florence of Worcester.   [3] *Ibid*.   [4] Chron.

[5] *Ibid*. ; W. Malm., *G. R.* ii. 471.

[6] Wace, *Roman de Rou* (ed. Andresen), 10366.

[7] *Ibid*. 10371.   [8] *Ibid*. 10373.

[9] Wace, 10423 ; Orderic, iv. 113.

[10] Chron.

[11] Sym. of Durham, i. 138. This is doubtful. Cf. Orderic, iv. 116, and *Annals of Winchester*.   [12] Orderic, iv. 111.

[13] Gervase of Canterbury (*Decem Script*. ii, col. 1338). Possibly she was born in February 1102. Cf. *Annals of Winchester, s.a.* 1110.

[14] Eadmer, p. 128. The court was probably at Windsor.

[15] *Ibid*. p. 131.

[16] Possibly arranged in three columns in the original document.

Robert of Chester, Ralph of Chichester, and John of Tusculum, papal legate.

(2) Earl Henry of Warwick, Simon earl of Northampton, William earl of Warenne, Roger Bigot, Eudes the sewer, Hamon the sewer, Robert Maleth, Nigel the constable, Alan Fitz-Flaald, William Maleth, William the butler.

(3) the abbots, Gilbert of Westminster, Serlo of Gloucester, Henry of Battle, Stephen of York, Aldwin of Ramsey, Richard of St. Albans, and Richard of Ely; Roger the chancellor, Herbert the chamberlain, Evrard the chaplain, Roger the chaplain.

' Facta est hec donatio anno ab incarnatione domini millesimo centesimo primo, mense Septembris, [in die] ordinationis beati pape Gregorii, apud Wyndesores.' [1]

26. The king grants to Bishop Herbert and his monks the manor of Thorp with sac and soc, &c. ' Facta est igitur hec donatio anno ab incarnatione domini millesimo centesimo primo, indictione nona, epacta XVIII, concurrente i, luna vi, tertio nonas Septembris' &c. The signatories are : King Henry, Queen Matilda, Robert duke of Normandy, ' frater regis Henrici '.

Nomina archiepiscoporum et episcoporum : The archbishops Anselm and Gerard, the bishops, Gundulf of Rochester, Maurice of London, John of Bath, Osbert of Exeter, Robert of Chester, Robert of Lincoln, Ralph of Chichester, Samson of Worcester, Ranulf of Durham (*sic*), John of Frascati, papal legate, and Tiberius, chamberlain of Pope Paschal. In the month of September on the [day of the] ordination of blessed Pope Gregory ; at Windsore.

Nomina primatum et principum : Robert count of Pontieu (' de Pontinio ' [2]), Stephen count of Brittany, Robert count of Meulan, Eustace count of Boulogne, Henry earl of Warwick, Simon earl of Northampton, William earl of Warenne, William count of Mortain, Count Roger the Poitevin, Eudes the sewer, Hamon the sewer, William the butler, Richard de Retvers, Robert Fitz-Hamon, Alan Fitz-Flaald, Gilbert Fitz-Richard, Robert Maleth, Roger Fitz-Richard.

Nomina abbatum et clericorum : The abbots Gilbert of Westminster, Serlo of Gloucester, Henry of Battle, Stephen of York, Aldwin of Ramsey, Odo of Chertsey, Richard of St. Albans, Richard of Ely, Roger the chancellor, Evrard the chaplain, Robert Peschal the chaplain, Thomas the chaplain, Winfrid the chaplain, Robert the chaplain, Osbern the chaplain, Herbert the king's chamberlain, Waldric the chaplain, Peter of Valoignes, William de Warelwast.[3]

27. Anselm confirms the ordination of the church of the Holy Trinity, Norwich, and the monks there, at the prayer of Herbert bishop of Norwich. The signatories are : Archbishop Anselm, and the bishops, Gundulf of Rochester, Maurice of London, Ralph of Chichester, William of Winchester,

---

[1] *Mon. Anglic.* iv. 15 b, n. 3 ; from Bodl. Libr., MS. Laud. Misc. 675.

[2] For ' Pontivo '.

[3] Reyner, *Apostolatus Benedictinorum in Anglia*, tract. ii, § 6, p. 146 ; *Mon. Anglic.* iv. 16 b, n. 5.

. . . of Salisbury (*sic*), Sampson of Worcester, John of Bath, Osbern of
Exeter, Robert of Chester, Robert of Lincoln, and Ranulf of Durham ;
and the abbots, Gilbert of Westminster, Serlo of Gloucester, Richard of
Ely, Richard of St. Albans, Stephen of York, Henry of Battle, Rycher of
Holme, Guntard of Thorney, and Aldwin of Ramsey.[1]

28. The king renews and confirms the gift of William his brother[2] of
the city of Bath to the church of St. Peter and John bishop of Bath, and
appoints that church to be the mother church of the see of Somerset.
' Facta est autem hec donaωio anno ab incarnatione Domini M⁰. C⁰. primo,
indictione IX, epacta nulla, concurrente I,' in the presence of Queen
Matilda and the illustrious men, both religious and lay, of all England.
Confirmed in the second year of the king's reign. The signatories and
witnesses are : Queen Matilda, Anselm archbishop of Canterbury, Gerard
archbishop of York, the bishops, Maurice of London, William of Winchester, Osbern of Exeter, Robert of Lincoln, Robert of Chester, Herbert
of Norwich, Gundulf of Rochester, Sampson of Worcester, Ralph of
Chichester, Ranulf of Durham (*sic*) and John of Frascati ; Tiberius sewer
and legate,[3] Grimbald the physician ;[4] the abbots, Gilbert of Westminster,
Richard of St. Albans, Odo of Chertsey, Serlo of Gloucester, Stephen of
York, Henry of Battle, Aldwin of Ramsey, Walter of Evesham, Gerold
of Tewkesbury, and Richer of Holme ; Rainhelm the queen's chancellor,
Arnulf the chaplain, Robert duke of Normandy, the king's brother,
Robert count of Pont(ieu), Eustace count of Boulogne, Robert count of
Meulan, Henry earl of Warwick, Stephen count of Brittany, Earl Simon
(of Northampton), William earl of Warenne, William count of Mortain,
Robert Fitz-Hamon, Eudes the sewer, Roger Bigod the sewer, Hamon
the sewer,[5] Robert de Montfort, Robert Malet, Herbert the chamberlain,
Roger the chancellor ' qui hanc cartam dictavi ',[6] Evrard the chaplain,
William de Warelwast, Roger the chaplain, Herbert the chaplain, Waldric
the chaplain, Osbern the chaplain, Robert Pecc(he) the chaplain, Humphrey
the chaplain, Robert the chaplain, Walter the chaplain, Richard de Orival,
Roger de Martinwast, Thomas the chaplain, William de Aubigny, Nigel
his brother, William de Curci the sewer, W(illiam) de Barba[7] the sewer,
Urse de Abbetot, Gilbert Fitz-Richard, Roger his brother, Walter his
brother, Winebald de Baalun, Hamelin his brother, Patric de Chaources,
Robert Fitz-Baldwin, Aiulf the chamberlain,[8] W(alter) Hosate, Roger de
Nunant, Alvred de Nicole, Henry de Port, Walter Fitz-Ansger, W(alter)

---

[1] *Ibid.* p. 20 ; from an exemplification made in 1281 by John Peckham, archbishop
of Canterbury.

[2] See Davis, *Regesta Regum Anglo-Norman.*, i, n. 315.

[3] Here the *Bath Abbey Chartul.* (Somerset Rec. Soc.), n. 40, runs on with the
abbots, in different order.

[4] ' Grimbaldus capellanus' : *ibid.*, where his name follows that of the chancellor,
and is again followed by Evrard, William de Warelwast, and nine other chaplains.
Then comes Robert, duke of Normandy.

[5] Here the order again changes ; *ibid.*

[6] These four words occur in *Bath Abbey Chartul.*, where the chancellor's name
follows the abbots' names.

[7] Leland, *Collectanea* (ed. Hearne), i. 30.

[8] ' Aiulfus vicecomes' : *Bath Abbey Chartul.*

Fitz-Edward.[1] 'Confirmatio huius carte facta est apud Wyndlesoram in die Ordinationis Sancti Gregorii, iii nonas Septembris, luna sexta.'[2]

Oct. After remaining two months in England with his brother, Duke Robert returns to Normandy shortly after Michaelmas, accompanied by William de Warenne and others, whom Henry has deprived of their English estates.[3]

6 Oct. Ralph, abbot of St. Benet's, Holme, dies on 2 nones of October, 1101 (*sic*).[4]

c. Oct. Henry is at Winchester, whither Anselm comes at his invitation. The bishops and magnates assembled there advise the dispatch of a joint embassy to Rome on behalf of the king and primate respectively. Thereupon Anselm sends Baldwin, a monk of Bec,[5] and Alexander a monk of Canterbury ;[6] the king dispatches on his behalf the newly invested archbishop of York, who also goes to obtain the pall, Herbert bishop of Norwich, who goes with the further intention of recovering the lost jurisdiction of his see over St. Edmund's abbey, and Robert bishop of Chester.[7]

29. Confirmation to the canons of St. Wlaur the confessor, in Boulogne, at the prayer of Ida, countess of Boulogne, of the manor of Nutfield, co. Surrey, which she had held of the king's father and then of the king. The signatories are : [Ellis ?] de St. Saens, King Henry, Anselm archbishop of Canterbury, Queen Matilda, Robert bishop of Lincoln, William the chamberlain (*cubicularius*), Mary the queen's sister, William de Evreux, Roger the chancellor, Guy de Balliol, Evrard the scribe.[8] [Easter or 3 Sept. 1101–Mich. 1102.]

30. Writ addressed to Osbert sheriff of Lincoln and Ranulf Meschin to cause Robert bishop of Lincoln to enjoy his lands, men, and possessions ' cum magno honore ', and the king wills that he shall not plead about the lands of which his ancestor was seised at his death, nor about the churches which he has held until now. It is attested by Urse de Abetot ; at Lacock.[9] [1100–1110.]

Possibly during the late autumn, or winter, Henry visits Newnham-on-Severn (?).

31. Writ addressed to all barons, sheriffs, and ministers acquitting the property of the abbot and monks of St. Peter's, Gloucester, of toll. It is attested by Roger the chancellor and Eudes the sewer ; ' apud Niweham '.[10] [Same as 29.]

25 Dec. At Christmas the king holds his court at Westminster.[11]

32. On the same day he grants and confirms to Eudes, his sewer, the city of Colchester with the keep and castle. The charter is addressed to Maurice bishop of London, Hugh de Bocheland, and the barons of Essex.

---

[1] Leland, *Collectanea*, i. 30.

[2] *Cal. of Chart. Rolls*, iii. 470 ; Charter Roll, 6 Edw. III, n. 18 ; *Dep. Keeper' Rep.* xxx, app. 6, p. 205.

[3] Orderic, iv. 116 ; Hen. of Huntingdon, pp. 233–4.

[4] *Mon. Anglic.* iii. 63 ; Cott. MS. Nero D. ii, fo. 215. This date may be a year too late. Richer was abbot in Sept. 1101.

[5] Cf. 15 Aug. 1100.   [6] *Ibid.*

[7] Eadmer, pp. 132–3.   [8] Cart. Antiq. roll A, n. 30 ; *Mon. Anglic.* vi. 1114.

[9] Vesp. E. xvi, fo. 7 d, n. 14 ; *Mon. Anglic.* vi. 1273, n. 27.

[10] *Chartul. of St. Peter's, Gloucester*, ii. 134.   [11] Chron.

It is attested by Robert bishop of Lincoln, William Giffard, bishop elect of Winchester, Robert count of Meulan, Earl Henry his brother, Roger Bigot, Gilbert Fitz-Richard and Roger his brother, Robert Fitz-Baldwin and Richard his brother. 'Et hec concessio facta fuit apud Westmoster in primo Natali post concordiam Roberti comitis, fratris mei, de me et de illo.' [1]

33. Confirmation, addressed generally, in favour of the canons of Colchester. It is attested by the bishops, Maurice of London and Robert of Lincoln ; and by Eudes the sewer ; 'apud Westmonasterium, per Matildem reginam.' [2] [Nov. 1100–Sept. 1107.]

34. Writ addressed to Maurice bishop of London, Hugh de Bocheland, Eudes the sewer, and the barons of Essex, in favour of the same canons, and confirming land given by Count Eustace of Boulogne. It is attested by Count Eustace himself, Eudes the sewer, Roger Bigot, and Roger de Sumeri ; at Westminster. [3] [1101–7.]

1102.

35. Precept directed to Gotselin de la Riviere to do to Faritius, abbot of Abingdon, the service (of three knights' fees at Beedon) which his brothers had formerly done to Abbot Adelhelm. It is attested by Robert Fitz-Hamon, (and is issued) by W(illiam) de la Rochelle ; at London. [4] [1101–2.]

At the time of the dedication [5] of the church of St. Mary, Monmouth, by Hervey bishop of Bangor, Bernard the king's chaplain obtains, by the command of King Henry, the custody of the see of Hereford. [6]

36. 8 Feb. The king, by charter addressed generally, restores to Eudes his sewer the lands which the same Eudes held at the late king's death. It is attested by Robert count of Meulan and Earl Henry his brother ; 'apud Westburiam, in prima die Sabati post Purificationem Sancte Marie post concordiam inter me et Robertum fratrem meum.' [7]

6 Apr. At Easter the king holds his court at Winchester. [8]

37. By charter addressed to Archbishop Anselm, William bishop of Winchester, Henry de Port the sheriff, and the lieges of Hampshire, the king grants Hayling (Island) to the abbey of Jumièges. It is attested by Robert count of Meulan, Henry earl of Warwick, Robert Fitz-Hamon, Richard de Retviers and Robert Fitz-Anschetill; at Winchester, at Easter. [9]

38. Writ addressed to Robert bishop of Coventry, Richard (son of Gotse), the sheriff, Count Roger (the Poitevin), William Peverel, Robert de Ferrers, and the lieges of Nottinghamshire and Derbyshire, notifying them of the king's grant to the church of Lincoln of the churches of Derby and Wirksworth, for a prebend. It is attested by the queen, Robert Fitz-Hamon, Hamon the sewer, Urse de Abetot, and Osbert the sheriff of Lincoln. [10] [Before July 1102.]

---

[1] *Chartul. of Colchester* (Roxburghe Club), i. 27.
[2] *Cal. of Pat. Rolls*, 1422–9, p. 415, n. 8.
[3] *Ibid.* n. 4.   [4] *Chron. of Abingdon*, ii. 92.
[5] Some time about 18 March 1101, or the same day in 1102.
[6] Round, *Cal. of Documents, France*, nn. 1136, 1138.
[7] *Chartul. of Colchester*, i. 26.   [8] Chron.
[9] Round, *Cal. of Documents, France*, n. 154 B. ; *Mon. Anglic.* vi. 1088 *b.*
[10] Vesp. E. xvi, fo. 8 *d*, n. 22 ; *Mon. Anglic.* vi. 1274, n. 35.

39. Queen Matilda addresses to Hugh de Bocheland and the lieges of Berkshire a charter granting to Faritius, abbot of Abingdon, the houses and buildings of the isle of St. Mary (*sic*) for the repair of the monastery of St. Mary (at Abingdon). It is attested by Roger the chancellor and Grimbald the physician.[1] [Same as 29.]

40. Matilda also directs a writ to Hugh de Bocheland to permit Faritius, abbot of Abingdon, to have the lead of the houses of Andresey for the use of his church of Abingdon. It is attested by Ralph de Tiuu[2] and Bernard the clerk; at Sutton.[3] [Same as 29.]

41. The king grants to Abbot Faritius and the monastery of Abingdon the chapel of St. Andrew's isle with the lead, stones, and timber of the houses, for the use of the monastery, and the isle or holme itself. The charter is addressed to Hugh de Bocheland, sheriff of Berkshire, the barons and lieges of that shire, and it is attested by Queen Matilda, Roger the chancellor, Herbert the chamberlain, Nigel de Oillei, Urse de Abetot, and Ralph Basset; at Windsor.[4] [Same as 29.]

25 May. At Whitsuntide the king and queen are at Westminster.[5]

42. Queen Matilda, by her writ, notifies Osbert the sheriff of Lincoln and the king's barons (of Lincolnshire) of her gift to St. Mary's, York, of £6 worth of land yearly in Belton. It is attested by R(einhelm) the queen's chancellor; at Westminster, at Whitsuntide.[6]

c. June. Robert of Bellême is summoned to answer to the king and his justices for treason to the crown and innumerable acts of oppression. He throws himself into his castle of Bridgenorth.[7]

The king advances with his forces to Arundel castle, which Robert of Bellême has munitioned against him.[8]

18 June. Henry, abbot of Battle, dies on 14 kalends of July.[9] During this month Foucher, brother of Ranulf Flambard, is consecrated bishop of Lisieux.[10]

15 July. Walter Giffard, earl of Buckingham, dies.[11]

Henry leads his forces to Bridgenorth and besieges the castle for three weeks,[12] at the end of which time it is surrendered by Ulger the huntsman, who had been placed in command of the garrison by Robert of Bellême.[13] Meantime Earl Robert betakes himself to Shrewsbury; but, after a siege of thirty days, the town is surrendered by the townsmen, who deliver up the keys to Henry by the hand of Ralph, abbot of Sées.[14] Earl Robert receives a safe-conduct to the sea-coast.[15]

---

[1] *Chron. of Abingdon*, ii. 51.

[2] Mr. H. E. Salter suggests 'Tiuu', in place of 'Tuiu', as in the printed Chartulary.

[3] *Chron. of Abingdon*, ii. 51.   [4] *Ibid.* p. 52.

[5] *Cal. of Pat. Rolls*, 1396–9, p. 75.

[6] *Ibid.*   [7] Orderic, iv. 170; W. Malm., *G. R.* ii. 472.

[8] Orderic, iv. 170; Florence of Worcester, *s. a.*   [9] *Mon. Anglic.* iii. 234 *b*.

[10] Orderic, iv. 116.   [11] Orderic, iv. 183 and note.

[12] *Ibid.* p. 172; Chron.; W. Malm., *G. R.* ii. 472. Orderic speaks of the siege as having taken place in the autumn. Possibly the castle was surrendered during August.

[13] Orderic, iv. 175.   [14] W. Malm., *G. R.* ii. 472.

[15] Orderic, iv. 176; W. Malm., *ut supra*.

Earlier in the rising Earl Robert with his brother Arnold, or Arnulf, and a large body of Norman retainers and Welsh levies devastate Staffordshire ; [1] but Henry puts William Pantulf, an upright knight whom Earl Robert had ousted from his estates, in charge of Stafford castle with a force of 200 knights to hold the neighbouring country.[2]

During these operations it is possible that Henry visits Cannock.

43. Notification to Robert bishop of Chester, Richard de Belmers, and all barons and lieges, of the royal confirmation to Fulchred, abbot of Shrewsbury, of the manor of Baschurch, to hold as beneficially as Robert of Bellême ever held it in his demesne. It is attested by Queen Matilda and Robert count of Meulan ; at Cannock (' Lecanot ').[3] [June 1102–Whitsun, 1108.]

c. July-Aug. Possibly after the surrender of Shrewsbury the king moves north towards Blythe, near Tickhill castle, late the *caput* of the fee of Roger de Builli, or Busli. This castle had been garrisoned by Earl Robert, and Bishop Bloet had been sent with part of the royal army to reduce it at the time of the king's advance to Bridgenorth.[4] Upon the king's approach to Tickhill the defenders, having no heart to oppose the forces which he is leading in person, come out to meet him, surrender the castle, and do homage.[5]

44. Mandate, addressed to Roger Bigot, Osbert the sheriff, Richard son of Gotse, and all the sheriffs in whose bailiwicks the monks of Blythe have lands, notifying them of the king's confirmation to the same monks of the tithes and customs which they had in the time of Roger de Builli, and particularly the tithes of Appleby and ' Assinton '. It is issued at Blythe (' apud Blidam ').[6] [1100-7.]

After the banishment of Earl Robert of Bellême Henry seizes the fee of Ives de Grentemesnil, sheriff of Leicestershire, and those of Earl Robert's brothers, Count Roger the Poitevin, lord of the honor of Lancaster, and Arnulf, lord of Pembroke and Holderness, who are likewise banished. Robert Malet and Robert de Lascy, son of Ilbert, lord of Pontefract and Clitheroe, retain their respective fees by the payment of heavy fines.[7]

46. Writ addressed to Roger sheriff (of Huntingdon) and Richard Engaine to cause Aldwin abbot of Ramsey to have his woodlands and customs, as in the time of the king's father. It is attested by Roger Bigot and Urse de Abetot ; at Brampton.[8] [Aug. 1100-Mich. 1102.]

47. Writ addressed to Roger de Huntendon and all the sheriffs and ministers in whose bailiwicks Aldwin, abbot of Ramsey, has lands, directing that the same abbot and his men shall plead as in the time of the kings, Edward and William I. It is attested by Urse de Abetot and Roger Bigot ; at Brampton.[9] [Same as 46.]

48. Writ directing Hugh de Bocheland and William sheriff of Oxford

---

[1] Florence of Worcester.   [2] Orderic, iv. 173.

[3] *Cal. of Chart. Rolls*, ii. 82 ; *Chartul. of Salop Abbey*, n. 14 ; Eyton, *Hist. of Shropshire*, x. 132.

[4] Florence of Worcester, *s. a.*   [5] Orderic, iv. 171.

[6] Chartul. of Blythe, Harl. MS. 3759, fo. 99 *d*.

[7] Orderic, iv. 161. The chronicler is mistaken in stating that the banishment of Malet and Robert de Lascy occurred at this time : *ibid.* p. 167. See below, *s. a.* 1111.

[8] *Chartul. of Ramsey*, ii. 82.   [9] Add. Ch. 33641.

to cause the men of their county (court) to give a true verdict between the abbey of Abingdon and Rualuc of Avranches. It is attested by Roger the chancellor and (is issued) by . . . agen Basset ; at Cambridge (' Grentebruge ').[1] [Easter 1101–Sept. 1102.]

49. Writ addressed to Herbert bishop (of Norwich), Roger Bigot, and the sheriffs in whose bailiwicks St. Edmund has lands, directing that the demesnes of St. Edmund shall be quit of gelds and scots, as in the time of King Edward and William I. It is attested by R(oger) Bigot and Urse de Abetot ; at Newport (' Neuport ').[2] [1100–7.]

Aug.–Sept. The envoys to Paschal return. Henry summons a council of the magnates at London.[3] A temporary agreement on the subject of investiture is patched up between the king and Anselm. Henry nominates Roger, his larderer, to the vacant see of Hereford, and Roger (le Poer), his chancellor, to that of Salisbury.[4]

50. 26 Sept. Notification to Ralph the chaplain, A(   ) the prior, and the lieges of the abbey of St. Edmund of the confirmation to St. Edmund's of land at Halstead (co. Essex), which Odo and his wife gave to the monastery for wine for the service of the altar. It is attested by Roger bishop elect of Salisbury ;[5] at Westminster, on 6 kalends of October.[6] [1102–5.]

29 Sept. Anselm, with the king's approval, holds a council in the abbey church of Westminster,[7] at which are present, besides the king and the primate, Gerard archbishop of York, and the bishops, Maurice of London, William elect of Winchester, Robert of Lincoln, Sampson of Worcester, Robert of Chester, John of Bath, Herbert of Norwich, Ralph of Chichester, Gundulf of Rochester, Hervey of Bangor, and the two newly invested bishops of Salisbury and Hereford. Osbert bishop of Exeter is prevented by sickness from attending.[8] The acts of the council are known as the ordinances of the council of London. The following abbots are deposed : Guy of Pershore, Wimund of Tavistock, Aldwin of Ramsey ; and certain who had not yet been consecrated, namely, Godric of Peterborough, Hamon of Cerne, Egelric of Milton (Abbas) ; and, for divers other causes, Richard of Ely, Robert of St. Edmund's, and the abbot (unnamed) of Muchelney.[9]

51. Writ addressed to Richard de Belmeis, Foucher (' Fulquius ') the sheriff, and the barons of Shropshire directing that the monks of St. Rémi (Rheims) shall hold their lands in Shropshire in as beneficial a manner as in the time of the king's father and brother. It is attested by Waldric the chaplain ; at Westminster, ' in consilio '.[10]

[1] *Chron. of Abingdon*, ii. 84.   [2] *Ante*, xxiv. 426 (11).

[3] Eadmer, p. 137.   [4] *Ibid.* pp. 140–1.

[5] Florence of Worcester, *s. a.* Roger's election followed on the ides of April 1103 ; *Flores Histor.* ii. 36.

[6] Chartul. of St. Edmund's, Camb. Univ. Lib., fo. 25 (46) ; Add. MS. 14847, fo. 34.

[7] ' . . . Londoniis in ecclesia sancti Pauli, praesente rege et suffraganeis episcopis, circa festum sancti Michaelis' : M. Paris, *Chron. Mai.* ii. 123 ; cf. *Flores Histor.* ii. 36.

[8] Eadmer, p. 141 ; Florence of Worcester.

[9] Eadmer, p. 142 ; Florence of Worcester, *s. a.*

[10] *Mon. Anglic.* vi. 1099 ; cf. 1043, n. 5.

52. Writ addressed to the barons and the sheriffs in whose bailiwicks the canons of St. Paul's, London, have lands, in favour of the said canons. It is attested by Roger the chancellor and Eudes the sewer ; at Westminster, ' post festivitatem sancti Michaelis '.[1] [1101–2.]

53. Notification to R(ichard) de Belmeis, Hugh de Falaise, and the barons of Sussex, of the restoration to Ralph bishop of Chichester of land by the city-wall of Chichester, as the bishop held it in the time of Robert of Bellême, &c. It is attested by William de Werelwast ; at Westminster, ' in concilio '.[2] [1102–7.]

Oct. Roger, the king's late larderer, who was recently invested in the bishopric of Hereford, is taken ill and dies in London. Reinhelm, the queen's chancellor, is nominated in his stead.[3]

The king summons Archbishop Gerard to London to consecrate the three recently invested bishops. William Giffard declines consecration at the hands of the archbishop of York,[4] and afterwards goes out of the kingdom ;[5] Reinhelm also resigns his see.[6]

Robert prior of Westminster is appointed abbot of St. Edmund's.[7]

54. Writ addressed to Archbishop Anselm, Hamon the sewer, the barons and lieges of Kent, notifying them of the confirmation to St. Andrew's, Rochester, of lands, &c., given by William de Aubigny. It is attested by Bishop Roger and the (?) chancellor ;[8] at Winchester.[9] [1102–3, 1107–9.]

55. Writ addressed to William Peverell, Richard (son of Gotse), the sheriff, and the barons of Nottinghamshire directing that Archbishop Gerard shall have his customs, as his ancestor Thomas had the same, ' de equitibus et de sochemannis et de villanis ', as in the time of the king's father and brother. It is attested by Richard de Revers ; at ' Wyncestre '.[10] [1101–Aug. 1108.]

56. The king notifies Robert bishop of Lincoln, Earl Simon, and all the sheriffs in whose bailiwicks the abbey of Ramsey has lands of his grant to Bernard, the monk of St. Albans, of the abbey of Ramsey. It is attested by Queen Matilda, Archbishop Gerard, Robert bishop of Lincoln, Robert count of Meulan, ' et aliis baronibus ' ; at Reading.[11]

25 Dec. At mid-winter the king is at Westminster.[12]

57. He expedites a general charter of confirmation and restoration to Abbot Faritius and the monastery of Abingdon of the demesnes of the monastery. It is addressed to the bishops, Roger of Salisbury and Robert of Lincoln ; Hugh de Bocheland, William de Oxeneford, and the barons of Berkshire and Oxfordshire, and is attested by the queen, Roger bishop

---

[1] *Hist. MSS. Comm. Rep.* ix, p. 61 ; Harl. roll i, n. 6 ; *Cal. of Chart. Rolls*, iii. 292 ; Simpson, *Reg. Statut.*, p. 114.

[2] *Mon. Anglic.* vi. 1168, n. 28.   [3] Eadmer, p. 142 ; *Flores Histor.* ii. 35.

[4] Eadmer, p. 145 ; *Flores Histor.* ii. 36.

[5] Soon after mid-winter : Chron.   [6] *Flores Histor.* ii. 36.

[7] *Ibid.* p. 37. According to Eadmer he was consecrated by Anselm on 15 August 1107: *op. cit.* p. 188.

[8] ' T[este ?] Rogero episc[opo] et canc[ellario].'

[9] *Cal. of Chart. Rolls*, ii. 195 ; *Mon. Anglic.* i. 164, n. 18.

[10] *Cal. of Chart. Rolls*, v. 479.

[11] *Chartul. of Ramsey*, i. 237, n. 158 ; ii. 293, n. 418   [12] Chron.

of Salisbury, Rainald the chancellor, and William de Werelwast; at ' Westmuster ', at the Nativity of our Lord.[1]

58. Writ addressed to Herbert bishop of Norwich, the barons, lieges, and ministers of Norfolk and Suffolk in favour of the monastery and borough of (Bury) St. Edmunds, touching their liberties and privileges. It is attested by Archbishop Anselm, the bishops Maurice of London and Roger of Salisbury, Robert Fitz-Hamon, Roger Bicot, and Aubrey de Ver; at Westminster.[2] [Sept. 1102–Easter 1103.]

1103.

12 Jan. William de Bréteuil (son of William Fitz-Osbern) dies at Bec on 2 ides of January, and is buried at the abbey of Lire, which his father founded.[3]

59. 13 Jan. On the ides of January, being the octave of the Epiphany 1103, an agreement is made at Salisbury, in the presence of King Henry and Queen Matilda, attended by many barons, between William abbot of Fécamp and Philip de Braose. There are present, besides the king and queen, the bishops, Robert of Lincoln, Roger of Salisbury, and John of Bath; Robert Fitz-Hamon, Hamon his brother, Eudes the sewer, Richard de Redviers, Roger Bigot, Humphrey de Bohun, William de Aubigny, Gilbert Fitz-Richard, Roger de Nunant, Waldric the chancellor, Henry de Port, Pain Peverel and Ansger Fitz-Walter, with others on behalf of the respective parties to the agreement.[4]

60. Writ addressed to Archbishop Anselm, Maurice bishop of London, Hugh de Bocheland, and the barons of London, confirming to St. Peter of Cluny and St. Martin des Champs nine dwelling-houses in London, which Bishop Odo gave to William Giffard, and the said William bishop of Winchester gave to St. Martin. The signatories are the king and queen, William Giffard, bishop of Winchester, Eudes the sewer, Robert Bloet, bishop of Lincoln, Roger Bigod, Roger bishop of Salisbury, and William de Werelwast.[5] [Sept. 1102–April 1103.]

61. Writ addressed to Archbishop Gerard, Bertram de Verdun, and the barons of Yorkshire in favour of Hugh abbot of Selby. It is attested by Robert bishop of Lincoln and Urse de Abetot; at Salisbury, in the council.[6]

29 Jan. Foucher bishop of Lisieux, and brother of Ranulf Flambard, dies.[7]

62. After 2 Feb. Writ addressed to Hugh de Bocheland in favour of St. Paul's, London, acquitting 24 hides ' de sceolanda ' of this present geld and all other gelds. It is attested by Waldric the chancellor; at London, after the Purification.[8] [1103–4.]

---

[1] *Chron. of Abingdon*, ii. 86; *ibid.* p. 87; *Mon. Anglic.* i. 521, n. 18.
[2] Chartul. of St. Edmund's, Harl. MS. 743, fo. 60; *Cal. of Chart. Rolls*, ii. 258.
[3] Orderic, iv. 185.
[4] *Mon. Anglic.* vi. 1083.   [5] *Ibid.* v. 200 n.
[6] *Cal. of Pat. Rolls*, 1301–7, p. 487. Cf. n. 161.
[7] Orderic, iv. 116. The obituary of Lisieux gives the date as 29 January 1102; *ibid.* p. 116 n.
[8] *Hist. MSS. Comm. Rep.* ix, p. 45.

63. The king notifies the sheriffs, in whose bailiwicks the alms of the poor of Westminster have lands, that he has released the land of the said alms, namely Paddington, Fanton, Cleygate, and what it had T. R. E. in the wood of Ditton, of pleas, scots, and aids, 'pro salute anime mee et Mathildis regine uxoris mee et subolis mee'. It is attested by Queen Matilda; at London, after the Purification of St. Mary.[1] [1103-4.]

64. An acquittance similar to the last is also attested by Queen Matilda, at London.[2] [Same as 63.]

65. A third charter combines the privileges of the two preceding documents and is issued ' precatu regine ' and attested by the queen; at London.[3] [Same as 63.]

66. The king notifies H(ugh) de Bocheland, W(illiam) the chamberlain, W(illiam) de Magnevill, and the lieges of Middlesex of his confirmation to St. Peter's, Westminster, and Abbot Gilbert of the land of Eye (in Westminster), which had been given by Geoffrey de Magnevill and his wife. It is attested by Queen Matilda and W(aldric ?) the chancellor; at London.[4] [1100-1, 1103-6.]

8-10 Mar. At Mid-Lent the king visits Canterbury, on his way, so it is reported, to Dover to treat about the compact which was still in force between him and Robert count of Flanders. He remains at Canterbury until the third day.[5]

67. The king notifies Hamon the sheriff, Gilbert de Tunebrigge, and the barons of Kent of his confirmation of the gift made by Archbishop Anselm to the nuns of Malling of the manor of Little Malling. It is attested by Robert bishop of Lincoln, Robert Fitz-Hamon, and William de Aubigny; [at Canterbury ?].[6] [1101-7.]

68. The king notifies Archbishop Anselm, Hamon the sheriff, and the barons of Kent of his grant at the request of his wife ' Mahaldis ', the queen, to the nuns of Malling of a weekly market in their town of Malling. It is attested by ' Mahald ' the queen, Robert bishop of Lincoln, Robert Fitz-Hamon, Alan son of Flathald, and William de Aubigny; at Canterbury.[7] [1101-3.]

69. Notification addressed generally to all of the realm, of the confirmation to the church of St. Andrew the Apostle in the city of Rochester of various possessions. The signatories are : the king, Archbishop Anselm, Bishop Gundulf, Queen Matilda, Robert bishop of Lincoln, Waldric the chancellor, William de Werelwast, Robert count of Meulan, Henry earl of Warwick, Gilbert de Tonebrigge, Robert Fitz-Hamon, Robert Fitz-Baldwin, William de Aubigny, Robert de Montefort, Eudes the sewer, and Alan Fitz-Flathald. ' Anno ab incarnatione Domini M⁰C⁰III⁰ '.[8]

70. Notification, addressed to Archbishop Anselm and generally to all

[1] Westm. Abbey Ch., n. 29; Chartul., fo. 482 ; Robinson, *Gilbert Crispin*, p. 144.

[2] Westm. Abbey Ch., n. 30; Chartul., fo. 482; Chartul. Faust. A. iii, fo. 75 d ; *Gilbert Crispin*, p. 143.

[3] Chartul., fo. 482 ; *Gilbert Crispin*, p. 144.

[4] Chartul. of St. Peter's, Westminster, Faust. A. iii, fo. 73 d ; *Gilbert Crispin*, p. 142.   [5] Eadmer, p. 146.

[5] *Mon. Anglic.* iii. 383 b ; *Cal. of Chart. Rolls*, v. 56, n. 6.

[6] *Cal. of Charter Rolls*, v. 56, n. 8.

[7] Hearne, *Textus Roffensis*, p. 224, c. 211 ; *Mon. Anglic.* i. 163, n. 8.

ministers, &c., of the confirmation of certain liberties to Bernard, abbot of Ramsey. It is attested by Earl Simon, Roger Bigot, and Urse de Abetot ; at Dover.[1] [Oct. 1102–Mar. 1104.]

29 Mar. At Easter Henry holds his court at Winchester.[2] Anselm decides to go to Rome at Henry's suggestion and by the advice of the magnates present at the Easter council.[3] After Easter he returns to Canterbury, where he remains only four days. From Dover he takes ship to Witsand, which he reaches on 5 kalends of May (27 April).[4]

71. Notification to the archbishops, Anselm and Gerard, and generally, of the grant to Robert bishop of Lincoln of the toll of the fairs at Stow. It is attested by Roger bishop of Salisbury, (Robert) count of Meulan, (Waldric ?) the chancellor, Roger Bigot, and Hamon the sewer ; at Winchester.[5] [1103–Mar. 1104, or April–June 1107.]

72. Writ addressed to Ranulf Meschin, Osbert the sheriff, and the barons of Lincolnshire, confirming to Robert bishop of Lincoln a gift made by Roger Bigot. It is attested by Roger bishop (of Salisbury), Waldric the chancellor, Robert count of Meulan, Henry (earl) of Warwick, Roger (Bigot),[6] and Hamon the sewer ; at Winchester.[7] [Same as 71.]

73. Writ to Roger bishop of Salisbury, Hugh de Bocheland, and the lieges of Berkshire notifying them that the king has released five hides of land at Worth of the monks of Abingdon of gelds and pleas. It is attested by the queen and Robert Fitz-Hamon, (and is issued) by Reiner de Kerisburc ; at Chute (' Ceat ').[8] [1102–7.]

27 Apr. Anselm reaches Witsand.[9] He is accompanied by William Giffard, bishop elect of Winchester, and the deposed abbots, Richard of Ely and Aldwin of Ramsey.[10]

William de Warelwast, the king's envoy, departs for Rome not much later than June, bearing news of the birth of the king's son. He arrives at Rome before Anselm.[11]

Anselm is at Chartres at Whitsuntide and, returning later to Bec, remains there until the middle of August. He probably arrives at Rome before November and departs after the 16th of that month. Warelwast remains some little time longer and leaves after 23 November.[12] They approach Lyons about Christmas time.[13] Warelwast arrives again in England about February 1104.

74. A charter of Robert duke of the Normans in favour of the abbey of St. Stephen, Caen, is issued possibly about this time. The witnesses are : Count Robert (of Bellême), Eustace of Breteuil ; and among others Ranulf bishop of Durham, William (de Tancarvill) the chamberlain, William earl of Warenne, Robert de Montfort, Gilbert de Aquila, William de Ferrers, Ralph Taisson, Robert Marmion, Robert de Grentemesnil, and Robert Doisnel.[14] [1101–4.]

---

[1] *Chartul. of Ramsey*, i. 238.
[2] Chron.   [3] Eadmer, p. 148.   [4] *Ibid.* p. 149.
[5] Vesp. E. xvi, fo. 7 *d*, n. 21 ; *Mon. Anglic.* vi. 1274, n. 34.
[6] ' ipso Rogero '.   [7] Vesp. E. xvi, fo. 8, n. 18 ; *Mon. Anglic.* vi. 1273, n. 31.
[8] *Chron. of Abingdon*, ii. 94. See no. 274 below.
[9] Eadmer, p. 149.   [10] Florence of Worcester.   [11] Eadmer, pp. 152–5.
[12] *Ibid.* pp. 152–7.   [13] *Ibid.* p. 157.
[14] Round, *Cal. of Documents, France*, n. 451.

c. June. Duke Robert unexpectedly visits Henry to plead for his friend William de Warenne. He succeeds in obtaining Warenne's pardon and the restoration of his English fee.[1] Before returning to Normandy Duke Robert is persuaded—by the queen, it is said—to forgo his yearly pension of 3,000 marks.[2]

75. 29 June. Writ in favour of St. Peter's, Bath, and John bishop of Bath, addressed to the archbishops, Anselm and Gerard ; the bishops, Maurice of London, Robert[3] of Lincoln, Sampson of Worcester, Robert of Chester, Osbern of Exeter, William of Winchester,[4] Ralph of Chichester,[4] Gundulf of Rochester, and Herbert[5] of Norwich ; Herlwin abbot of Glastonbury, William count of Mortain, Robert Fitz-Hamon, Aiulf the chamberlain, and the barons of Somerset and England The witnesses are : the bishops, Maurice of London, Robert of Lincoln, and Samson of Worcester ; Henry earl of Warwick, Robert Fitz-Hamon, Urse de Abetot, Aiulf the chamberlain, William de Aubigny, and Walter Hosate ; at Geddington,[6] on the day of Peter and Paul, the Apostles.[7]

c. June–July. A son is born to the king.[8] He is named William.

21 Oct. Matthias abbot of Peterborough dies on 12 kalends of November. He had been received at Peterborough, after the deposition of Abbot Godric, on or about the same day in the preceding year.[9]

Possibly about this time the king sends Robert count of Meulan to suppress the disorders which were occurring in Normandy, and to summon Duke Robert and the Norman magnates to take steps for the amelioration of the state of the duchy.[10]

There is evidence of a royal visit to the neighbourhood of Oxford during the autumn.

76. Manasser Arsic makes a gift to the church of Fécamp whilst he is at Cogges, co. Oxon., on 3 nones of November 1103 ; ' sub testimonio et confirmatione regis Henrici ', &c.[11]

At Christmas Henry holds his court at Westminster.[12]

77. Notification, addressed to Archbishop Gerard, Osbert the sheriff (of York), Richard sheriff of Nottingham, and the barons of the archbishopric of York, of the grant to St. Peter's, York, of the church of Laughton(-en-le-Morthen) for a prebend. It is attested by Bernard the chaplain and Robert Malet ; at Westminster, at Christmas.[13] [1102–3, 1105, 1107.]

78. Writ addressed to Herbert bishop (of Norwich), Roger Bigot, Robert Malet, and the lieges of Norfolk and Suffolk, directing that Robert, abbot of St. Edmund's, shall have warren in his demesne

[1] Orderic, iv. 161–2.   [2] Chron. ; W. Malm., *G. R.* ii. 461.

[3] ' Remigius ' in *Mon. Anglic.*   [4] Not in *Bath Abbey Chartul.*

[5] ' Hereveo ' : *Bath Abbey Chartul.*   [6] ' apud Bedintonam ' : *ibid.*

[7] *Two Bath Chartul.* (Somerset Rec. Soc.), n. 45 ; *Dep. Keeper's Rep.* xxx, app. 6, p. 206 ; *Mon. Anglic.* ii. 268.

[8] Eadmer, p. 155.   [9] Chron.

[10] Orderic, iv. 190.

[11] Cart. Antiq. roll S, n. 9 ; *Mon. Anglic.* vi. 1003, n. 2 ; Round, *Cal. of Documents, France*, no. 120, note 8.

[12] Chron.

[13] *Historians of the Church of York*, iii. 30.

lands. It is attested by Waldric the chancellor; at Westminster, at Christmas.[1]

79. Another writ in favour of the same monastery is addressed to Bishop Herbert, Roger Bigot, and the barons of Norfolk and Suffolk. It is attested by Robert Malet; at Westminster, at Christmas.[2] [Same as 77.]

1104.

20 Jan. Walter abbot of Evesham dies on 13 kalends of February.[3]

80. Possibly during the first quarter of 1104 the king spent some time in the New Forest. There, in response to a complaint made by Wihenoc, a monk of St. Florence of Saumur, against Alvric the reeve of Andover, the king sent his mandate to Henry (de Port) sheriff of ' Hantunsira ' and Gerald the reeve of Winchester to summon the hundred (court) of Andover and make inquiry as to the property which belonged to the church of Andover. The hundred met and returned a verdict in the house of Edwin the old reeve, on the feast of St. Lucy (13 December), and thereof were witnesses: Wihenoc and two other monks; of laymen Henry de Port and thirteen others. An agreement was also made before Henry (de Port) the sheriff and Croc the hunter, between the monks of St. Florence and Edward de Foscote, touching the church of Andover and chapel of Foscote. The king's confirmation of these acts was sealed ' apud Storuuellam in Nova Foresta ', the witnesses being Robert bishop of ' Nicole ', Waldric (' Galdricus ') the chancellor, ' who received therefor one rouncey ', Rainulf abbot of St. Vincent of Le Mans, Alan Fitz-Fleald, Gilbert the monk, William Fitz-Baderon, Rainulf Pevrel, and Drew, who was the keeper of the seal.[4] [1102–6.]

c. Feb.–Mar. William de Warelwast returns from Rome and reports to the king the course of the proceedings in the dispute with the primate. Henry takes the temporalities of the see of Canterbury into his own hands.[5]

William Giffard probably returns from Rome with Warelwast. He is reinstated in the see of Winchester.[6]

81. Writ addressed to Herbert bishop of Norwich, Roger Bigot, Hugh [Fo]lyoth, R(alph) Passelewe, the barons of Norfolk and Suffolk, and all sheriffs in whose bailiwicks St. Edmund and Abbot Robert have lands, directing that the abbot's demesne shall geld as heretofore, and shall be quit of this (isto) geld and all other gelds, as in the time of the king's father and brother. It is attested by William bishop of Winchester and Roger Bigot; at Canterbury.[7] [1104–7.]

82. Writ, addressed to Maurice bishop of London, Hugh de Bocheland, and the barons and lieges of London, notifying them of the restoration to Otho ' iuvenis ' of his father's office of stamping coins in the mint (' cuneo-

---

[1] Add. MS. 14847, fo. 33 d; ante, xxiv. 426, n. 9.

[2] Chartul. of St. Edmund's, Camb. Univ. Lib., fo. 28 d, n. 104.

[3] Sym. of Durham, ii. 236.

[4] Mon. Anglic. vi. 992; Cal. of Pat. Rolls, 1313–17, p. 307.

[5] Eadmer, p. 159.

[6] ' Episcopatum suum suscepit ': Annals of Winchester, p. 42.

[7] Ante xxiv. 426 (12).

rum') and particularly of his land of 'Lislestona' (Lisson Green, in Marylebone). It is attested by Robert count of Meulan, William de Warenne, and William de Aubigny; at Arundel.[1] [1102–7.]

3 Mar. Serlo abbot of St. Peter's, Gloucester, dies on 5 nones of March.[2]

6 Mar. Herewald bishop of Glamorgan (Llandaff) dies on 2 nones of March.[3]

17 Apl. At Easter the king holds his court at Winchester.[4]

83. Writ addressed to Archbishop Gerard, Osbert the sheriff, and the barons of Yorkshire in favour of the church of Beverley. It is attested by Waldric the chancellor, (and is issued) by Evrard son of Earl Roger; at Winchester, at Easter.[5] [1103–4.]

84. Writ addressed to Roger Picot, directing him to cause the monks of St. Albans to have their customs (at Tynemouth) in as beneficial a manner as Earl Robert had them. It is attested by William de Werelwast and Nigel de Aubigny; at Winchester, at Easter.[6] [1101–4.]

85. Writ addressed to Hamon the sewer and the ministers (of Kent) in favour of the men of St. Augustine's touching the aid of the borough of Canterbury. It is attested by Waldric the chancellor; at Winchester, at Easter.[7] [1103–4.]

86. Notification to William bishop of Winchester, Roger the sheriff, and the barons and lieges of Surrey and Southwark of a grant in favour of the monks of Bermondsey. It is attested by Waldric the chancellor, William de Werelwast, the sewers Eudes and Hamon; William de Aubigny, and Roger sheriff of Surrey; at Winchester, at Easter.[8]

87. Writ addressed to Hugh de Bocheland, William sheriff of Oxford and the lieges of Berkshire and Oxfordshire directing that the monks of Abingdon shall hold in demesne the land in Wytham, which Ranulf bishop of Durham held, and this notwithstanding any grant which the king may make of the land of Stanton. It is attested by Robert bishop of Lincoln, at Winchester, at Easter (and is issued) by William de Oxeneford.[9] [1101–4.]

88. Notification to the bishop of Exeter, Richard de Retvers, G(eoffrey) de Magnevill, the barons and lieges of Devonshire, of the grant to the monks of St. Nicholas, Exeter, of the land of Harald of Exeter. It is attested by Robert bishop of Lincoln, W(aldric ?) the chancellor, William de Warelwast and Gilbert de Aquila; at London.[10] [1103–7.]

Serlo bishop of Sées and Ralph abbot of Sées take refuge in England from the oppressions of Robert of Bellême.[11]

5 June. At Whitsuntide Henry holds his court at Westminster.[12]

[1] *Cal. of Pat. Rolls*, 1370–4, p. 363.

[2] *Chartul. of St. Peter's, Gloucester*, i. 13; 'quarto nonas': Sym. of Durham, ii. 236.

[3] *Annals of Margan*.   [4] Chron.

[5] Farrer, *Early Yorkshire Charters*, i, n. 90.

[6] Craster, *Hist. of Northumb.* viii. 55, note 5.

[7] *Dep. Keeper's Rep.* xxx, app. 6, p. 199, n. 17.

[8] *Cal. of Chart. Rolls*, iv. 182.   [9] *Chron. of Abingdon*, ii. 84.

[10] Chartul. of St. Nicholas, Vitell. D. ix, fo. 28 and fo. 66 d; *Mon. Anglic.* iii. 377 b.

[11] Orderic, iv. 192.   [12] Chron.

89. Notification, addressed generally, of the confirmation to St. Augustine's, Canterbury, of sac and soc, &c., as granted and confirmed by William I and William II. It is attested by William de Werelwast [1] and Thurstan the chaplain ; at Westminster, at Whitsuntide.[2]

90. Notification to Robert bishop of Lincoln, R(anulf) Fitz-Ranulf, and the barons of Lincolnshire that in the king's presence Hugh de Evremou has surrendered to St. Peter's, Westminster, and Abbot Gilbert the manor of Doddington (co. Linc.) which he had received from the abbot in the time of William II in exchange for the manor of Duxford (co. Camb.). The king has restored Duxford to Count Eustace and has given Hugh an exchange. It is attested by Robert bishop of Lincoln, Henry earl of Warwick, Gilbert Fitz-Richard, and William de Werelwast ; at Westminster, at Whitsuntide.[3] [1102 or 1104.]

91. Notification to Herbert bishop (of Norwich), R(oger) Bigot, R(alph) Passelewe, and the lieges of Norfolk and Suffolk of the gift to St. Edmund of the land of Stanham, which Ailbold the priest held, and the service of the land. It is attested by Wald(ric) the chancellor ; at Westminster, at Whitsuntide.[4]

92. Possibly at this Whitsuntide court the king expedites a charter confirming the foundation of the church of St. John, Colchester, as a monastery, by Eudes his sewer and Rohaise wife of Eudes, and the endowments by them bestowed upon it. The charter contains this clause : ' Nunc itaque consilio archiepiscoporum meorum, episcoporum, abbatum, comitum, ducum, et universorum procerum meorum, auctorizo et regia potestate confirmo ', &c. The signatories are : Queen ' Mahald ', Eudes the sewer and founder of the alms, Waldric the chancellor, Gilbert Fitz-Richard, (Archbishop) Gerard, the bishops, Maurice of London, Samson of Worcester, Gundulf of Rochester, Herbert of Norwich, Robert of Lincoln, Robert of Chester, and Ralph of Chichester ; the abbots, Gilbert of Westminster, Richard of St. Albans, Stephen of St. Mary's, York, Ralph of Sées, and Gunter of Thorney ; Richard earl of Chester, Henry earl of Warwick, William count of Mortain, and Roger Bigot.[5]

93. Writ addressed to Robert bishop of Lincoln, Earl Simon, Roger sheriff of Huntingdon, and the sheriffs in whose bailiwicks Bernard abbot of Ramsey has lands, directing *inter alia* that Abbot Bernard shall admeasure the services of his vavasors and recover the lands of his demesne which Abbot Aldwin gave or exchanged. It is attested by Robert bishop of Lincoln and Waldric the chancellor ; at Windsor, on the octave of Whitsuntide.[6] [1103–4, 1106.]

94. Notification to Urse de Abetot and the barons of Worcestershire of the confirmation to St. Peter's, Westminster, of the land of Comberton,

---

[1] ' Welerwast ' in MS.

[2] *Cal. of Pat. Rolls*, 1461–7, p. 404 ; *Hist. S. Aug. Cantuar.* p. 361 ; Cart. Antiq. roll I, n. 9 (15) ; Exch. K. R., Misc. Bks. 27, n. 4 ; *Dep. Keeper's Rep.* xxx, app. 6, p. 197.

[3] Chartul. of St. Peter's, Westminster, Faust. A. iii, fo. 74 ; Robinson, *Gilbert Crispin*, p. 145.

[4] Chartul. of St. Edmund's, Camb. Univ. Lib., fo. 25 (49).

[5] *Chartul. of Colchester* (Roxburghe Club), pp. 11–14.

[6] *Chartul. of Ramsey*, i. 238 ; Add. Ch. 33642.

which Robert the dispenser gave. It is attested by Robert bishop of Lincoln; at Windsor.[1] [1101–10.]

95. Writ addressed to Ranulf Meschin, Osbert sheriff of Lincoln, and the lieges of Lincolnshire in favour of Robert bishop of Lincoln and his canons. It is attested by Waldric the chancellor, and Urse de Abetot; at Newbury ('Niweberia').[2] [1103–7.]

96. Writ addressed to Roger Bigot and Ralph Passelewe to cause Herbert bishop of Norwich to have his land and men of Brisley ('Brusela'), &c. as on the day when William II died. It is attested by Eudes the sewer; at Newbury.[3] [1104–7.]

97. Writ addressed to Roger bishop of Salisbury, Hugh de Bocheland, and the barons of Berkshire directing that Abbot Faritius and the monks of Abingdon shall hold the hundred of Hormer as in the preceding reigns. It is attested by Robert Fitz-Hamon and Roger Bigod; at (Bessels) Leigh ('apud Legam').[4] [1102–6.]

98. Notification addressed to William bishop of Winchester and Henry de Port of the grant to Hadewis, wife of William Malduit,[5] of her full dower in her husband's lands in Shaldern ('Sceldedena') and Hartley Mauduit ('Herleia') and two messuages in Winchester outside the gate, and land in the Fullers' street, as her husband held the same in the time of the king's father and brother. It is attested by William de Werelwast, Eudes the sewer, Robert Fitz-Hamon, Roger Bigot, Hamon the sewer, William Fitz-Humphrey; at (Bessels) Leigh ('apud Legam').[6] [1101–6.]

99. Writ addressed to W(illiam) sheriff of Oxford and the foresters of Oxfordshire, acquitting the abbot of Eynesham and his men of Eynesham of the service of standing in the forest to drive the deer ('ad stabilitatem') at such time as the royal household is lodging there. It is attested by Robert bishop of Lincoln, and William de Warelwast; at Handborough ('Haneberga').[7] [Same as 88.]

c. June. During the early summer Duke Robert becomes reconciled with Robert of Bellême, contrary to the understanding between the duke and King Henry.[8]

William count of Mortain leaves England and takes up arms in Normandy against Henry, who forthwith deprives him of his English fief.[9]

100. 31 July. At the prayer of Queen Matilda, the king grants to Robert bishop of Lincoln the manor of Nettleham (co. Linc.). The charter is attested by Queen Matilda and Roger Bigod; at Winchester, on the feast of St. German the bishop in the first year of King Henry.[10] [1101.]

101. The queen notifies Osbert sheriff of Lincoln, Ranulf Meschin, the barons and lieges of Lincolnshire that the king, her lord, at her prayer,

[1] Chartul. of St. Peter's, Westminster, Faust. A. iii, fo. 74; Robinson, *Gilbert Crispin*, p. 147.

[2] *Mon. Anglic.* vi. 1273, n. 29.   [3] Cott. charter ii. 6.

[4] *Chron. of Abingdon*, ii. 115.

[5] See Round, *The Commune of London*, pp. 81–2; *The Ancestor*, v. 205–10.

[6] Add. MS. 28024, fo. 28.

[7] *Cal. of Pat. Rolls*, 1377–81, p. 61.   [8] Chron.; Orderic, iv. 192.

[9] Chron.; Hen. of Huntingdon, p. 234.

[10] *Cal. of Chart. Rolls*, ii. 271. Cf. Chartul. of St. Mary, Lincoln, Vesp. E. xvi, fo. 6, n. 1; *Mon. Anglic.* vi. 1271, n. 8.

has made the last-named grant. The writ is attested by Hamon the sewer and Urse de Abetot ; at Winchester.[1] [1101–10.]

5 Aug. Peter, prior of St. Peter's, Gloucester, is elected abbot of that monastery on the nones of August.[2]

After 4 Aug. In this, the fifth year of his reign, the king crosses to Normandy with a large force and proceeds to Domfront, the only Norman town which was reserved to him in the treaty made with his brother Robert. He is joined by many of the Norman feudatories, who possess fees in England, namely : Robert count of Meulan, Richard earl of Chester, Stephen count of Aumâle, Henry of Eu, Rotrou of Mortain, Eustace of Breteuil, Ralph de Conches, Robert Fitz-Hamon, Robert de Montfort, and Ralph de Mortemer.[3]

15 Aug. Whilst Henry is in Normandy, the queen, in journeying beyond Abingdon, rests there for the feast of the Assumption as the guest of Abbot Faritius.[4] She consents to accept a gift of alms made to her (by Robert Gernon) for the benefit of the monastery.

102. This she later confirms by charter addressed to Robert bishop of Lincoln, Hugh de Bocheland, and the barons of Buckinghamshire. It is attested by Roger de Courcelles, Robert Malet, and Odo Moire ; at London.[5] [1104 or 1106.]

103. Apparently soon after the issue of the last charter, Roger de Courcelles, who had attested it, crosses to Normandy and attests the king's confirmation of Matilda's gift by charter addressed similarly to the queen's. It is issued at Lyons-la-Forêt (' apud Sanctum Dionisium in Leons ').[6] [1104 or 1106.]

24 Aug. The incorrupt body of St. Cuthbert is exhumed at Durham.[7]

14 Sept. The translation of St. Cuthbert's body takes place at Durham in the presence of Bishop Flambard, Ralph abbot of Sées, Turgot prior of Durham, William (de Curbeuil) clerk of Bishop Flambard, Alexander earl (of Lothian), brother of the king of Scots, Richard abbot of St. Albans, Stephen abbot of York, Hugh abbot of Selby, and others.[8]

Henry summons his brother Robert to his court [9] and reproaches him for his misgovernment of Normandy.[10] Duke Robert resigns to his brother the homage of William count of Evreux with the comté of Evreux.[11]

104. Queen Matilda addresses a charter to Richard son of Gotse, Roger de Lovetot, and the barons of the honor of Blythe, granting to St. Peter's, York, the church of Laughton(-en-le-Morthen) for a prebend. It is attested by Hervey bishop (of Bangor), Bernard the chaplain, John of Bayeux, John of Sées, Ern(   ) the chaplain, Robert Malet, and Ald(helm) the chamberlain ; at Evreux.[12] [1104–6.]

105. The king addresses a writ to his officers of the comté and forests

[1] *Cal. of Chart. Rolls*, ii. 271.
[2] *Chartul. of St. Peter's, Gloucester*, i. 13.   [3] Orderic, iv. 199.
[4] *Chron. of Abingdon*, ii. 97.   [5] *Ibid.* p. 98.   [6] *Ibid.* p. 99.
[7] Sym. of Durham, i. 249.
[8] *Ibid.* pp. 258–61. If the date of the translation was 14 September 1104, then St. Cuthbert resigned his see on 2 March 686 : *ibid.* p. 261.
[9] Perhaps at Evreux.   [10] Orderic, iv. 199.   [11] *Ibid.* p. 200.
[12] *Regist. Magn. Album*, i. 63 ; *Historians of York*, iii. 30, where ' Ald. com.' is given in error for ' Ald. cam.'

of Arques and Alihermont notifying them of his gift to the monks of Bec
serving at Envermou of certain woodlands. It is attested by Hugh de
Envermou; in the siege before Arques ('in obsidione ante Archas').[1]
[1104–6.[2]]

106–7. Writs are issued by the king and Queen Matilda respectively.
They are addressed to William Peverel of Nottingham, Richard son of
Gotse, and Roger de Lovetot, and forbid the monks of Blythe to interfere
with the enjoyment of the church (of St. Peter) of York of the tithes
which belong to the church of Laughton(-en-le-Morthen). The king's writ
is attested by William de Aubigny (and is issued) by John of Sées; at
Lillebonne ('apud Juliibonam'). The queen's writ is attested by John of
Sées and Bernard the chaplain; at Lillebonne.[3] [1104–9.]

The king returns to England ' before winter '.[4]

25 Dec. At Christmas he holds his court at Windsor.[5]

1105.

108. 1 Jan. Writ addressed to Osbert the sheriff and the barons of
Yorkshire in favour of the churches of York and Beverley and the lands
of the archbishopric. It is attested by the count of Meulan and (is issued)
by Thurstan the chaplain; at Windsor, on the Circumcision of our Lord.[6]
[1101–14.]

109. Notification, addressed generally for England, of the confirmation
to St. Peter's and the monks of Chertsey of four manors, namely Chertsey,
Egham, Thorpe, and Chobham, with liberties, as the kings, Edward and
William I, granted the same to them. It is attested by Roger bishop of
Salisbury, Waldric [7] the chancellor, and Eudes the sewer; at Windsor.[8]
[1103–6.]

Robert Fitz-Hamon and others of the king's entourage (*familia*) are
seized by Gontier d'Aunai, constable of Bayeux, and Rainald de Warenne,
and are incarcerated with a view to ransom being obtained for their
release.[9]

110. Confirmation to the abbey of St. Vincent of Le Mans of certain
gifts made by Winebald de Balaon ('Baladone'). The signatories are the
king and queen, Waldric ('Gaudricus') the chancellor, Roger bishop (of
Salisbury), William Peverel ('Piperellus'), Robert Peche, Herlewin abbot
of Glastonbury, Humphry 'Aureis Testiculis', Waldric son of Roger de
Curcelle, Winebald (de Ballon) and Elizabeth his wife, Hamelin de Ballon
and Agnes his wife, William son of Hamelin, and Matthew son of the same
Hamelin.[10] [1103–7.]

111. Writ addressed to Herbert bishop (of Norwich), Robert Malet,

---

[1] Round, *Cal. of Documents, France*, no. 393.

[2] Cf. Robert of Torigny, *s. a.* 1105, p. 84.

[3] Regist. Magn. Album, i. 63, ii. 83–4; *Historians of York*, iii. 31; *Mon. Anglic.*
vi. 1179, n. 19. Professor Haskins assigns these writs to the date 1106–7; *Norman
Institutions*, p. 310.

[4] Orderic, iv. 201.   [5] Chron.

[6] Farrer, *Early Yorkshire Charters*, no. 129; *Mon. Anglic.* vi. 1179, n. 21.

[7] 'Walter' (*sic*).

[8] Chartul. of Chertsey, Vitell. A. xiii, fo. 54 *d*.   [9] Orderic, iv. 203.

[10] Round, *Cal. of Documents, France*, no. 1048.

D

and Ralph de Belfou, directing that the monks of Eye shall hold Fersfield and 'Pelecoc' in as beneficial a manner as they held it at the death of the king's father. It is attested by Ranulf bishop of Durham, (and is issued) by (William) de Hocton; at Winchester.[1] [1104–6.]

112. Writ addressed to Herbert bishop of Norwich, Roger Bigot, R(alph) Passelewe, the barons and lieges of Norfolk and Suffolk, directing that the church of St. Edmund and abbot R(obert) shall hold in peace their 8½ hundreds, as abbot Baldwin held them. It is attested by Waldric the chancellor, (and is issued) by William de la Rochelle ('de Rochela'); at Winchester.[2] [1104–6.]

For some days before and after the beginning of Lent the king and court are at Romsey,[3] awaiting a favourable passage to Normandy.

113. 13 Feb. Notification, addressed generally, of the confirmation of gifts made by Roger Bigot to the monastery of Thetford. It is attested by the bishops, Robert 'Bloiet' of Lincoln and Roger of Salisbury; Waldric[4] the chancellor, Hamon the sewer, Robert Malet the chamberlain, Urse de Abetot, William de Tornei,[5] William de Reines,[6] and William de Magnevill; at Romsey, 'in transitu regis', on the day next before the feast of St. Valentine the martyr.[7]

114. Feb.–Mar. The king by charter restores to the monastery of Abingdon, with the consent of Queen Matilda, certain lands at Sparsholt held by Hugh Fitz-Thurstan, the dispenser of the king's court.[8] It is attested by the bishops, Ranulf of Durham, John of Bath, Hervey of Bangor, Robert of Lincoln, and Roger elect of Salisbury; William de Werelwast, Waldric the chancellor, Grimbald the physician, the sewers, Eudes, Roger Bigod, and Hamon; Urse de Abetot, Walter Fitz-Richard, and Roger de Oilei the constable. 'Hoc actum est anno Dominicae Incarnationis M.C.V., indictione XIII., anno vero Henrici serenissimi regis V., in curia eiusdem regis apud Romesei.'[9]

115. Feb.–Mar. Notification to Maurice bishop of London, Hugh de Bocheland, sheriff of Hertfordshire, and all his lieges, that Richard, abbot of Ely, has deraigned against Ranulf, bishop of Durham, the manor of Haddenham 'in my court at Romsey, before me and my barons'. The witnesses are: the bishops, Robert of Lincoln, William Giffart of Winchester,[10] John of Bath, and Ralph of Chichester; Waldric the chancellor, David the chaplain, Evrard the chaplain, son of earl (Roger), John of Bayeux the chaplain, Thomas the chaplain, Audin the chaplain, the sewers, Eudes, Hamon, and Roger Bigot; Walter Fitz-Richard, Robert Malet, Henry de Port, Osbert the sheriff, Robert Peche, Hugh de Bocheland, Roger de Ouili, Peter de Valoignes, Geoffrey Ridel, Alfred of Lincoln,

---

[1] *Cal. of Chart. Rolls*, v. 363.

[2] Cart. Antiq., roll P, n. 15 (8); *ante*, xxiv. 427, n. 14.

[2] Chron. Ash Wednesday fell on 22 February.

[4] 'Waltero' (*sic*).   [5] Cf. *Cal. of Chart. Rolls*, iii. 310.

[6] Cf. Round's *Calendar*, no. 665.   [7] *Mon. Anglic.* v. 149 *b.*

[8] Cf. Round, *The King's Serjeants*, p. 188.

[9] *Chron. of Abingdon*, ii. 126.

[10] In the original charter William Giffard's description is clearly *ep'o Wintonie* and not *electo*, although he was not consecrated until more than two years later. See the facsimile of the charter, *ante*, xxvi. 488.

William Peverel of Dover, William Peverel of London, Harding Fitz-Alnod, and Edward the chamberlain ; ' apud Romesi, quinto anno coronationis Henrici regis '.[1]

116. Feb.–Mar. Writ addressed to William, sheriff of Oxford, in favour of the church of Abingdon, respecting a hide of land given by Drew de Andelci. It is attested by Waldric the chancellor and Grimbald the physician ; at Romsey.[2]

26 Mar. Pope Paschal II notifies Anselm that he has published a sentence of excommunication upon the count of Mortain and his accomplices for having impelled King Henry to the crime of investiture of ecclesiastics.[3]

2–8 Apr. In the last week of Lent the king lands at Barfleur.[4]

8 Apr. On Holy Saturday he reaches Carentan.[5]

9 Apr. Serlo bishop of Sées conducts the service on Easter Sunday at Carentan.[6]

13 Apr. Henry attacks and burns Bayeux. Prior to the sack of the town, Gontier d'Aunai, the constable, goes over to the king, bringing with him Robert Fitz-Hamon, whom he has released from imprisonment, in the hope of obtaining the king's favour.[7]

Later, the people of Caen, fearing a like fate to those of Bayeux, hasten to meet the king, with whom they make terms by a payment of money, and deliver the town to him.[8]

117. Mandate to Hugh de Bocheland to put Eudes the sewer in possession of three manors which belonged to William de Magnevill's town of Waltham. It is attested by Richard de Redvers ; at Caen.[9] [1105–7.]

The king arrives before Falaise. In an engagement which ensues before the town Roger of Gloucester is wounded,[10] and Robert Fitz-Hamon receives a dangerous wound in the head from the thrust of a pike, by which his reason becomes temporarily impaired.[11]

118. Notification to Samson bishop of Worcester and Walter sheriff of Gloucester, and the barons of Gloucestershire, of the gift and confirmation to the church of St. Peter of Gloucester of the manor of Coln (' Culna '), as Roger de Glocestra gave it. Witnesses : Girmund abbot of Winchelcumb, Roger de Glocestra, and Hugh Parvus.[12]

28 May–3 June. During Whitweek Henry and his brother Robert meet at Cintheaux, between Caen and Falaise. After negotiations extending over two days they part without having achieved anything.[13]

About this period David, brother of Edgar king of Scots, comes to England on a visit to his sister, Queen Matilda.[14]

22 July. At the king's desire Anselm comes to Laigle to meet him. They are reconciled, and the king restores to the archbishop the temporalities of his see.[15]

---

[1] Facsimile and transcript by the Rev. H. E. Salter, *ante*, xxvi. 487–9.
[2] *Chron. of Abingdon*, ii. 70. See nos. 122 and 166 below.
[3] Eadmer, p. 163.   [4] Orderic, iv. 204.
[5] *Ibid.*   [6] *Ibid.*   [7] *Ibid.* p. 219.   [8] *Ibid.*
[9] *Chartul. of Colchester*, i. 24.
[10] Orderic, iv. 220 ; W. Malm., *G. R.* ii. 475, 521 n.   See no. 131 below.
[11] W. Malm., *G. R.* ii. 475.   [12] *Ibid.* p. 521.   [13] Orderic, iv. 220.
[14] Roger of Wendover, *s. a.*   [15] Eadmer, pp. 165–6.

In August the king returns to England.[1]

119. Notification to Archbishop Anselm, Roger bishop of Salisbury, Robert Fitz-Hamon and Hugh de Bocheland, sheriffs, the barons and officers of London and Kent, of the grant of certain privileges to the abbey of St. Peter, Ghent. It is attested by Robert count of Meulan, Count Eustace (of Boulogne), William earl of Warenne, Earl David, and William de Aubigny ; at Westminster.[2]

120. 29 Aug. Notification to Robert bishop of Lincoln of a grant in favour of the church of St. Albans and Abbot Richard. It is attested by Waldric the chancellor, Robert count of Meulan, David the queen's brother, Stephen of Aumâle, and Haldene (the chamberlain ?) ; at St. Albans, on 4 [3] kalends of September.[4]

121. Notification to Robert bishop of Lincoln, Hugh de Bocheland, and the lieges of England of the grant to the monastery of St. Albans of an eight days' fair at St. Albans. It is attested by Waldric the chancellor, Roger Bigot, William de Aubigny, Nigel de Aubigny, William de Werelwast, and Audin the chaplain ; at St. Albans.[5] [1103–6.]

27 Sept. Robert Fitz-Hamon, Sibil his wife, and Mabel their daughter are present at the ordination of the monastery of Tewkesbury on 5 kalends of October in the year of the incarnation of our Lord 1105, ' quo eodem Henricus rex Anglorum destruxit Baiocas incendio '.[6]

Oct. William de Warelwast and Baldwin, a monk of Tournay, are respectively sent on behalf of the king and Anselm on a mission to Rome.[7]

121 A. Henry notifies Anselm that he has sent William de Warelwast to him after Michaelmas, to proceed to Rome as his envoy. It is attested by Waldric the chancellor ; at High Wycombe (' apud Wiccombam ').[8]

121 B. Writ addressed to Anselm directing him to send Baldwin the monk with William de Warelwast to Rome, in order that peace may be made between the king and the primate. It is attested by Waldric the chancellor, Robert count of Meulan, and Eudes the sewer ; at Pontefract.[9]

121 C. Notification to Gerard archbishop of York, Osbert the sheriff, and the barons (of Yorkshire) of the confirmation to the monks of Marmoutier of the gifts made to them by Ralph Paynel of the church of the Holy Trinity, York, and other possessions. It is attested by Ralph Paynel, Eudes the sewer, William de Aubigny and his brother, Nigel de Aubigny, Ralph de Roilly, Alan Fitz-Flahald, and Ranulf the treasurer ; at York.[10] [1101–6.]

121 D. Notification addressed generally of the confirmation to the church of the Holy Trinity, York, of all the churches, lands, and tithes given by Ralph Paynel (' Paganellus '). It is attested by Nigel de Aubigny, Robert de Brus, Hamon (' Simon ') the sewer, Ralph de Roilly (' de Rolliaco '), Alan Fitz-Fleald, and Ranulf ' our treasurer ' ; at York.[11] [Same as 121 C.]

[1] Hen. of Huntingdon, p. 235.   [2] Round, *Cal. of Documents, France*, no. 1377.
[3] The date is 3 kalends of September in *Mon. Anglic.* iii. 290 ; and Nichols's *Leicestershire*, ii (1), 24 note.
[4] Hist. MSS. Comm., *Duke of Rutland's MSS.*, iv. 98.
[5] *Cal. of Chart. Rolls*, iii. 20.   [6] *Mon. Anglic.* ii. 81 *b*.
[7] Eadmer, p. 171.
[8] Anselm, *Epistolae*, iv. 63 (Gerberon, p. 443).
[9] *Ibid.* p. 64 (Gerberon, p. 443).   [10] Round, *Cal. of Documents, France*, no. 1225.
[11] Patent Roll, 30 Edw. III, pt. 3, m. 13 ; *Mon. Anglic.* iv. 683 *b*, n. 5.

121 E. Writ addressed to Guy de Baileol prohibiting him from hunting in the forests of Ranulf bishop of Durham. It is attested by Waldric the chancellor ; at Barton upon Humber.[1]

122. Notification to Robert bishop of Lincoln, William the sheriff of Oxford, and the barons (of Oxfordshire) of the confirmation to Abbot Faritius and the church of Abingdon of a hide of land given by Drew de Andelei. It is attested by the queen and Geoffrey Peche ; at Aylesbury.[2] [1105–6.]

123. Mandate to William de Cahaines, the sheriff, and the monks of Peterborough (' Burg ') that no toll shall be taken for the stone carried for building the church of St. Edmund ; the ships which have been detained are to be released. It is attested by Peter de Valoignes ; at Brill (' Brohella ').[3] [1103–7.]

124. Writ addressed to Hugh de Bocheland, Aubrey (de Ver ?), and the barons of Berkshire in favour of Faritius, abbot of Abingdon. It is attested by Roger Bigod, (and is issued) by Walter Hosate ; at Brill.[4] [1101–7.]

125. 18 Oct. Notification to Robert bishop of Lincoln, William sheriff of Oxford, and the barons of Oxfordshire of the confirmation of a grant made by William de Curci, the king's sewer, to the monks of Abingdon. It is attested by Ranulf bishop of Durham, and Roger Bigod, (and is issued) by Geoffrey Peche ; at Cornbury on the day of St. Luke the Evangelist.[5]

126. Notification, addressed as above, of the confirmation to the same monastery of land which has been restored to the monks by Nigel de Oilli. It is attested by the queen, Eudes the sewer, William de Curci, Urse de Abetot, Robert Malet, and Aubrey de Ver; at Cornbury.[6] [1100–6.]

127. Notification to Sampson bishop of Worcester, Walter sheriff of Gloucestershire, and the barons of that county of the confirmation to Abbot Faritius and the monks of Abingdon of land in Dumbleton (near Winchcomb) given by Walter Fossatarius. It is attested by the bishops, Robert of Lincoln, and Ranulf of Durham ; Roger Bigod, David the queen's brother, Nigel de Oili, Roger de Oili, William de Hoctun, and Drew (' Drocus ') the huntsman ; at Cornbury.[7] [1105–7.]

128. Notification to Maurice bishop of London, Gilbert abbot of Westminster, Hugh de Bocheland, and the barons of London and Middlesex, of the confirmation to the monastery of Abingdon, in the time of abbot Faritius, of the church of Kensington with land there given by Aubrey de Ver (the elder), for the welfare of his deceased (and first-born) son, Geoffrey. It is attested by the queen, Eudes the sewer, William de Curci, Nigel de Oilei, Urse de Abetot, and Robert Malet ; at Cornbury.[8] [1100–6.]

129. Notification to Roger bishop of Salisbury, Hugh de Bocheland,

---

[1] Leland, *Collectanea*, ii. 389 ; from the manuscript account of the church of Lindisfarne.

[2] *Chron. of Abingdon*, ii. 68. See no. 116 above and no. 166 below.

[3] Vet. Reg. of St. Edmund's, Add. MS. 14849, fo. 33 *d* ; Chartul. of St. Edmund's, Camb. Univ. Libr., fo. 25, n. 43. See no. 284 below.

[4] *Chron. of Abingdon*, ii. 90.   [5] *Ibid.* p. 54.   [6] *Ibid.* p. 74.

[7] *Ibid.* p. 105.   [8] *Ibid.* p. 56   *Mon. Anglic.* iv. 100, n. 3.

and the barons of Berkshire, of the grant to Abbot Faritius and the monks of Abingdon of the custody of the wood of Cumnor and Bagley. It is attested by the bishops, Robert of Lincoln and Ranulf of Durham, Roger Bigod, Nigel de Oilli, David the queen's brother, Roger de Oilli, Geoffrey Ridel, Drew the huntsman, and William de Hocton; at Cornbury.[1] [1105–7.]

130. Writ addressed to Archbishop Gerard, Osbert the sheriff, Helgot the sheriff, and the barons of Yorkshire and Nottinghamshire, in favour of the monks of Blythe. It is attested by Nigel de Oili, and is issued by Carbonell the staller (*stabularius*) ; at Cornbury.[2] [1102–8.]

130A. Letter from Henry informing Anselm of the news of a papal schism at Rome and consulting him as to whether the legates, William and Baldwin de Tournay, should go to Rome, as intended, or remain until the situation is clearer. It is attested by Robert bishop of Lincoln and Robert count of Meulan (no place named).[3]

131. Notification to Sampson bishop of Worcester and Walter sheriff of Gloucester of the confirmation to the church of St. Peter of Gloucester of the manor of Coln (' Culna '), as Roger de Gloucester gave it and as he held it, and of the exchange of the monks' garden, in which the king's tower stands, as Walter sheriff of Gloucester made livery to them. Signatories : the king, Queen Matilda, Waldric the chancellor, the bishop of Durham, Robert bishop of Lincoln, Richard de Reveis (*recte* Reveriis), David, Robert count of Meulan.[4]

132. Notification to Roger bishop of Salisbury, Hugh de Bocheland, Aubrey (de Ver), and the barons of the shire-moot [5] of Berkshire of a grant in favour of Pain Peverel. It is attested by Waldric the chancellor ; at Handborough.[6] [1103–6.]

133. Writ addressed to Ulger, Geoffrey de Borton,[7] and the foresters of Shropshire in favour of the abbot of Shrewsbury. It is attested by Robert bishop of Lincoln, (and is issued) by Bernard the chaplain ; at Handborough.[8] [1101–7.]

134. Writ addressed to W(illiam) the sheriff of Oxford to permit the church of Abingdon to have its customs. It is attested by Urse de Abetot ; at Wallingford.[9] [1102–10.]

Dec. Before Christmas Robert of Bellême comes over seas from Normandy to treat with Henry.[10]

About 200 priests come to London and petition the king at his palace (of Westminster) for redress of their grievances.[11]

25 Dec. At Christmas the king holds his court at Westminster. During the week Robert of Bellême returns to Normandy, unreconciled with Henry.[12]

---

[1] *Chron. of Abingdon*, ii. 113 ; *Mon. Anglic.* i. 523, n. 24.

[2] Chartul. of Blythe, Harl. MS. 3759, fo. 99 *d*. Another writ on fo. 120 is similarly addressed and attested.

[3] *Epistolae*, iv. 67 (Gerberon, p. 444).

[4] *Notes and Queries*, 12 S., v. 17 ; *Chartul. of St. Peter's, Gloucester*, i. 235.

[5] ' de comitatu '.   [6] ' Apud Hanebergam ' : *Cal. of Chart. Rolls*, iv. 290.

[7] ' Gorton ' : *Cal. of Chart. Rolls*, ii. 82.

[8] *Ibid.* iv. 286.   [9] *Chron. of Abingdon*, ii. 80.   [10] Chron.

[11] Eadmer, p. 173.   [12] Chron.

135. Writ addressed to Henry earl of Warwick and William sheriff (ot Oxford) in favour of a tenant of the monastery of Abingdon. It is attested by Waldric the chancellor and Grimbald the physician; at Westminster, at Christmas.[1] [1102–3 or 1105.]

136. Notification to Sampson bishop (of Worcester), Walter sheriff of Gloucester, and the barons of Gloucestershire, of the grant to the church of St. Martin of Troarn of lands, late of Mabel the countess (of Shrewsbury), given by the king's father for the health of her soul. It is attested by Waldric the chancellor and Robert count of Meulan; at Westminster, at Christmas.[2] [Same as 135.]

137. Writ addressed to all sheriffs and ministers of England in favour of the monastery of St. Augustine, Canterbury, directing that the serjeants of the abbey shall have acquittance of toll on what they purchase for the use of the monks. It is attested by Waldric the chancellor; at Westminster, at Christmas.[3] [Same as 136.]

During the year Henry imposes levies of money upon both the clergy and the laity for the expenses of his past and projected expeditions to Normandy.[4]

1106.

About this time Archbishop Gerard, and the bishops, Robert of Chester, Herbert of Norwich, Ralph of Chichester, Sampson of Worcester, and William elect of Winchester address a letter to Anselm, begging him to return to his see.[5]

Anselm bids them await the return of the mission to Rome, declaring that he cannot yet return because the king would not consent to his doing so.[6]

138. Writ addressed to G. the chaplain,[7] R(obert) de Lacy, and Richard son of Gotse, directing that the monks of Blythe shall have the tithes of Laughton(-en-le-Morthen) as fully as they had them on the day on which the king received to his own use the castle of Blythe, and as Roger de Builli granted those tithes to them. It is attested by Robert Fitz-Hamon and Waldric the chancellor; at Westminster.[8] [1103–Aug. 1106.]

139. Notification to all sheriffs and ministers of the grant to the church of Ely of acquittance of toll. It is attested by Roger Bigot; at Sawtry.[9] [Same as 138.]

140. Another writ, in the same terms, for the church of Ely is attested by W(aldric) the chancellor, at Sawtry.[9] [Same as 138.]

141. Writ addressed to Nicholas sheriff of Stafford, summoning him ' ut in die in initium Quadragesime sis ad curiam nostram ' if he desires to deraign the land of Cotes against the abbot of Burton. It is attested by W(aldric) the chancellor, Henry earl of Warwick, and W. de [blank]; at (King's) Cliffe.[10]

---

[1] *Chron. of Abingdon*, ii. 93.   [2] Round, *Cal. of Documents, France*, no. 469.

[3] *Dep. Keeper's Rep.* xxx, app. 6, p. 198.

[4] Chron.; Eadmer, pp. 171–5.   [5] *Ibid.* p. 173.   [6] *Ibid.* p. 174.

[7] Possibly an error for ' Gerard the archbishop '.

[8] Chartul. of Blythe; Harl. MS. 3759, fo. 120.

[9] Lib. Eliensis; Bentham, *Hist. of the Church of Ely*, app. 18*.

[10] ' Apud Clivam ': *Chartul. of Burton* (Salt Arch. Soc.), v (1), 8. See no. 204 below.

142. Writ addressed to Archbishop G(erard), Bishop R(anulf), the sheriffs, barons, and lieges of England, directing that the land and men of St. Cuthbert and his monks shall be quit of shires and hundreds ; and that if they have been dispossessed of any property after the death (*sic*) of Bishop R. they shall be reinstated. It is attested by Robert bishop of Lincoln, Robert count of Meulan, Roger Bigot, and Urse de Abetot ; at (King's) Cliffe.[1] [1104–7.]

1–7 Feb. Henry is at Northampton before Lent. Here his brother Robert comes to petition for the restoration of the lands in Normandy which Henry has taken from him. His request is not granted and he returns to Normandy threatening reprisals.[2]

142 A. Henry notifies Anselm that his brother, Count Robert, has interviewed him in England and has returned satisfied ; that he himself will be at a seaport on Ascension Day (3 May) ready to pass over seas ; that meanwhile Anselm shall decide, when William de Warelwast and the other legates return from Rome, whether they cross to England before his passage thence, or remain with Anselm, pending their meeting to discuss matters. Witness : W(aldric) the chancellor ; at Northampton.[3]

143. Notification to the justices, foresters, and ministers of Essex, of a grant in favour of the monks of Colchester. It is attested by Robert bishop of Lincoln, William Giffard, elect of Winchester, Robert count of Meulan, Henry earl of Warwick, Roger Bigot, Gilbert FitzRichard, and Roger his brother ; at Northampton.[4] [1101–7.]

144. Writ addressed to Hugh de Bocheland, Godric, and the barons of Berkshire in favour of the church of Abingdon, and indefinitely postponing a plea about a ' hay ' at Winkfield brought against the church by Godric, the reeve of Windsor. It is attested by Roger Bigod and Grimbald the physician ; at Northampton.[5] [1101–7.]

145. Writ addressed to Roger Bigot, and the ministers of Suffolk, for the men of the abbey of Ramsey at Lawshall. It is attested by Waldric the chancellor ; at Northampton.[6] [1103–6.]

146. Writ addressed to Robert bishop of Lincoln, and Osbert the sheriff, directing them to restore to the abbot of Ramsey ½ carucate of land in Threckingham[7] (co. Linc.). It is attested by Roger Bigot and Urse de Abetot ; at Brigstock.[8] [1101–7.]

147. The queen addresses a charter to the abbot of Peterborough, Earl Simon, Robert de Pavilli the sheriff, Michael de Hamesclape, and the barons of Northamptonshire, granting the manor of Tixover (co. Rutland) to Robert bishop of Lincoln. It is attested by Waldric the chancellor, Bernard the chaplain, Eudes the sewer, William Pevrell of Nottingham, and Michael de Hamesclape ; at Rockingham.[9] [1104–6.]

148. Notification to the abbot of Peterborough, Earl Simon, Michael

---

[1] Durham Treasury, 2da 1^ae *Regalium*, H. i, n. 8 ; *Journ. of the Brit. Arch. Assoc.* xxix. 256.

[2] Chron. ; Florence of Worcester.   [3] *Epistolae*, iv. 77 (Gerberon, p. 446).

[4] *Chartul. of Colchester*, i. 20.   [5] *Chron. of Abingdon*, ii. 87.

[6] *Chartul. of Ramsey*, i. 249, n. 179. Cf. *ibid.* n. 180.

[7] Cf. *Domesday Book* i. 346 b ; *Chartul. of Ramsey*, i. 258, 281 ; ii. 262.

[8] ' Apud Brichestoche ' : *Chartul. of Ramsey*, i. 237.

[9] *Cal. of Chart. Rolls*, iv. 102.

de Hamesclape, Robert de Pavilli, and the lieges of Northamptonshire, of the confirmation of the queen's grant of the manor of Tixover (as above). It is attested by W(aldric) the chancellor, Eudes the sewer, and William Peverel of Nottingham ; at Rockingham.[1] [1104–6.]

149. Writ addressed to Robert Gernun to permit the tenant of the land (at Colnbrook) which the said Robert had given to the queen, who gave it to Abingdon,[2] to enjoy his land and property in peace. It is attested by the queen and Robert count of Meulan ; at Rockingham.[3] [1104–7.]

150. Writ addressed to Robert bishop of Lincoln and Osbert the sheriff in favour of Rumfare [4] of Lincoln. It is attested by the queen, Nigel de Oilei, and Osbert the sheriff ; at Rockingham.[5] [1100–15.]

151. Notification to Osbert the sheriff, the barons and burgesses of Lincoln of the royal grant to Bishop Robert and the canons of Lincoln of the king's garden (*vinia*) in Lincoln. It is attested by W(aldric) the chancellor, Eudes the sewer, and Urse de Abetot ; at Stamford.[6] [1103–6.]

152. Writ addressed to Roger Bigot, Ralph Passeleu, and all of Norfolk and Suffolk, notifying them that the manor of Thorpe (St. Andrew) is quit of aids and scots, as it was when it was in the king's hands and in his demesne. It is attested by Robert bishop of Lincoln ; at Norwich.[7] [1104–7.]

153. Notification to Maurice bishop of London, Hugh de Bocheland, and the barons and lieges of Essex and Hertfordshire, granting conditionally to Eudes the sewer the manors in Sawbridgeworth, Wealdham and Walden, to hold until William de Magnevill shall pay to him his debt of £2,210 3*s.*, which he owes to the king. It is attested by the queen, Waldric [8] the chancellor, Robert count of Meulan, and Richard de Retvers ; at Norwich.[9] [1103–6.]

154. In a record of the foundation of Norwich cathedral with its priory of monks by the grant of King William, King Henry his brother, Anselm archbishop of Canterbury, &c., it is stated that the ordinations were signed with the cross by Henry the king, Matilda the queen, Waldric the chancellor, Roger (Bigot),[10] Eudes the sewer,[11] Robert Malethe, Nigel (de Oilli) the constable, and William (de Aubigny) the butler.[12] No place named. [1103–6.]

155. Writ addressed to Herbert bishop of Norwich, Roger Bigot, Ralph Passelewe, and the lieges of Norfolk and Suffolk notifying them that the land which Peter of Bourges (*Bituricensis*) held of St. Edmund's shall be in the demesne of St. Edmund's. It is attested by Roger de Courcelles ; at St. Edmund's (Bury).[13] [1104–7.]

156. Writ addressed to Bishop Herbert,[14] R(oger) Bigot, R(alph) Passelewe, the lieges of Norfolk and Suffolk, and Otho the goldsmith of

---

[1] *Mon. Anglic.* vi. 1271, n. 9.   [2] Cf. no. 102 above and no. 174 below.
[3] *Chron. of Abingdon*, ii. 99.   [4] Cf. *Cal. of Chart. Rolls*, iii. 115–16, 120.
[5] *Cal. of Pat. Rolls*, 1396–9, p. 75.   [6] *Mon. Anglic.* vi. 1272, n. 21.
[7] *Cal. of Chart. Rolls*, iv. 439.
[8] ' Waltero ' in the printed chartulary.   [9] *Chartul. of Colchester*, i. 22.
[10] Manuscript torn ; supplied from Rot. Cott. ii. 21.   [11] *Ibid.*
[12] Cott. MS., Aug. ii. 103 ; Rot. Cott. ii. 21.
[13] Chartul. of St. Edmund's, Camb. Univ. Lib., fo. 24 *d* (38).
[14] ' Herv.' in manuscript.

London, notifying them of the king's grant that St. Edmund shall have his moneyer at St. Edmund's (Bury) with all customs of money, as he had them in the time of the king's father, and as his brother, King William, granted by his writ (*breve*). It is attested by Roger de Courcelles; at St. Edmund's (Bury).[1] [1104–7.]

157. A writ of general protection for the abbey of St. Edmund's is attested by Urse de Abetot; at St. Edmund's (Bury).[2] [1100–10.]

158. Notification to Maurice bishop of London, Hugh de Bocheland, the barons and lieges of Essex of the grant to the canons of Colchester of tithes of the royal manor of Hatfield. It is attested by the queen, Robert bishop of Lincoln, and Eudes the sewer; at Bergholt ('Berchold').[3] [1102–7.]

159. A charter of similar purport to the last is addressed to Bishop Maurice, Hugh de Bocheland, Alfred (of   ) and the barons of Essex. It is attested by Queen Matilda, Robert bishop of Lincoln, Eudes the sewer, Roger Bigot, William Malet, and William Baiard; at Bergholt.[4] [1102–7.]

160. Writ addressed to Robert bishop of Chester, Nicholas sheriff of Stafford, and Richard de Belmeis, sheriff of Shropshire, prohibiting them from summoning the monks of St. Rémi of Rheims to hundred and shire courts save by their reeves or men. It is attested by Henry earl of Warwick; at Waltham.[5] [1100–May 1108.]

12 Mar. On St. Gregory's day the king, being at Tunbridge, receives Anselm's protest against his acceptance of fines from those priests who had neglected to put away their concubines, in accordance with the edict of the London synod.[6] He promises to send his reply to the archbishop after consultation with his barons at a council intended to be held on Ascension Day (3 May).[7]

25 Mar. At Easter the king holds his court at Bath.[8]

161. Writ addressed to Archbishop Gerard, Osbert the sheriff, the barons and lieges of Yorkshire, in favour of Hugh abbot of Selby. It is attested by Waldric the chancellor; at Alveston.[9] [1103–6.]

162. The king now sends a reply to the primate's letter and intimates that it is his intention to cross to Normandy ere long. His letter is issued by Waldric the chancellor; at Marlborough.[10]

163. Writ addressed to Hugh de Bocheland and all sheriffs and ministers of England directing that the goods of the monastery of Abingdon, bought or sold by their officials, shall be quit of toll, &c. It is attested by the chancellor, at Marlborough.[11] [1103–6.]

164. Writ addressed to the bishop of Winchester, the sheriff, barons and lieges of Hampshire, in favour of the abbey of Romsey, and granting

---

[1] Add. MS. 14847, fo. 33 *d*; *ante*, xxiv. 427 (13).

[2] Chartul. of St. Edmund's, Camb. Univ. Libr., fo. 28 *d* (107).

[3] *Mon. Anglic.* vi. 105.   [4] *Cal. of Pat. Rolls*, 1422–9, p. 414.

[5] *Mon. Anglic.* vi. 1099; *ibid.* p. 1043, n. 7.

[6] Eadmer, p. 176.   [7] *Ibid.*   [8] Chron.

[9] 'Apud Allouestan': *Chartul. of Selby* (Yorks. Rec. Soc.), n. 29.

[10] Eadmer, p. 177.

[11] *Chron. of Abingdon*, ii. 79. Cf. Chartul. of St. Peter's, Westminster, fo. 76; Robinson, *Gilbert Crispin*, p. 149.

licence to Stephen son of Arard to give a rent of 20*s.* to the monastery with his daughter. It is attested by Waldric the chancellor, Ralph the sewer, and Geoffrey the chamberlain ; at Ludgershall (' Lotegarsal ').[1] [1103–6.]

13 May. On Whitsunday the king is at Salisbury, ' because he would not hold a court on his departure over sea '.[2]

165. Writ, addressed to Roger bishop of Salisbury, A(iulf) the chamberlain, and the lieges of Dorset, notifying them of the confirmation to the abbot of Abbotsbury of his liberties and customs ; and mandate to Bishop Roger and Alfred of Lincoln to protect the abbot. It is attested by Alfred of Lincoln and Croc the huntsman ; at Salisbury.[3] [1100–16.]

166. On Whitsunday in the sixth year of Henry's reign Richard earl of Chester and the countess Ermentrude his mother, being at Abingdon, confirm to Abbot Faritius and the monastery the hide of land at Weston, co. Oxon., which Drew de Andelei had given.[4]

c. June. William de Warelwast and Baldwin of Tournay, the envoys sent to Paschal on behalf of the king and Anselm, return by way of Rouen, bearing the pope's letters dated 10 kalends of April (23 March).[5]

Warelwast makes his report to the king, and after a few days' delay hastens to Bec to deliver the royal mandate to Anselm, recalling him to England. He finds Anselm ill.[6]

c. July. Commencing his journey to England Anselm reaches Jumièges. There he is again seized with illness which prevents the continuation of his journey for about one month. In the meantime messengers arrive, who inform him of the king's intention to cross to Normandy in a brief time (' in proximo '). Anselm then returns to Bec, where he again becomes so seriously ill that his death is hourly expected. He recovers unexpectedly.[7]

Henry directs a letter to Anselm expressing his grief at the latter's ill health and announcing his early arrival in Normandy. Witness : Waldric (the chancellor) ; at Windsor.[8]

Before August the king goes over sea to Normandy.[9]

During the course of this year the king commissions Robert bishop of Lincoln, Ralph Basset, Geoffrey Ridel, Ranulf Meschin, and Peter de Valoignes to go to York (and Ripon) and inquire what were the customs of the church of St. Peter, York, which Archbishop Gerard alleged had been much infringed by Osbert the sheriff of Yorkshire. To this end the king's justices called before them the most prudent Englishmen of that county, whom they caused to swear by the fealty which they owed to the king to declare the truth. These were Uctreth son of Alwin, Gamel son of Swartecol, Gamel son of Grim, Norman the priest, William son of Ulf, Freuger (?) the priest, Uctreth son of Turkill, Norman son of Basing, Thurstan son of Turmot, Gamel son of Orm, Morcar son of Ligulf, and Ulvet son of Forne, who, by right of inheritance, was the lagaman of the city of York, and was at that time also prefect (?). These testified before

---

[1] *Cal. of Chart. Rolls*, ii. 102.   [2] Chron.

[3] *Cal. of Chart. Rolls*, ii. 132. See no. 248.

[4] *Chron. of Abingdon*, ii. 69. See nos. 116 and 122.

[5] Eadmer, pp. 177–9.   [6] *Ibid.* pp. 181–2.   [7] *Ibid.*

[8] *Epistolae*, iv. 75 (Gerberon, p. 445).   [9] Chron.

the king's justices, Ansketil de Bulemer, reeve of the North Riding, being their interpreter, what they remembered to be the customs of the church of York.[1]

7 Aug. The bishop of Lincoln and other justices of the king are said to have dealt with judicial matters at York on Tuesday next after the feast of the translation of St. Thomas, A.D. 1106, being the sixth year of the reign of King Henry, brother of William, son of the Conqueror.[2]

15 Aug. On the feast of the Assumption the king comes to Bec, and after mass he effects a final agreement with Anselm touching the matters which have not been decided by Paschal's letter and declaration.[3]

The primate then passes over to England by way of Dover.[4]

Aug. Henry, supported by many of the nobles of Normandy and Anjou with the power of England and Brittany, lays siege to the castle of Tinchebrai.[5]

Aug.–Sept. Reginald de Warenne and Robert de Stutevill, the younger, hold the castle of St. Pierre-sur-Dive against Henry on behalf of Duke Robert. The king takes the fortress by assault and makes them prisoners.[6]

28 Sept. Henry defeats Duke Robert, Robert of Bellême, William of Mortain, Robert de Stutevill, the elder, William de Ferrers, and William Crispin in a pitched battle fought at Tinchebrai.[7] Robert of Bellême escapes ; the others named are taken prisoners, namely the duke, by Waldric the chancellor,[8] and Eadger Atheling, who had joined the duke not long before.[9] William de Aubigny, the Breton, greatly distinguishes himself.[10]

Oct. At the suggestion of Duke Robert the king sends William de Ferrers to secure the possession of the castle of Falaise, whither he himself proceeds shortly after.[11] Later he moves to Rouen, where Hugh de Nonant, by the duke's command, surrenders the castle.[12]

In mid-October the king holds a great council at Lisieux. He takes into his own hands all the Norman fees which had belonged to his father.[13] From this date Henry adopts the style of ' King of the English and duke of the Normans '.

167. 7 Nov. In the year 1106, indiction 15, 7 ides of November, a dispute or claim is terminated before Henry king of the English, and now duke of the Normans, at Rouen, in the chamber of Archbishop William and in his presence, between the monks of St. Taurin (at Evreux) and the church of Fécamp. Besides the king, there are present at this cause or plea, on behalf of the king : William, archbishop of Rouen, the bishops, Turold of Bayeux, Gilbert of Evreux, William Giffard of Winchester, and Ranulf of Durham ; the abbots, Helgot of St. Ouen, Arnulf of Troarn,

[1] Southwell Lib. Alb. p. 18 ; Thoroton, *Hist. of Notts.* (ed. Throsby), iii. 77 ; *Memorials of Ripon* (Surtees Soc.), i. 34. See no. 239 below.

[2] *Memorials of Ripon* (Surtees Soc.), i. 58.   [3] Eadmer, p. 182.

[4] *Ibid.* p. 183.   [5] Roger of Wendover.

[6] Orderic, iv. 222–3 ; *Annals of Winchester*, ii. 42. Cf. *Gallia Christiana*, xii, instr., col. 155.

[7] Orderic, iv. 226–31 ; Florence of Worcester ; Eadmer, p. 184.

[8] Orderic, iv. 230.   [9] Chron.

[10] Roger of Wendover ; Matth. Paris, *Chron. Mai.* ii. 132.

[11] Orderic, iv. 231–2.   [12] *Ibid.* p. 233.   [13] *Ibid.* p. 234.

Urse of Jumièges, Walter of the Holy Trinity of the Mount ; Benedict, Fulbert, and Richard, archdeacons of the church of Rouen, and Robert archdeacon of Evreux ; of the barons : Robert count of Meulan, Richard de Redvers, William de Aubigny, Walter son of Richard de Vernun, and Waldric, who then was the king's chancellor.[1]

167 A. William archbishop of Rouen confirms, with Henry's assent, to St. Mary's, Bec, the church of Notre-Dame of Ermentrudisvilla, as Abbot William and the monks of the same place deraigned it in the chapter of Notre-Dame of Rouen before the archbishop, bishops, and barons of Normandy, namely Turold bishop of Bayeux, Turgis bishop of Avranches, Robert of Bellême, Robert count of Meulan, Eustace (count) of Boulogne, Henry count of Eu, and the archdeacons, Fulbert, Benedict, Richard, and Ursell.[2]

168. 30 Nov. Notification to Archbishop Anselm, Herbert bishop of Norwich, Roger Bigot, (Robert) abbot of St. Edmund's, and the barons of Suffolk, of the confirmation to the Benedictine nunnery of Malling of the gift of the manor of Cornard made by Robert Fitz-Hamon with his daughter. It is attested by Waldric the chancellor, Hamon the sewer, William de Aubigny, and William Peverel of Dover ; at Rouen, on the feast of St. Andrew.[3]

1107.

Jan. The king holds a council of the barons at Falaise.[4]

6 Jan. Eadgar, king of Scots, dies on 8 ides of January. He is succeeded by his brother, Alexander.[5]

After 24 Feb. Waldric, the late chancellor, is consecrated bishop of Laon.[6]

Mar. The king holds a council at Lisieux, whereat, by the advice of his barons, he publishes edicts for the better preservation of order in Normandy and for the remedy of the late disorders.[7]

John archdeacon of Sées, who was a refugee in England in 1106, is appointed bishop of Lisieux.[8] Possibly at this time Richard son of Samson, bishop of Worcester, is appointed bishop of Bayeux.

Mar. Robert Fitz-Hamon dies ' diebus Marcii anno gratie M.C.VII. regis Henrici primi, scilicet, anno septimo '.[9]

Mar.–Apl. Henry returns to England during Lent.[10]

169. Notification to Richard de Belmeis (' Belmers '), the reeve of Chichester, and the barons of Sussex, of the grant to the church of Chichester of an eight days' fair to be held on the days which shall be fixed by Bishop

---

[1] *Gallia Christiana*, xi, instr., p. 127. Cf. Haskins, *Norman Institutions*, p. 87.

[2] Archives of the Seine-Inférieure ; MS. Lat. 13905, fo. 18 d ; Haskins, *Norman Institutions*, p. 293.

[3] *Cal. of Chart. Rolls*, v. 56, n. 7 ; *Mon. Anglic.* iii. 384. Cf. Davis, *ante*, xxvi. 88.   [4] Orderic, iv. 269.

[5] Florence of Worcester. ' On the ides of January (13th) ' : Chron. His obit was kept at Durham on 5 ides January (9th) : *Liber Vitae*, p. 149.

[6] Guibert of Nogent, iii. 4 ; *ante*, ii. 109–10.

[7] Orderic, iv. 269.   [8] *Ibid.* p. 273.   [9] *Mon. Anglic.* ii. 60 b.

[10] Chron. ; Eadmer, p. 184 ; Hen. of Huntingdon, p. 236.

Ralph. It is attested by Ranulf the chancellor, and Robert count of Meulan; at Portsmouth.[1]

Robert count of Meulan at this time obtains a grant of the earldom of Leicester with the third penny of the county.[2]

170. A charter is issued in favour of the abbey of Tewkesbury confirming the gifts made by Robert Fitz-Hamon. It is subscribed by the king, Waldric (sic) the chancellor, Archbishop Gerard, the bishops, Robert of Lincoln, Samson of Worcester, William of Exeter, Roger of Salisbury and Urban of Llandaff; the abbots, (Herlwin) of Glastonbury, Hugh (of St. Augustine's, Canterbury?), Gormund (of Winchcomb), Nigel (of Burton), and Pharisius (of Abingdon); Robert count of Meulan, Thomas the king's chaplain, Robert Fitz-Nigel, Humphrey de Bohun, Hamon the sewer, and Roger de Pistris (sic): 'Facta est hec carta anno ab origine mundi vᵒcccᵒxiᵒ (sic),[3] ab incarnatione Domini Mᵒ centesimo viiᵒ, apud Wintoniam.' [4] [Spurious.]

171. Notification to William bishop of Exeter and the barons and lieges of Devonshire, of the confirmation to St. Nicholas's, Exeter, of the church of South Tawton, and of the gift made by Robert Foliot of the church of North Tawton. It is attested by Roger bishop of Salisbury, Robert bishop of Lincoln, W(aldric?) the chancellor, and Gilbert de Aquila; at Winchester.[5] [Spurious.]

14 Apr. At Easter the king holds his court at Windsor.[6] A conference with Anselm is postponed until the Whitsuntide court, pending the return of William de Warelwast and Baldwin of Tournay from Troyes, to which place they had been summoned by Paschal.[7] On the same day (18 kalends of May) Norman the prior founds a monastery in Christ's Church, London.[8]

172. Notification to Robert earl of Leicester,[9] Ranulf Meschin, Osbert the sheriff, and the lieges of Lincolnshire, of the confirmation to the church of Lincoln for a prebend of certain houses in Lincoln, which Robert de Stutevill gave, to be held as freely as Hugh Fitz-Baldric held them in the time of William I. It is attested by the queen, Robert earl of Leicester, Earl Henry, Roger Bigot, and William de Aubigny; at Windsor.[10] [April– Sept. 1107.]

21–5 May. A council is held at Troyes by pope Paschal.[11]

2 June. At Whitsuntide the king holds his court at Westminster.[12] Anselm is unable to be present, being detained by sickness at Bury St. Edmund's until the octave (9 June). A day is given him on the kalends of August (1 Aug.) to meet the king.[13]

---

[1] *Cal. of Chart. Rolls*, iv. 440; *Hist. MSS. Comm., Var. Collections*, i. 181.

[2] See Orderic, iv. 168–9; G. E. C., *The Complete Peerage*, v. 40, and note g.

[3] recte 'vM ' cᵒ xiᵒ'.

[4] *Cal. of Chart. Rolls*, ii. 490; *Mon. Anglic.* ii. 66; *Dep. Keeper's Rep.* xxx, app. p. 204; cf. another confirmation, *ibid.* p. 203, where the names of the witnesses occur in different order.   [5] *Chartul. of St. Nicholas*, Vitell. D. ix, fo. 28.

[6] Chron.   [7] *Eadmer*, pp. 184–5.   [8] *Flores Histor.* ii. 40.

[9] Cf. Orderic, iv. 169. This description of Robert count of Meulan removes Mr. Round's doubts as to the count ever having been styled 'earl of Leicester'. See *Dict. of Nat. Biogr.*, s. t. 'Beaumont'.   [10] *Mon. Anglic.* vi. 1274, n. 39.

[11] Mas Latrie, *Trésor de Chronologie*, cols. 1087, 1289.

[12] Chron.   [13] Eadmer, p. 185.

173. Notification to the bishop of Salisbury, W(alter) the sheriff, the barons and lieges of Wiltshire, of the confirmation to the abbess and church of Romsey of lands given by William Escuet with his daughters. It is attested by Count Eustace, David the queen's [1] brother, Urse de Abetot, and Walter Hosate ; at Westminster, at Whitsuntide.[2] [1104, 1107-9.]

174. Notification to Robert bishop of Lincoln, Nigel de Oili, Hugh de Bocheland, William sheriff of Oxford, the barons and lieges of Oxfordshire and Buckinghamshire, of the confirmation to the monks of Abingdon of certain gifts made by William Fitz-Aiulf, Robert Fitz-Hamon, Miles Crispin, and Robert Gernun.[3] It is attested by the bishops, William of Winchester and Roger of Salisbury ; the sewers, Eudes and Hamon ; [4] Roger Bigod, William de Curci, Nigel de Oili, and Roger Fitz-Richard ; at Westminster, at Whitsuntide.[5]

175. A confirmation to Abingdon of a gift made by Robert Fitz-Hamon is attested by William bishop of Winchester, the sewers, Eudes and Hamon ; Roger Bigot, Roger Fitz-Richard, and William de Curci ; at Westminster, at Whitsuntide ; Robert Bloet being bishop of Lincoln and William sheriff of Oxfordshire.[6]

176. Writ addressed to Archbishop Gerard, Osbert the sheriff of Yorkshire (' Euerwicsira '), and the barons of Yorkshire, notifying them of an exchange of lands in Yorkshire made by the king with Robert de Brus. It is attested by Robert count of Meulan,[7] Nigel de Aubigny, Roger Fitz-Richard, and David the queen's brother ; at Windsor, at Whitsuntide.[8] [1104 or 1107.]

177. Writ addressed to the sheriffs of Yorkshire and Northumberland, notifying them of the confirmation to St. Oswin's, and the monks of Tynemouth, of their court and customs, to hold as fully as earl Robert had them before his forfeiture. It is attested by Peter de Valoignes ; at Westminster, at Whitsuntide.[9] [Same as 173.]

178. Queen Matilda notifies Roger Picot of her grant to St. Alban and St. Oswin of Tynemouth, and Abbot Richard of the land of Archil Morel. The writ is attested by Bernard (the queen's) chancellor, at London.[10] [1102-c. 1107.]

16 June. Richard, abbot of Ely, dies on 16 kalends of July.[11]

179. Writ addressed to Archbishop Gerard, Robert de Lacy, the sheriff, and Roger Picot, confirming the grant made by Queen Matilda to St. Albans of the land of Archil Morel. It is attested by Queen Matilda ; at Ludgershall.[12] [1101-8.]

180. Notification to Robert bishop of Lincoln, Osbert the sheriff, and the lieges of Lincolnshire of the confirmation of an agreement, made between the abbot of Selby and Nigel de Aubigny, touching the land of

---

[1] ' fratre Reginaldi ' incorrectly in *Cal. of Chart. Rolls,* ii. 103. [2] *Ibid.*
[3] Cf. nos. 102, 149. [4] ' Raimero ' : *Chron. of Abingdon,* ii. 107.
[5] *Ibid.* [6] *Ibid.* p. 96.
[7] ' comite Deivell ' : *Cal. of Pat. Rolls.*
[8] *Cal. of Pat. Rolls,* 1377-81, p. 319.
[9] *Mon. Anglic.* iii. 313, n. 8. See a writ similarly issued and attested in *Hist. of Northumb.* (ed. Craster), viii. 55, n. 4.
[10] Gibson, *Tynemouth Priory,* ii, app., n. 19. [11] *Mon. Anglic.* i. 462.
[12] Craster, *Hist. of Northumb.* viii. 54 n.

Crowle, co. Lincoln. It is attested by the count of Meulan, at Ludgershall? ('apud Lod .. .').[1] [1100–15.]

181. Notification to Ranulf Meschin, Osbert the sheriff, and the barons of Lincolnshire of a grant in favour of Robert bishop of Lincoln and his church of St. Mary, Lincoln. It is attested by Eudes the sewer, Roger Bigot, Hamon the sewer, Urse de Abetot, and Osbert the sheriff; at Cirencester ('apud Cirecestria').[2] [1100–7.]

182. 24 June. Notification to Ranulf bishop of Durham, Roger Picot, and the lieges and ministers of Northumberland of a grant to Richard D'Orival ('de Aurea Valle'), the king's chaplain, of certain churches in Northumberland. It is attested by Robert bishop of Lincoln, William de Werlewast, Evrard son of earl (Roger), and Thomas the chaplain; at Cirencester, on the Nativity of St. John the Baptist.[3] [1104 or 1106–7.]

183. Notification to Ranulf bishop of Durham, and his barons and ministers, of the grant to St. Oswin and the monks of Tynemouth, of Tynemouth with the church and other possessions. It is attested by Queen Matilda; at Cirencester ('[apud Cire]cestriam').[4] [1104–16.]

184. Writ, addressed generally, directing that the men of the monks of Gloucester, their victuals and property, shall be quit of toll, custom, and passage. It is attested by Ranulf the chancellor; at Cirencester.[5] [1107–16, 1120–2.]

185. Notification to Richard bishop of Bayeux and the chapter that Godfrey the priest has deraigned his church of St. Saviour in the market-place of Caen in the king's court before his bishops and clergy. John bishop of Lisieux, (Serlo) bishop of Sées, (Turgis) bishop of Avranches, Archdeacon Fulbert,[6] and the chapter of Rouen are witnesses. It is attested by Ranulf the chancellor; at Cirencester ('apud Cyrecestriam').[7] [April 1107–22.]

186. Writ addressed to Richard de Belmeis, the sheriffs, barons, and ministers generally, directing that the property of the abbot of Shrewsbury shall be free from all customs as in the time of Roger de Muntgomery, Hugh, and Robert of Bellême. It is attested by Ranulf the chancellor; at Gloucester.[8] [April 1107–May 1108.]

187. Writ addressed to Osbern the sheriff and the ministers of Yorkshire directing them to restore (*resaisiare*) to Ranulf bishop of Durham lands which belonged to the bishopric of Durham, and particularly the land of Cleveland which Copsig gave to St. Cuthbert. It is attested by Urse de Abetot; at Hereford.[9] [1104–10.]

188. Writ addressed to Osbert the sheriff and the ministers of Yorkshire concerning the churches of the royal demesne in Yorkshire. It is attested by Robert bishop of Lincoln; at Worcester.[10] [1101–15.]

---

[1] *Chartul. of Selby*, n. 31. Mr. Davis in his *Regesta* wrongly ascribes this writ to William II.

[2] *Vesp. E. xvi*, fo. 9, n. 27; *Mon. Anglic.* vi. 1274, n. 40.

[3] *Mon. Anglic.* vi. 144; *Memor. of Hexham* (Surtees Soc.), i, p. ix.

[4] Craster, *Hist. of Northumb.* viii. 55 n., n. 13.

[5] *Chartul. of St. Peter's, Gloucester*, ii. 132.

[6] Archdeacon in 1074: *Gallia Christiana*, xi, instr., c. 17; Davis, *Regesta*, i, n. 77.

[7] *Livre Noir de Bayeux*, n. 38.   [8] *Cal. of Chart. Rolls*, ii. 81.

[9] *Mon. Anglic.* i. 241, n. 9.   [10] Farrer, *Early Yorkshire Charters*, no. 428.

189. Writ addressed to Robert bishop of Lincoln, Ranulf Meschin, Osbert the sheriff, and the barons and lieges of Lincolnshire, in favour of the church of St. Mary, Lincoln. It is attested by Ranulf Meschin; at Worcester.[1] [1101–15.]

190. Writ addressed to Osbert the sheriff and the barons of Yorkshire in favour of Archbishop Gerard. It is attested by Robert bishop of Lincoln and (Robert) count of Meulan; at Bushley ('apud Biselegam ').[2] [1101–8.]

191. Writ addressed to Gilbert sheriff of Surrey in favour of St. Peter's, Westminster, and Abbot Gilbert (Crispin). It directs that the land of the abbey which is in the royal demesne within the park and forest of Windsor and eight hides of the manor of Piriford shall always be free from geld and scot, and particularly ' de novo geldo propter hidagium '. It is attested by Roger Bigot; at Bushley (' apud Bisselegam ').[3]

It is possible that during his visit to the west the king nominates Urban, archdeacon of Llandaff, to the see of Llandaff, commonly called the bishopric of Glamorgan.[4] Urban is consecrated by Anselm on 3 ides of August (11th), 1107.[5]

1 Aug. The king holds a great council in London at the royal palace (of Westminster). During three days, pending Anselm's arrival, the subject of ecclesiastical investiture is discussed by Henry and the bishops.[6] On the fourth day Archbishop Gerard makes profession of obedience to Anselm.[7] A number of preferments to bishoprics and abbacies in England and Normandy are made by the king.[8]

Ralph, sometime prior of Rochester, is elected abbot of Battle.[9]

192. A confirmation is issued to the abbey of St. Mary of Montebourg of various gifts made by Richard de Redvers, and of other possessions of the abbey. The signatories are: Queen Matilda, Archbishop Anselm, the bishops, Roger of Salisbury, Herbert of Norwich, Robert of Lincoln, William of Winchester, Samson of Worcester, William of Exeter, and Ralph of Chichester;[10] the abbots, Richard of St. Albans, Roger (sic) of Abingdon, and Herlewin of Glastonbury; Richard de Redvers, Earl Simon, Ranulf the chancellor, Baldwin Fitz-Richard de Redvers, and William, brother of the same Baldwin.[11]

193. Richard de Redvers executes a charter of confirmation in favour of the same monastery. The signatories are: Henry and Queen Matilda, Baldwin Fitz-Richard de Redvers, William Fitz-Richard de Redvers, Count Eustace, Earl Simon (of Northampton), Earl William (de Warenne), Humphrey de Bohun, Roger de Magnevill, Richard de Lestre, Richard de . . ., Alfred of Lincoln, the bishops, Robert of Lincoln, Ralph of Chichester, and Ralph (sic) of Durham; and Anselm, archbishop of Canterbury.[12] [1104–7.]

---

[1] *Mon. Anglic.* vi. 1273, n. 32.   [2] Farrer, *Early Yorkshire Charters*, n. 15.

[3] Chartul. of St. Peter's, Westminster, Faust. A. iii, fo. 67 ; Robinson, *Gilbert Crispin*, p. 141.

[4] Florence of Worcester, *s. a.* 1107.

[5] Eadmer, p. 187.   [6] *Ibid.* p. 186.   [7] *Ibid.* p. 187.

[8] Chron.   [9] *Mon. Anglic.* iii. 234 *b*.

[10] ' Ricardi + de Redveriis ' occurs here in *Cartul. Normand.*

[11] *Cal. of Chart. Rolls*, iv. 157 ; Delisle, *Cartul. Normand.*, no. 737.

[12] *Gallia Christiana*, xi., instr., col. 232.

E

194. Notification to H(erbert) bishop (of Norwich), Roger Bigot, and generally, of a confirmation to St. Mary's, Binham, of various liberties, and a grant of a market at Binham. It is attested by Archbishop Anselm and R(anulf) the chancellor; at Westminster.[1]

195. Notification to Bishop Herbert, Roger Bigot, and generally, of the confirmation to the monastery of Binham of various possessions. It is attested by Archbishop Anselm and R(anulf) the chancellor; at Westminster. It also bears the following signatories:[2] (1) Henry king of the English, Queen Matilda, the archbishops, Anselm and Gerard; the bishops, Maurice (of London), William (of Winchester), Ralph (of Chichester), Robert (of Lincoln), Herbert (of Norwich), Hervey (of Bangor), Samson (of Worcester), and Ranulf (of Durham); the abbots, Gilbert (of Westminster), Ernulf (of Peterborough), (2) 'Farizo' (of Abingdon), Peter (of Gloucester), Stephen (of York), and Nigel (of Burton); Robert count (of Meulan), Simon earl (of Northampton), Richard earl (of Chester), Henry earl (of Warwick), Stephen count (of Aumâle), Ranulf the chancellor, Peter de Valoignes, Roger son of Peter (de Valoignes), Haïmon the sewer, (3) William de Aubigny, Nigel de Aubigny, Nigel de Oillei, Roger Fitz-Richard, Roger de Oilnei (*sic*), Humphrey de Aubigny, David (the queen's brother), William de Curci, Walter Fitz-Richard, William Pevrell of London, Pain Pevcrell, Othuer (son of Earl Hugh), William Pevrell of Dover, Oine the chaplain, Walter Fitz-Ansger, Hamon Pevrell.[3]

196. Notification, addressed generally, of the confirmation to the monks of St. Andrew's, Northampton, of the gifts made by Earl Simon (of Northampton) and Matilda his wife. It is attested by the queen, Archbishop Anselm, the bishops, Robert of Lincoln, Robert of Chester, John of Lisieux, John of Bayeux (*sic*), Gundulf of Rochester, and Maurice of London; Ranulf the chancellor, William earl of Warenne, Robert count of Meulan, David the queen's brother, and Robert de Ferrers; at Westminster.[4]

197. The charter of Simon earl of Northampton and Matilda his wife, reciting their gifts to St. Andrew's monastery, Northampton, terminates with this clause: 'laudante hoc et confirmante Henrico Anglorum rege octavo imperii sui anno, coram subscriptis testibus:' [viz.] King Henry, Queen Matilda, Archbishop Anselm, the bishops, Robert of Lincoln, Robert of Chester, John of Lisieux, Samson (of Worcester), John of Bayeux (*sic*), Gundulf of Rochester, and Maurice of London; Ranulf the chancellor, Henry earl of Warwick, William earl of Warenne, Nigel de Oily, Robert de Ferers, Eudes the sewer, William de Aubigny, William de Curcy, Robert count of Meulan, David the queen's brother [who each made the sign of the cross on the charter].[5]

11 Aug. Anselm consecrates at Canterbury the five bishops: William of Winchester, Roger of Salisbury, Reinhelm, who has lately been restored

---

[1] Cart. Antiq. roll N, n. 13 (41).

[2] In three columns.

[3] Chartul. of Binham, Claud. D. xiii, fo. 38 *d*. Cf. *Mon. Anglic.* iii. 351, n. 15.

[4] Chartul. of St. Andrew's, Northampton, Cott. MS. Vesp. E. xvii, fo. 13 *d* (old fo. 10 *d* and fo. 12 *d*).

[5] From the Chartul. of St. Andrew's; *Mon. Anglic.* v. 191.

to the see of Hereford, William de Warelwast elect of Exeter, and Urban elect of Glamorgan, i.e. Llandaff. The primate was assisted by the bishops, Robert of Lincoln, John of Bath, Herbert of Norwich, Ralph of Chichester, and Ranulf of Durham.[1]

15 Aug. Robert, formerly prior of St. Peter's, Westminster, is consecrated abbot of St. Edmund's by Anselm.[2]

198. 1 Sept. Notification to Archbishop Anselm, Hamon the sheriff, and the barons of England of the grant to the monks of St. Augustine's, Canterbury, of a fair at Canterbury. It is attested by Thurstan the chaplain and Hamon the sewer ; at London, on the kalends of September.[3] [1101–3 or 1107.]

8 or 15 Sept. On the Nativity of St. Mary Roger Bigot the sewer dies at Earsham, near Bungay, and later is buried at Thetford.[4]

Within the year Richard de Redvers dies and is buried at Montebourg ; [5] Miles Crispin of Wallingford also dies.[6]

199. A charter of Roger Bigot, by which he grants to the church of Cluny the church which he has begun to build at the town of Thetford, is attested by the bishops, Herbert (of Norwich), Gundulf (of Rochester), and Robert Bloet (of Lincoln) ; Alfred archdeacon (of Norwich ?), Geoffrey archdeacon (of Suffolk ?), Rotold son of the earl, Ranulf the chancellor, Eudes the sewer, William Malet, Eustace de Breteuil ('Brettevill') 'et aliis, dum rex moram fecit apud Thetfordiam, ubi et hoc + signum sancte crucis et sigillum suum in testimonium apposuit '.[7]

200. Writ addressed to Archbishop Gerard, Osbert the sheriff, and the barons of Yorkshire in favour of the abbey of Selby. It is attested by R(anulf) the chancellor, Thomas the chaplain, Nigel de Aubigny, and Humphrey de Aubigny ; at Trumpington.[8] [April 1107–May 1108.]

16 Sept. Robert, late prior of Westminster, abbot of St. Edmund's (el. 1102), dies on 16 kalends of October. The abbey then remains void for a period of seven years.[9]

26 Sept. ? Maurice bishop of London dies.[10]

201. Notification to Archbishop Gerard, Robert de Lascy, and the barons of Yorkshire of the grant to St. Mary's, York, of the land of Ousefleet and (Great) Armin, co. York. It is attested by Ranulf bishop of Durham, Nigel de Aubigny, and William Peverel of Nottingham ; at Winchester.[11] [1104–8.]

202. Notification to Archbishop Anselm, Hamon the sewer, and the barons of Kent of the confirmation to St. Augustine's and Abbot Hugh of land which the said abbot deraigned against Wybert (de Taenet) in

---

[1] Eadmer, p. 187.

[2] *Ibid.* p. 188. Robert was elected in 1102.

[3] Charter Rolls, 20 Edw. II, m. 2, n. 16 ; *Dep. Keeper's Rep.* xxx, app., p. 198, n. 15.

[4] *Mon. Anglic.* v. 153 ; Orderic, iv. 276–7. The Reading Calendar gives the date as 28 July : Vesp. E. v.

[5] Orderic, iv. 276.

[6] *Ibid.* He was reported to be sick in 7 Henry I : *Chron. of Abingdon,* ii. 97.

[7] MS. Cotton, Vitell. F. iv ; *Mon. Anglic.* v. 148.

[8] *Chartul. of Selby,* n. 19.

[9] *Mon. Anglic.* iii. 155 b.

[10] Le Neve, *Fasti Eccles. Anglic.*

[11] *Cal. of Chart. Rolls,* i. 461.

Thanet. It is attested by the bishops, Roger of Salisbury and William of Exeter; at Winchester.[1] [July 1107–July 1108.]

203. Confirmation to St. John's, Colchester, and Abbot Hugh of land given by William Peverel of London. It is attested by Ranulf the chancellor; at Winchester.[2] [1107 ?]

204. Mandate to R(ichard) son of G(otse), sheriff (of Nottingham), to do right between Nigel[3] abbot (of Burton) and Nicholas de Stafford, sheriff (of Stafford), touching the land of Cotes. It is attested by W(illiam) Giffard, bishop of Winchester, and R(anulf)[4] the chancellor; at Westminster.[5] [1107–*c.* 1108.]

25 Dec. The king keeps the feast of the Nativity of Our Lord at Westminster.[6]

205. Mandate to Osbert sheriff of York to cause Archbishop Gerard to have the tithes of the past August which belonged to certain churches of the royal demesne in Yorkshire, lately given to him by the king. It is attested by Roger bishop of Salisbury; at Westminster 'in Natale Domini'.[7] [1105 or 1107.]

1108.

206. Confirmation to the abbot and monks of Evesham and grant, at the prayer of Ranulf the chancellor, of a weekly market at Stow-on-the-Wold ('Eadwardestowe'). It is attested by the archbishops, Anselm and Gerard; Samson bishop (of Worcester), Robert count of Meulan, Henry earl of Warwick, and Urse de Abetoth; at Westminster.[8] [April 1107–May 1108.]

207. Notification, addressed generally, of the grant to the same monastery of the hundred of Blakhurst. It is attested by the same witnesses as the last; at Westminster.[9] [Same as 206.]

c. 19 Feb. At the beginning of Lent Henry was possibly at Westminster. Anselm comes nigh to London ('iuxta Lundoniam') to have a conference with the king about the consecration of Hugh, monk of Bec, to the abbey of St. Augustine, Canterbury.[10]

7 Mar. Gundulf, bishop of Rochester, dies on the nones of March.[11]

5 April. At Easter the king is at Winchester[12] in accordance with his usual practice. The attendance of the sheriffs and other ministers of the crown at the half-yearly audit at the Exchequer within a month after Easter may have necessitated the royal presence at Winchester during that period, as also in October.

The king publishes enactments against the excesses which were often

---

[1] *Hist. S. Aug. Cantuar.* p. 360. The Chronologia assigns this writ to the year 1107.　　　　　　　　　　　　　　[2] *Chartul. of Colchester*, p. 26.

[3] 'Nicholas' in the manuscript.　　　　　　[4] 'Regis' in the manuscript.

[5] *Chartul. of Burton* (Salt Arch. Soc.), v (1), p. 9, also p. 12. See no. 141 above.

[6] Chron.

[7] Regist. Magn. Album, i. 63 *d*; Farrer, *Early Yorkshire Charters*, no. 427. Cf. Hugh the Chantor in *Histor. of York*, ii. 111.

[8] *Cal. of Chart. Rolls*, i. 257; Chartul. of Evesham, Harl. MS. 3763, fo. 82 *d*.

[9] Campbell ch. xviii. 12.　　　　　　　　　　　　　[10] Eadmer, p. 188.

[11] Roger of Howden, i. 165; cf. Eadmer, p. 192.　　　[12] Chron.

committed by the rabble which usually followed the court; and also against thieves and the coiners and utterers of bad money.[1]

208. Writ to Osbert sheriff (of Lincoln) and Richard son of Gotse ('Gozo', 'Gero') in favour of Gerard, archbishop of York, touching pleas and judgements of moneyers and thieves in his court, and his right to administer the royal statute recently enacted touching such pleas. It is attested by Robert bishop of Chester; at Winchester, at Easter.[2]

209. Notification to Roger bishop of Salisbury, Walter Hosate, and the barons of Wiltshire, of the confirmation to the abbess of Romsey, of property given by Ernulf Deschuit, when he placed his daughter in the abbey. It is attested by William Fitz-Humphrey and Urse de Abetot; at Winchester, at Easter.[3]

210. Notification to William bishop of Winchester, William earl of Warenne, Ralph Fitz-Nigel, and the barons and lieges of Surrey, of the confirmation to St. Saviour's, Bermondsey, and Prior Petreius, of the gift made by Nigel de Munivill of land at Balham,[4] and of land at Bermondsey which his wife bestowed in the presence of William bishop of Winchester, William Malet, and Manasser Arsic. It is attested by Robert bishop of Lincoln; at Winchester in the council.[5] [1103–10.]

21 May. Archbishop Gerard dies (at Southwell) on his way to attend a synod in London.[6]

24 May. A synod is held in London at Whitsuntide in which the king and the lay barons assisted.[7] The question of the elevation of the abbey of Ely to the degree of a bishopric is discussed.[8] Thomas elect of York takes part in issuing the decrees of the synod.[9] Richard de Belmeis is elected bishop of London.[10]

211. Notification to Archbishop Anselm and the canons of St. Martin's, Dover, Hamon the sewer, and the barons of Kent, of the confirmation to St. Augustine's, Canterbury, and Abbot Hugh of a prebend for one canon in the church of St. Martin, Dover, which he deraigned in the king's court. It is attested by Roger bishop of Salisbury and William bishop of Exeter; at Westminster, at Whitsuntide.[11]

212. Writ addressed to all the sheriffs in whose baliwicks Gundulf the bishop used to hold lands directing that the lands of the bishopric (of Rochester) shall be in peace and pay no more geld than in the days of the king's father and brother. It is attested by William bishop of Exeter; at Westminster, at Whitsuntide.[12]

213. Notification to Archbishop Anselm, the bishops, earls, and barons of England of the grant to Thomas, the king's chaplain, of the archbishopric

---

[1] Eadmer, pp. 192–3; Sym. of Durham, ii. 239.

[2] *Cal. of Pat. Rolls*, 1338–40, p. 166; Regist. Magn. Album, pt. ii, fo. 5. Cf. *Mon. Anglic.* vi. 1180, n. 27; *Histor. of York*, iii. 22.

[3] *Cal. of Chart. Rolls*, ii. 103.

[4] *Chron. of Bermondsey, Annales Mon.*, iii. 430.

[5] *Cal. of Chart. Rolls*, iv. 182.

[6] Eadmer, p. 193; Hugh the Chantor, p. 111.   [7] Eadmer, pp. 193–4.

[8] *Ibid.* p. 195; cf. *Mon. Anglic.* i. 483, n. 20.

[9] Eadmer, p. 194.   [10] *Ibid.* p. 196.

[11] Exch. K. R. Misc. Bks. 27, n. 1; *Dep. Keeper's Rep.* xxx, app., p. 197; *Hist. S. Aug. Cantuar.*, p. 357.   [12] *Regist. Roffense* (ed. Thorp), p. 34.

of York. It is attested by Anselm, Samson of Worcester, and the other bishops of England, Ranulf the chancellor, Robert count of Meulan, Henry earl of Warwick, William de Warenne and the other earls of England, Hamon the sewer, William de Aubigny, Thomas de St. John, William Bigod, and William de Pirou ; at Westminster, at Whitsuntide.[1]

214. At this Whitsuntide court a dispute between Peter, abbot of St. Peter's, Gloucester, and Reinhelm, bishop of Hereford, is settled in the presence of the king, Archbishop Anselm, Robert count of Meulan, and many bishops, abbots, and nobles ; the judgement of the court being announced by Robert of Meulan.[2]

215. Notification, addressed generally, of the grant to St. Andrew's priory, Rochester, of the customs which Christ Church, Canterbury, enjoyed. It is attested by Robert bishop of Lincoln, Tur(old) de Evermou, and Hamon the sewer ; at London.[3] [1105–9.]

After Whitsuntide Anselm addresses letters to Paschal, petitioning for the erection of an episcopal see at Ely.[4]

1 June. Anselm ordains Richard, elect of London, a priest, ' ieiunio quarti mensis '.[5] The elect is Richard de Belmeis, late viceroy of Shropshire under Urse de Abetot.

216. Notification addressed to Robert bishop of Lincoln, Earl Simon, Gilbert the sheriff, and the lieges of Huntingdonshire of an agreement made before the king between Aldwin abbot of Ramsey and William the king's dispenser, touching the land of Ellington. It is attested by Ranulf the chancellor, William de Curci, Roger de Oilli, William the chamberlain of Hohtun, Ailric le Moyne (*monachus*), Reinald le Moyne (*monachus*), Ingelram de Ou, and Guy the sewer of Bishop Herbert ;[6] at Weybridge Wood. ' Hec conventio facta erat apud nemus Wardberga.'[7] [April, 1107–1113.]

217. At the same time and place an agreement is made before the king between Abbot Aldwin and William of Lincoln (Nicholiensis '), the king's chaplain, touching land at Stukeley. It is addressed to, and attested by, the same persons respectively. ' Hec conventio facta erat apud Wardeberg nemus.'[8] [Same as 216.]

218. Notification to the lieges of Norfolk and Suffolk that the altar of St. Edmund's shall have all that Peter (of Bourges),[9] the clerk of Amiens, held in churches, tithes, &c. It is attested by (Robert) count of Meulan ; at Brampton.[10] [1106–10.]

219. Notification to Earl Simon, Hugh (de Leicestre) the sheriff, and the barons of Northamptonshire of the confirmation to Robert bishop of Lincoln of a gift made by Gilbert de Gant of the church of Empingham, and mandate that if (Henry) count of Eu has disseised the bishop, Aubrey the chamberlain shall restore seisin to him. It is attested by Osbert the sheriff ; at Brampton.[11] [1106–10.]

[1] *Mon. Anglic.* vi. 1180, n. 29.   [2] *Chartul. of St. Peter's, Gloucester,* i. 13–14.
[3] *Regist. Roffense,* p. 34 ; *Dep. Keeper's Rep.* xxx, app., p. 199.
[4] Eadmer, p. 195.   [5] *Ibid.* p. 196.
[6] He occurs in 1108 ; *Mon. Anglic.* iii. 348, n. 6.
[7] Add. Ch 33250. Cf. *Chron. of Ramsey Abbey,* p. 215 ; *Chartul. of Ramsey,* no. 156.
[8] *Ibid.* no. 155.   [9] Cf. no. 155 above.
[10] Chartul. of St. Edmund's, Camb. Univ. Libr., fo. 24 *d* (37), *s. t.* Hemgrave.
[11] *Mon. Anglic.* vi. 1273, n. 33.

220. Notification to Robert bishop of Lincoln, Aldwin abbot of Ramsey, and his convent, Hugh de Bocheland, and the lieges of Bedfordshire and Hertfordshire of the confirmation of an agreement made between Aldwin abbot of Ramsey and Reinald de Argentuem concerning the mills of Icklesford. It is attested by Gerald de Calz and Robert Gerbert; at Brampton.[1] [1107–13 ?]

221. Writ addressed to Archbishop Anselm, Hamon the sewer, and the barons and ministers of Kent directing them to give effect to a judgement obtained in the king's court by Abbot Ansbold and the monks of Ghent against Robert de Baantun. It is attested by Robert bishop of Lincoln and Robert count of Meulan; at Lincoln.[2]

29 June. Ralph D'Escures, abbot of Sées, is appointed bishop of Rochester by Anselm on the feast of the apostles Peter and Paul, and on 9 August he is consecrated.[3]

222. Writ addressed to the archbishop of Canterbury, Ralph bishop of Rochester, and Hamon the sheriff, in favour of A(vice) abbess of Malling. It is attested by Roger bishop of Salisbury and Ranulf the chancellor; at Westminster.[4] [July 1108, or June 1109–April 1114.]

223. Notification to Archbishop Anselm and Richard bishop of London, of a grant in favour of St. Paul's, London, touching the disposition of the prebends. It is attested by the bishops, (Roger) of Salisbury, (Robert) of Lincoln, and William of Exeter; R(anulf) the chancellor, and (Robert) count of Meulan; at Windsor.[5] [May–Aug. 1108.]

Early in July the king is at one of the royal manors near Portsmouth, awaiting a favourable opportunity for taking passage over seas. Anselm is staying at a place which is separated by an arm of the sea from the king's residence. The archbishop is too ill to travel across the bay to bestow his blessing on the king; wherefore the king sends William bishop of Winchester and the bishop of Exeter to escort his son William to Anselm, into whose charge he delivers his son, together with the affairs of the kingdom during his absence.[6]

Before August the king crosses to Normandy.[7]

29 July. Philip king of the French dies,[8] and is succeeded by Louis. 'There were afterwards many strifes betwixt the king of France and him of England while he abode in Normandy.'[9]

Anselm summons Thomas, archbishop of York, to come to Canterbury on 6 September to make subjection.[10] Thomas, by letter and by William his clerk, requests an extension of time, which the primate concedes, namely to 27 September;[11] but Thomas disregards the summons and is given a further date on 8 November to come to Canterbury to make subjection.[12] Later Anselm sends the bishops of London and Rochester to

---

[1] *Chartul. of Ramsey*, ii. 60; *Mon. Anglic.* ii. 570, n. 36.

[2] Round, *Cal. of Documents, France*, no. 1378.   [3] Eadmer, pp. 196, 198.

[4] *Cal. of Charter Rolls*, v. 56, n. 4.

[5] *Hist. MSS. Comm. Rep.* ix, app. 61; Simpson, *Reg. Statut.*, p. 119.

[6] Eadmer, p. 197.

[7] Chron.; Eadmer, p. 197; Robert of Torigny, i. 134.

[8] Orderic, iv. 284. On 5 April according to *Flores Historiarum*, ii. 41.

[9] Chron.   [10] Eadmer, p. 199.

[11] *Ibid.* p. 201.   [12] *Ibid.* p. 203.

interview Thomas. They find him at Southwell, but he defers his answer until the return of the envoys, whom he has sent to the king in Normandy. The king addresses a letter to Anselm postponing further action until his return at the ensuing Easter.[1]

Little is known of the movements of Henry and his court during this expedition to Normandy.

224. A confirmation is issued to the abbey of St. Pierre-sur-Dives (arr. of Lisieux). It is attested by the king, William archbishop of Rouen, Serlo bishop of Sées, Robert de Curci, and Fulk de Alnei ; at Argentan.[2]

21 Nov. Paschal issues letters to Henry to sanction the erection of the see of Ely. They are dated at Troie, 11 kalends of December.[3]

225. Confirmation of Henry, 'king of the English and duke of the Normans', to the priory of Longueville. It is executed 'in curia Henrici regis, presente magno procerum conventu apud Rothomagum', and is attested by the queen, Earl Simon, Roger Fitz-Richard, and William de Aubigny.[4] [Nov. 1106–13 ?]

226. Notification to William archbishop of Rouen and Robert de Candos and the lieges of the Roumois of the gift to the abbey of Jumièges of the land of Dudela in the forest of Roumare ; and mandate to Robert de Candos to give seisin. It is attested by Ranulf the chancellor, William the chamberlain, William de Aubigny, Nigel de Aubigny, and Walter Fitz-Anser ; at Caen.[5]

226 A. Mandate to Faritius abbot of Abingdon to Justice Hugh Fitz-Thurstan[6] (the dispenser) if he will not do boon-services on bridges and parks in respect of the land (of Sparsholt) which he holds of the abbot. It is attested by (Ranulf ?) the chancellor, at Pont de L'Arche ('apud Pontem Arcarum').[7] [1108 ?–Feb. 1117.]

25 Dec. Henry is in Normandy at Christmas.[8]

1109.

Mar. Henry leads his forces to Gisors on the Epte. King Louis advances against that place.[9]

Henry meets Louis at Neauples.[10]

226 B. Letter from Henry to Anselm referring to his interview with Louis of France and the breach between them. Also to the settlement of the affair (*negotium*) between himself and the Emperor. He commits affairs in England to his disposition and entrusts his son and daughter to his care. Witness : Ranulf the chancellor ; at Rouen.[11]

---

[1] Eadmer, pp. 204–5.

[2] *Gallia Christiana*, xi, instr., col. 156 ; Delisle, *Cartul. Normand.*, no. 1219 ; *Neustria Pia*, p. 503.

[3] *Mon. Anglic.* i. 482, n. 19 ; cf. *ibid.* n. 15.

[4] Round, *Cal. of Documents, France*, no. 219. Professor Haskins assigns this charter to 1106–7 : *Norman Institutions*, p. 310.

[5] Round, *Cal. of Documents, France*, no. 156.

[6] Round, *The King's Serjeants*, p. 187.

[7] *Chron. of Abingdon*, ii. 91.   [8] Chron.

[9] Suger, *Vita Ludovici*, c. 15 ; G. B. Adams, *Political Hist. of England*, ii. 156.

[10] Luchaire, *Louis VI*, n. 72 ; Haskins, *Norman Institutions*, p. 310.

[11] *Epistolae Anselmi*, iv, n. 93. Cf. Eadmer, p. 205.

227. Notification addressed generally of the render and grant to William de Albini, the king's butler of the manor of Snettisham with other possessions, to hold as beneficially as William II gave them to him. It is attested by William archbishop of Rouen, R(obert) count of Meulan, Earl Walter Giffard,[1] R(anulf) the chancellor, Gilbert de Aquila, William the chamberlain of Tancarvill ; at Rouen.[2]

21 April. Anselm dies at Canterbury on Wednesday, 11 kalends of May.[3]

25 April. Henry is in Normandy at Easter.[4]

c. 31 May–2 June. About Rogation days Henry returns to England.[5]

13 June. At the Whitsuntide court held at Westminster the king takes pledges from the envoys sent by Henry, the Roman emperor, who sought the hand of the king's daughter, Matilda, in marriage.[6]

The subject of the consecration of Archbishop Thomas is discussed, the count of Meulan taking particular part in it.[7] There are also present the bishops, Richard of London, William of Winchester, Robert of Lincoln, Herbert of Norwich, Roger of Salisbury, Ralph of Rochester, Reinhelm of Hereford, Robert of Chester, John of Bath, Ralph of Chichester, William of Exeter, and Samson of Worcester.[8] Thomas elect of York ultimately agrees to make a profession of obedience to Canterbury.[9]

227 A. Confirmation, addressed generally, of the priory (*canonicatum*) of canons regular in Christ Church, London, which Queen Matilda has instituted there, free from all subjection save to the bishop of St. Paul's. It is attested by Roger bishop of Salisbury and Robert bishop of Lincoln ; at Westminster.[10]

228. Mandate, addressed to Samson bishop (of Worcester), Urse de Abetot, and the barons of Worcestershire, concerning the holding of the county and hundred courts at the times and places which were customary in King Edward's days.[11] It is attested by R(ichard) bishop of London, Roger bishop (of Salisbury), Ranulf the chancellor, and Robert, count of Meulan ; at Reading.[12] [May 1108–Aug. 1111.]

27 June. Thomas elect of York is consecrated at St. Paul's, London,[13] and he receives the pall from the cardinal Ulric.[14] About this time (' inter hec ') Hervey bishop of Bangor is translated to the new see of Ely.[15]

229. Writ addressed to Richard bishop of London, Hugh de Bocheland, and generally, notifying them of a grant made to the queen that she may place canons regular in the church of the Holy Trinity, London, which is now discharged from subjection to the church of Waltham by

---

[1] A minor at the death of his father, Walter Giffard, on 15 July 1102.

[2] *Cal. of Pat. Rolls*, 1327–30, p. 20.

[3] Eadmer, p. 206 ; Sym. of Durham, ii. 241.   [4] Chron.

[5] Florence of Worcester.   [6] Hen. of Huntingdon, p. 237.

[7] Eadmer, p. 207.   [8] *Ibid.* p. 208.   [9] *Ibid.* p. 209.

[10] *Ancient Charters* (Pipe Roll Soc. x), n. 2 ; *Facsimiles of National Manuscripts*, pt. i, n. 7 ; *Mon. Anglic.* vi. 155.

[11] See the remarks of Professor George Burton Adams in *The Political Hist. of England*, ii. 151–3.

[12] *Foedera*, i. 12 ; Stubbs, *Constitutional Hist.* (ed. 1880), i. 445, and *Select Charters* (ed. 1870), p. 99 ; Liebermann, *Gesetze*, i. 524.

[13] Eadmer, p. 210.   [14] *Ibid.* p. 211.   [15] *Ibid.*

an exchange given by the queen in the presence of the king, Roger bishop of Salisbury, Thomas de St. John, and Jordan de Say ; at Dunstable.[1] [May 1108–16.]

230. 17 Oct. At a council held at Nottingham on the day of the Translation of St. Etheldreda, being the 16 kalends of November 1109, the erection of the see of Ely is duly constituted by Henry, by authority of Pope Paschal, and the transfer of the town of Spaldwick to Robert bishop of Lincoln and his successors, in compensation for the loss of an important part of his see, is approved, in the presence of these signatories:[2] (1) the king and queen, Matilda spouse of the king of the Romans, Hervey the first bishop of Ely, and the bishops, Roger of Salisbury, Richard of Bayeux, Herbert of Norwich, Reinhelm of Hereford, (2) Ralph of Rochester, Richard of London, Robert of Chester, William of Exeter, Ranulf of Durham, and Robert of Lincoln ; Ranulf the chancellor,[3] (3) Thomas archbishop of York,[4] Robert count of Meulan, William earl of Warenne, Earl Simon, Stephen (count) of Aumâle, Count Roger of Poitou, Gilbert de Aquila, William de Aubigny, and Nigel de Aubigny.[5]

231. A confirmation is issued to the church of Durham and Bishop Ranulf of certain lands and privileges in co. Durham, between Tees and Tyne. It is attested by Archbishop Thomas and the bishops Richard of London, William of Exeter, Robert of Chester, Herbert of Norwich, and Hervey of Ely, Gilbert abbot of Westminster, Robert count of Meulan, William de Warenne, Gilbert de Aquila, Nigel de Aubigny, Robert de Lacy, Humphrey de Bohun, Robert de Brus, Geoffrey Ridel, and Alfred of Lincoln. 'Hec donatio facta est anno ab incarnatione Domini millesimo cix° in concilio totius Anglie apud Notingaham.'[6]

232. A confirmation is issued to the Cluniac monks of Lenton of the gifts made by William Peverel of Nottingham. The signatories are : (1) the king and queen, William Peverel of Nottingham and Adelina his wife, William Peverel their son, and Robert the brother of William Peverel ; (2) the bishops, Roger of Salisbury, Robert of Lincoln, and Robert of Chester ; Ranulf the chancellor ; (3) Robert count of Meulan, Earl Simon (of Northampton), Stephen count of Aumâle, Gilbert de Aquila, and Herbert Peverel.[7]

233. Notification to the sheriff of Nottinghamshire and the barons of Nottinghamshire and Derbyshire of the confirmation to Archbishop Thomas of all liberties in Nottinghamshire, as in the time of the king's brother William II. It is attested by Roger bishop of Salisbury, Ranulf the chancellor, and (Robert) count of Meulan ; at Nottingham.[8]

---

[1] Chartul. of Holy Trin. Priory, London, Hunterian Mus., Glasgow ; *Mon. Anglic.* vi. 155 n., from Stevens's *Continuation.*

[2] Arranged in three columns.

[3] Placed after the bishop of Salisbury in Lib. Elien., MS. iii, c. 6.

[4] Omitted, *ibid.*

[5] Harl. ch. 43, C. 11 ; *Mon. Anglic.* i. 483 ; Bentham, *Hist. of the Church of Ely,* app. 13*.

[6] *Hist. Dunelm. Script. Tres* (Surtees Soc.), p. xxxii ; *Cal. of Chart. Rolls,* v. 454 ; *Dep. Keeper's Rep.* xxx, app. 6, p. 201 (corrupt) ; *Mon. Anglic.* i. 242.

[7] Round, *Cal. of Documents, France,* no. 1383 ; *Mon. Anglic.* v. 113, n. 2.

[8] *Cal. of Chart. Rolls,* v. 478.

234. Writ addressed to the justices, sheriffs, and barons of Yorkshire in favour of the monks of Selby. It is attested by Nigel de Aubigny; at ' Pontefratch '.[1] [1101–29.]

235. Notification to Archbishop Thomas, Nigel de Aubigny, Osbert the sheriff and all lieges of the confirmation to the brethren of Goathland (near Pickering) of the place of Goathland, &c. It is attested by Archbishop Thomas and Robert de Brus; at York.[2] [June 1108–Feb. 1114.]

237. Notification to Archbishop Thomas, Osbert the sheriff, the barons and lieges of Yorkshire and Northumberland of the confirmation to Ranulf, bishop of Durham, of a market on Sunday at Norton (near Stockton). It is attested by Robert bishop of Lincoln, Nigel de Aubigny, and Robert de Brus; at York.[3] [Same as 235.]

238. Notification to Herbert bishop of Norwich, the sheriffs, barons, and ministers of Norfolk and Suffolk, of the confirmation of a partition made by Robert abbot of St. Edmunds [4] of the rents of the abbey between himself and the prior and convent of St. Edmunds. It is attested by Thomas, archbishop of York (*no place named*).[5] [Same as 235.]

239. Notification to the archbishop of York and the sheriff and ministers of Yorkshire of a grant to the abbey of St. Mary, York, of tithe of the royal venison in Yorkshire. It is attested by Humphrey Bigot the chaplain and Eudes the sewer; at Pickering (' Picheringis ').[6] [1101–16.]

240. Notification to Thomas archbishop of York, Osbert the sheriff, Nigel de Aubigny, Anschetell de Bulmer, the barons, ministers, and lieges of Yorkshire, of the confirmation to William (de Percy), abbot of Whitby, and his monks of their forest, in return for their grant to the king of the beasts of the chase in their forest of Whitby. It is attested by (William) bishop of Exeter, Ranulf bishop of Durham, (Robert) count of Meulan, Henry earl of Warwick, Alan de Percy, and Robert de Brus (*no place named*).[7] [Same as 235.]

241. Confirmation, at the prayer of Henry count of Eu, of all his gifts to the church of St. Mary, Bec. It is attested by the queen, Ingram de Hastingues, Richard Fitz-Baldwin, Henry count of Eu, Gilbert Fitz-Richard, Ranulf the chancellor, William bishop of Exeter, William Peverel, Walter Fitz-Richard, Humphrey de Buhun, William earl of Warenne. ' Hec carta facta est apud mancrium quod vocatum est Fiseleia,' [8] i.e. Fishley, co. Norfolk. [1107–13.]

242. 30 Nov. Notification to Bishop Herbert, Ralph de Belfou, and the barons of Suffolk and Norfolk, of the confirmation of an agreement, or fine, made between Bishop Herbert and Peter de Valoignes in the king's court at Norwich, before the king and his barons, concerning

---

[1] *Chartul. of Selby*, n. 9.

[2] *Chartul. of Whitby*, n. 197 ; *Mon. Anglic.* iv. 544, n. 3.

[3] Original in the Durham Treasury, 3. 1. Regalium, Hi, n. 8 ; *Journ. of Arch. Assoc.* xxix. 253.

[4] Died 16 September 1107.

[5] *Mon. Anglic.* iii. 153, n. 14 ; *ante*, xxiv. 425.

[6] *Cal. of Chart. Rolls*, v. 471 ; *Mon. Anglic.* iii. 560 *b* ; Farrer, *Early Yorks. Charters*, no. 353.

[7] *Chartul. of Whitby*, n. 190 ; Add. MS. 4715, fo. 162 *d*.

[8] Round, *Cal. of Documents, France*, no. 1417.

Binham and Langham. It is attested by Roger bishop of Salisbury, William earl of Warenne, Gilbert de Aquila, William de Aubigny, Roger Fitz-Richard and Gilbert his brother, Otuer son of Earl (Hugh), and Simon de Molendinis ; at Norwich, on St. Andrew's Day.[1] [1109-16.[2]]

243. Notification to the barons of Norfolk and Suffolk, of the confirmation to Bishop Herbert and the church of Norwich of the gift made by Alan son of Flahald of the king's manor of Eaton (in Norwich) with soc, &c., as it was in the king's demesne. This the king will confirm ' when Alan comes to my court '. It is attested by Roger bishop of Salisbury, Gilbert de Aquila, William de Aubigny, and Ralph de Beaufou, at St. Edmund's (Bury), by John of Bayeux and Gilbert (' Gys.') the chaplain.[3] [1102-16.]

244. Writ addressed to Archbishop Thomas, Osbert the sheriff, Robert de Lacy, Nigel de Aubigny, and the barons of Yorkshire and Nottinghamshire, in favour of Robert bishop of Lincoln. It is attested by Ranulf bishop of Durham, (Ranulf) the chancellor, and Gilbert de Aquila ; ' per tres parmenos [4] quos ego ei dedi ' ; at Trumpington.[5] [1108-13.]

245. Writ addressed to Archbishop Thomas, Nigel de Aubigny, Osbert the sheriff, and the barons and lieges of Yorkshire, notifying them of a gift to Robert bishop of Lincoln of the churches of the king's three manors of Coxwold, Kirkby (Moorside), and Hovingham, co. York. It is attested by Nigel de Aubigny ; at Woodstock.[6] [1108-15.]

25 Dec. At Christmas the king holds his court at Westminster.[7] Archbishop Thomas attends the court with the intention of crowning the king and conducting mass in the place of the primate, but Richard bishop of London refuses to acquiesce in this interference with his prerogative.[8]

246. Confirmation to the monastery of Eynsham, upon the restoration thereof of land given by Robert bishop of Lincoln in exchange for Newark and Stow and of land given by others, including the gift of Harding of Oxford ' qui in Hierusalem ivit [9] et ibi mortuus est '. Done at Westminster, at Christmas, 1109, the 10th year of Henry's reign.[10]

247. Notification to Robert bishop of Lincoln, William sheriff of Oxfordshire, and the barons, of the grant to the monks of Abingdon (in the time of Abbot Faritius) of land in Oxford. It is attested by the bishops, Roger of Salisbury and Robert of Lincoln ; Hamon the sewer, William de Curci, William sheriff of Oxfordshire, Theold (' Hoeld ') [11] the chaplain, Ralph Basset, and Alfred of Lincoln ; at ' Westmuster '.[12] [1102-10.]

248. Notification to Roger bishop of Salisbury, Hugh de Bocheland, and the ministers and barons of Berkshire of the king's grant to

---

[1] Chartul. of Binham, Claud. D. xiii, fo. 20 *d* ; *Mon. Anglic.* iii. 348, n. 7. Cf. *Hist. MSS. Comm. Rep.* ix. 367.

[2] Possible years are 1109-10, 1113 or 1115. An agreement recorded in *Mon. Anglic.* iii. 348, n. 6, points to the year 1109.

[3] *Cal. of Chart. Rolls*, i. 153 ; *Mon. Anglic.* iv. 17, n. 6.

[4] i.e. ' pearmains '.   [5] *Cal. of Chart. Rolls*, iv. 138.

[6] *Mon. Anglic.* vi. 1272, n. 17.   [7] Chron.

[8] Eadmer, p. 212. See Round, *The King's Serjeants*, p. 319.

[9] Possibly in 1107 or 1108. Cf. Orderic, iv. 239, 242.

[10] *Mon. Anglic.* iii. 15 *b* ; *Chartul. of Eynsham*, ii. 36.

[11] ' Teoldus ' in Cart. Antiq. x, n. 3.   [12] *Chron. of Abingdon*, ii. 66.

Faritius, abbot of Abingdon, of liberty to cultivate certain waste
ground at Wallingford, which has been indicated to him by Croc the
huntsman[1] and Alfred of Lincoln. It is attested by Alfred of Lincoln,
Drew the huntsman, and Hugh de Falaise ; at ' Westmuster ', at Christmas.[2] [1102–10.]

249. Writ addressed to Croc the huntsman touching the same matter.
It is attested by Alfred of Lincoln ; at ' Westmoster '.[3] [1102–10.]

1110.

23 Feb. Henry gives his daughter Matilda in marriage to Henry, the
Roman emperor. He takes for her marriage an aid of 3s. from every hide
in England.[4] At the beginning of Lent, which was the 4 ides of April (*sic*),
he sends her from Dover to Witsand.[5]

250. Notification to Roger bishop of Salisbury, Hugh de Bocheland,
and the barons of Berkshire of the confirmation to the church of Abingdon
of land which Walter son of Josceline de la Rivière held of Humphrey de
Bohun, who rendered it before the king to the said church. It is attested
by Walter de Mayenne (' de Meduana '), Guy de Clermunt, Ralph de
Toeni, Drew de Moncei, Luhell de Brielval, Richard de Meri,[6] William
de Aubigny, Robert de Dunstanvill, Aretus the falconer, and Patric de
Chaources (' de Cadurcis ') ; at Romsey, in the year in which the king gave
his daughter to the emperor.[7]

251. Confirmation, addressed generally, of a grant made by R(einhelm ?) bishop of Hereford to Walter de Gloucester in fee of Little Hereford
and Ullingswick, to hold for the service of two knights' fees. It is attested
by R(anulf) the chancellor, Geoffrey de Clinton, and Richard son of
Ponce (or Pons) ; ' apud Cheddreholam ' (Cheddar cliffs ?).[8] [1107–15.]

10 Apr. At Easter the king is at Marlborough.[9]

252. Notification to Hervey bishop of Ely, Gilbert the sheriff, and the
barons of Cambridge, of the grant to the canons of Cambridge, at the
prayer of Pain Peverel, of land near the springs of Barnwell, for the site
of their church and monastery. It is attested by the bishops, Roger of
Salisbury, William of Exeter, and John of Bath ; Thurstan the chaplain,
and Hamon the sewer ; at Marlborough, at Easter.[10]

253. Writ addressed to the bishops, Roger of Salisbury, and Robert
of Lincoln ; Hugh de Bocheland, William sheriff of Oxford, and the
barons and ministers of each shire in favour of the monks of Abingdon.
It is attested by William bishop of Exeter, Eustace de Bréteuil, and
Patric de Chaources ; at Marlborough.[11] [1107–10.]

254. Notification, addressed generally, of the grant to the church of
Salisbury of the churches of Heytesbury and Godelming, which Ranulf

---

[1] See no. 165.   [2] *Chron. of Abingdon*, ii. 82.
[3] *Ibid.* p. 83.   [4] Hen. of Huntingdon, p. 237.
[5] Sym. of Durham, ii. 241 ; ' Quarto Idus Aprilis ' : *Flores Histor.* ii. 41. This
was Easter Day.
[6] Son of Humphrey de Bohun.   [7] *Chron. of Abingdon*, ii. 107.
[8] Cotton ch. xi. 60 (mutilated). See Mr. Round in *Ancient Charters* (Pipe Roll
Soc. x), p. 22.   [9] Chron.
[10] Cart. Antiq. roll K, n. 36 ; *Mon. Anglic.* vi. 87 ; J. Willis Clark, *Liber Memorand.
de Bernewelle*, p. 43.   [11] *Chron. of Abingdon*, ii. 95.

Flambard holds of the king and is henceforth to hold during his life as a canon of Salisbury. It is attested by the bishops, William of Winchester and Robert of Lincoln ; Pharicius abbot of Abingdon, Roger de Marte-wast,[1] and Alfred of Lincoln ; at Marlborough.[2] [1104–16.]

255. Mandate to Robert bishop of Chester, Robert de Ferrers, and Richard son of Gotse,[3] to restore to Robert bishop of Lincoln and his churches of the Peak the lands, tithes, and customs whereof he and his churches were seised on the day on which the king gave his lordship of the Peak to William Peverel, because he gave him none of those things whereof the said churches were seised. It is attested by (Robert) count of Meulan ; at Chute ('apud Ceat ').[4] [1106–14.]

256. Grant, addressed generally, in favour of the monks of Battle. It is attested by Robert bishop of Lincoln, William the chaplain, and Eudes the sewer ; at Wartling ('Wercling ').[5] [1100–16.]

15–18 May. The king's court was sitting in London at Rogations.[6]

257. 17 May. Henry meets Robert count of Flanders at Dover on the 16 kalends of June to discuss the terms of a further treaty, which was there made. On behalf of the king there are present : Robert bishop of Lincoln, John of Bayeux the chaplain, Count Eustace, Robert of Bellême, William de Warenne, Gilbert de Aquila, Hamon the sewer, Ranulf Meschin, and William Fitz-Richard. The sureties on behalf of the king for due performance of the treaty are : Count Eustace, Manasses de Ghuisnes, Robert de Bettun, Ranulf Meschin, Gilbert de Aquila, Henry count of Eu, Roger Fitz-Richard, William earl of Warenne, and Simon de Molines. Done at Dover, on the 16 kalends of June.[7]

258. Notification to Haimon the sewer and the barons of Kent of the king's grant to Ralph bishop of Rochester and Avice abbess of Mellings of warren in their land of Malling ('de Mellingis '). It is attested by Grimbald the physician ; at Canterbury ('Cantorberia ').[8] [June 1109–Aug. 1111, or July 1113–April 1114.]

259. Writ addressed to Osbert the sheriff of Lincoln, Picot (son of Colsuen), and Alan (of Lincoln), in favour of the canons of St. Mary's, Lincoln. It directs that Welton, near Lincoln, shall be quit of gelds and customs, and particularly of the aid then in course of collection. It is attested by Ranulf the chancellor ; at Perry Court ('Peri ').[9] [1107–15.]

29 May. The king holds his court at Whitsuntide at New Windsor which he has built.[10] He expels from the kingdom certain nobles who have injured him, namely Philip de Braose ('Brahuse '), William Malet, and William Bainard.[11]

---

[1] Cf. *Testa de Nevill*, p. 270 b.

[2] *Sarum Charters* (Rolls Ser.), p. 3 ; cf. *Reg. St. Osmund*, i. 200.

[3] He resigned office as sheriff in favour of Robert de Heriz before February 1114.

[4] *Cal. of Chart. Rolls*, iv. 139 ; Vesp. E. xvi, fo. 6, n. 3 ; *Mon. Anglic.* vi. 1272, n. 16.

[5] Chartul. of Battle, Vitell. D. ix, fo. 29 and fo. 86 ; *Mon. Anglic.* iii. 247, n. 17.

[6] See no. 261 below.

[7] Hearne, *Liber Niger*, p. 16 ; *Foedera* (ed. 1745), i, pt. i, p. 1.

[8] *Cal. of Chart. Rolls*, v. 56, n. 3.

[9] Chartul. of St. Mary's, Lincoln, Vesp. E. xvi, fo. 7 d, n. 15 ; *Mon. Anglic.* vi. 1273, n. 28.   [10] Hen. of Huntingdon, p. 237.

[11] *Ibid.* Possibly Robert de Lascy was banished at this time.

260. Writ addressed to Richard bishop of London, Hugh de Bocheland, and the barons of Hertfordshire, directing them to render to Hervey bishop of Ely the land of (Great) Hadham. It is attested by the bishops, William of Winchester, Roger of Salisbury, Robert of Lincoln, William of Exeter, Robert of Chester, John of Bath, and Ralph of Rochester; Ranulf the chancellor, Robert count of Meulan, Gilbert de Aquila, William de Aubigny, Hamon the sewer, and Nigel de Aubigny; at Windsor, at Whitsuntide, in the year in which the king's daughter was given to the emperor.[1]

261. Notification, addressed generally, that Hugh abbot of St. Augustine's, Canterbury, has deraigned in the king's court his lands of Ripple and Langdon against Manasser Arsic. It is attested by (Robert) bishop of Lincoln and (Robert) count of Meulan; 'at Windsor, at Whitsuntide, in the year in which the king gave his daughter to the emperor. This was deraigned at London in Rogations.'[2]

262. Notification to William de Pont de l'Arche the sheriff, Herbert the chamberlain, Henry de Port, and generally, of a grant in favour of Bishop William Giffard and the monks of the old minster at Winchester.[3] It is attested by the bishops, Roger of Salisbury and Robert of Lincoln; Ranulf the chancellor, Gilbert de Aquila, Hamon the sewer, and William de Aubigny. 'This gift was confirmed at Windsor, at Whitsuntide, when the king had returned from Dover after his colloquy with Robert count of Flanders.'[4]

263. Notification to the bishops, William of Winchester and Roger of Salisbury; the sheriffs of Wiltshire, Hampshire, Dorset, and Buckingham, and the barons and lieges of those shires, of the grant to the church of St. Mary of 'Sarum' of the tithes of the New Forest and of the royal forests in Wiltshire, Dorset, and Berkshire. It is attested by[5] Robert bishop of Lincoln, Ranulf the chancellor, Robert count of Meulan, and Hamon the sewer; at Northampton.[6] [1107–16.]

264. Mandate to Hugh de Bocheland to permit the monks of Wallingford to have their tithes of Moulsford and of the land of Henry the larderer, as they held them in the time of King William, the king's brother. It is attested by Ranulf the chancellor; at Northampton.[7] [1107–16.]

265. 5 July. Confirmation of certain gifts, made by Manasser Arsic in the years 1103 and 1107, to the church of Fécamp of property in England, namely at Sabrinton. It is attested by Robert bishop of Lincoln, Ranulf the chancellor, Gilbert de Aquila, William de Tanquervill, and Eudes son of Hubert the seneschal. On the part of Holy Trinity the signatories are: William Fitz-Gerard and Ingelram the seneschal. 'This was done at Stamford on the 3 nones of July, in the year of the Incarnation 1110.'[8]

266. Writ, addressed to John bishop of Lisieux, Roger de Magnavilla,

---

[1] *Lib. Eliensis*, MS. iii, c. 7; Bentham, *Hist. of the Church of Ely*, app. 17*.

[2] *Charter Rolls*, 20 Edw. II, m. 2, n. 14; *Dep. Keeper's Rep.* xxx, app., p. 198, n. 16; *Hist. S. Aug. Cantuar.* p. 362.

[3] Cf. Florence of Worcester, *s. a.* 1111; *Chron. of Abingdon*, ii. 111–12.

[4] *Cal. of Chart. Rolls*, iii. 351.   [5] Cf. nn. 268, 269.

[6] *Reg. of St. Osmund*, i. 206; also p. 201.   [7] Bodleian ch., Berks., n. 1.

[8] *Cart. Antiq.* roll S, n. 18 (8); *sub tit.* 'carta de Cogis'. See *Mon. Anglic.* vi. 1003 *b*; Round, *Cal. of Documents, France*, no. 221.

and William son of Ansger,[1] directing that Richard bishop of Bayeux shall have the jurisdiction (*iusticia*) of his bishopric, as fully as Odo his predecessor had it. It is attested by Roger bishop of Salisbury; at Stamford ('Stanfort').[2] [1107–c. 1116.]

267. Notification to Robert bishop of Lincoln, Gilbert the sheriff (of Huntingdon), the barons, lieges, and merchants generally of the grant in favour of St. Benet's of Ramsey and St. Ives of a yearly fair. It is attested by Robert bishop of Lincoln, Robert count of Meulan, Hamon the sewer, Gilbert the sheriff, and William de Houcton (the chamberlain); 'at Brampton, in the year in which the king gave his daughter to the emperor'.[3]

268. Grant to the same (in the same terms), attested by Robert count of Meulan, Robert bishop of Lincoln, Ranulf the king's chancellor, Earl Simon ('Simundus'), Robert, William (de Houcton) the king's chamberlain, and Gilbert the sheriff, at Brampton. 'Hec concessit ipse rex ipso anno quo dedit filiam suam Henrico imperatori, hoc est anno Incarnationis Domini millesimo centesimo decimo.'[4]

269. Notification to the archbishop of Canterbury, Ralph bishop of Rochester, Hugh abbot of St. Augustine's, Hamon the sewer, and the barons of Kent, of the confirmation to Hugh, abbot of St. Augustine's, of land which the monks of the Holy Trinity, Canterbury, gave them in exchange for land which they received for the enlargement of their cemetery. It is attested by the bishops, Roger of Salisbury and Robert of Lincoln; Ranulf the chancellor, Hamon the sewer, William de Aubigny, and Ranulf Meschin; at Brampton.[5] [Same as 258.]

270. Writ, addressed generally, for the monks of Tiron (arr. Perche). It is attested by Roger bishop of Salisbury and Walter de Gloucester; at Brampton.[6] [1102–c. 1116.]

271. Writ, addressed to Hugh de Bocheland and Haldene, in favour of St. Albans. It is attested by Eudes the sewer (and is issued) by Robert Doisnell;[7] at Brampton.[8] [1100–16.]

272. Notification to Ranulf bishop of Durham, Aluric and Ligulf sheriffs, and the barons of Northumberland, of the grant to St. Alban and St. Oswin and Abbot Richard of Graffard's land in certain places. It is attested by Robert bishop of Lincoln, Ranulf the chancellor, and Nigel de Aubigny; at Brampton.[9] [c. 1106–16.]

273. Notification to the county court of Berkshire, namely to Roger bishop of Salisbury, Hugh de Bocheland, and the lieges of Berkshire, of a grant in favour of the church of Abingdon. It is attested by the bishops, Roger of Salisbury, Robert of Lincoln, and John of Bath; William de

---

[1] Cf. Orderic, iii. 356; Round, *Cal. of Documents, France*, no. 167; *Liber Winton.* pp. 537 b, 538 b.

[2] *Livre Noir* of Bayeux, n. 29.

[3] *Chartul. of Ramsey*, n. 162; Add. Ch. 33670 (1).

[4] *Chartul. of Ramsey*, n. 80.   [5] *Hist. S. Aug. Cantuar.* p. 359.

[6] Round, *Cal. of Documents, France*, no. 1004.

[7] He held the serjeanty of the king's marshalsea at Huish, co. Wilt. Cf. *Red Book of the Excheq.* (Rolls Ser.), pp. 209, 486; *Testa de Nevill*, pp. 147 b, 155; *Rot. Chartarum* (Rec. Com.), p. 16.

[8] Math. Paris, *Chron. Mai.* vi. 40.

[9] Craster, *Hist. of Northumb.* ix. 54 n., and viii. 55, note 12

Curci, William de Aubigny the butler, Nigel de Oilli,[1] Thomas de St. John, Ralph Basset, Hugh de Bocheland, Walter de Gloucester, and Geoffrey de Clinton ; ' at Woodstock in the park, in the year in which the king gave his daughter to the Roman Emperor'.[2]

274. Writ addressed to R(oger) the bishop, Herbert the chamberlain, and Hugh de Bocheland, directing them to acquit Abbot Faritius of the aid, which the barons have given to the king, in respect of five hides at Worth, which he has granted quit for all time by another writ.[3] It is attested by the sewers, Eudes and Hamon, William de Curci, and Nigel de Oilli ; at Cornbury.[4] [1102–16.]

During the last three months of 1110, and until the king left England in August or September 1111, the movements of the court are almost wholly unknown. The bulk of the documents which follow, down to the time of the king's embarkation, are of uncertain date.

275. Confirmation to St. Peter's, York, of certain privileges and immunities. It is attested by Archbishop Thomas, the bishops, William Giffard of Winchester, Robert of Lincoln, and Ranulf Flambard of Durham; William earl of Warenne, Ralph Basset, Geoffrey Ridel, and Forne son of Sigulf ;[5] at Winchester.[6] [May–July 1108; June 1109–Aug. 1111; July 1113–Feb. 1114.]

276. Writ addressed to Osbert the sheriff directing that the land of Archbishop Thomas shall not geld otherwise than it used to do in the time of Archbishop Thomas I. It is attested by Nigel de Aubigny ; at Winchester.[7] [Same as 275.]

277. Notification to Samson bishop of Worcester, Walter (de Gloucester) sheriff, and the barons of Gloucestershire, of the confirmation to the monastery of Abingdon of a gift made by William Guizenboeth with the consent of (Robert) count of Meulan in the eighth year of Henry I.[8] It is attested by (Robert) count of Meulan, Utuer (son of Earl Hugh), Geoffrey Fitz-Pain, and Alfred of Lincoln; at Winchester.[9] [June 1109–May 1112.]

278. Notification to Roger bishop of Salisbury, the sheriff of Wiltshire, &c., of the confirmation to St. Mary's, Shaftesbury, of the land of Down-head. It is attested by Roger Fitz-Richard and Alfred of Lincoln ; at Winchester.[10] [1102–16.]

279. Writ addressed to Osbert the sheriff, and the barons of Yorkshire, directing that the land of St. John (of Beverley) shall not geld otherwise than it did in the time of King Edward. It is attested by Robert count of Meulan ; at Westminster.[11] [1100–15.]

280. Notification to Richard bishop of London, Hugh de Bocheland, and the barons of London and Middlesex, of the king's gift to Abingdon

---

[1] A benefactor to Eynsham Abbey before 1109 ; Salter, *Cartul. of Eynsham,* pp. viii, 36.

[2] *Chron. of Abingdon,* ii. 64.   [3] A reference to no. 73.

[4] *Chron. of Abingdon,* ii. 113. See no. 73 above.

[5] Lord of Greystoke, co. Cumb., and a tenant-in-chief in co. York.

[6] *Histor. of York,* iii. 34 ; *Mon. Anglic.* vi. 1180, n. 31.

[7] Farrer, *Early Yorkshire Charters,* n. 17.

[8] Cf. *Chron. of Abingdon,* ii. 102.   [9] *Chron. of Abingdon,* ii. 103.

[10] *Mon. Anglic.* ii. 482, n. 9.   [11] *Cal. of Chart. Rolls,* iii. 140.

and Abbot Faritius of the messuage late Aldwin's in 'Suthstret' (in Westminster), adjoining the said abbot's lodging. It is attested by Roger
bishop of Salisbury, Gilbert de Aquila, Otuer son of Earl (Hugh), Grimbald
the physician, and Walter de Beauchamp; at 'Westmoster'.[1] [May
1108–11.]

25 Dec. 'This year the king did not wear his crown at Christmas.'[2]
Possibly the king passed the last days of the year at Windsor.

1111.

281. Notification to R(ichard) bishop of London, Hugh de Bocheland,
the barons and lieges of London and Middlesex, of the confirmation to
the monastery of Abingdon and Abbot Faritius of their lodgings in London
in 'Westminstre stret'. It is attested by Grimbald the physician and
Nigel de Aubigny; at Windsor.[3] [May 1108–16.]

282. Confirmation, addressed generally, in favour of the monastery of
St. Albans. It is attested by the bishops, William of Winchester, Ranulf
(of Durham), and Roger (of Salisbury); William Peverel of Dover and
Nigel de Aubigny; at Sutton (Courtenay).[4] [1104–16.]

283. Writ addressed to Hugh de Bochelande and generally, wherever
St. Albans has lands, notifying them of the confirmation to St. Albans,
at the prayer of Abbot Richard, of the customs and privileges of the
monastery, to hold as beneficially as Stigand had them on the day when
King Edward died. It is attested by William bishop of Winchester,
Ranulf bishop (of Durham), Roger bishop[5] (of Salisbury), William Peverel
of Dover, and Nigel de Aubigny; at Sutton (Courtenay).[6] [1104–16.]

284. Notification to William Fitz-Walter,[7] Croc the huntsman, Richard
the serjeant,[7] and the ministers of the forest of Windsor, of the grant to
the church of Abingdon of plenary tithe of the venison to be taken in the
forest of Windsor. It is attested by Robert bishop of Lincoln and Eudes
the sewer; at Brill ('Bruhella').[8] [c. 1110–16.]

285. Notification to Thomas archbishop of York, bishop Samson, the
barons and lieges of Gloucestershire, of the grant to Walter de Gloucester
of land of the canons of St. Oswald lying in front of Gloucester Castle,
and mandate to Walter de Gloucester to give the canons land of the royal
demesne in exchange. It is attested by Roger bishop of Salisbury; at
Brill.[9] [May 1108–Aug. 1111.]

2 April. The king did not wear his crown at Easter.[10]

286. In the eleventh year of his reign the king sends a mandate to the
sheriffs of Berkshire and Oxfordshire to cause right to be done to the
abbey of Abingdon in respect of toll due to the abbey from shipping at
Oxford. Subsequently in a court held that year in the house of Harding

[1] *Chron. of Abingdon*, ii. 75. See no. 288 below.
[2] Chron.   [3] *Chron. of Abingdon*, p. 75. See nos. 280, 288.
[4] M. Paris, *Chron. Mai.* vi. 38 ; *Cal. of Chart. Rolls*, iii. 19.
[5] 'Rogero cancellario': MS. An error; M. Paris, *ut supra*, p. 38.
[6] M. Paris, *ut supra*, p. 38.   [7] *R. Mag. Pip.*, 31 Hen. I, pp. 127–8.
[8] *Chron. of Abingdon*, ii. 94.
[9] Duchy of Lanc., Royal Chart. n. 2 ; *Ancient Charters* (Pipe Roll Soc.), p. 4.
[10] Chron.

the priest, within the city of Oxford, before Thomas de St. John and Richard de Monte, sheriff of Oxfordshire, the right to levy this toll is adjudged to the church of Abingdon. In the ensuing year the church of Abingdon deraigns this custom in a court at which Richard de Monte, sheriff of Oxfordshire, and Walter, archdeacon of Oxford, are present.[1]

During the spring or summer the king sends for Geoffrey le Breton, dean of Le Mans, and nominates him to the see of Rouen.[2]

287. April–July. Confirmation, addressed generally, in favour of the church of Abingdon and its filiation, St. Andrew's, Colne. It is attested by Robert bishop of Lincoln, John of Bayeux (the king's chaplain), Gilbert the chaplain, Geoffrey de Dive, Hamon the sewer, Ranulf Meschin, William Peverel of Nottingham, and Hugh de Bocheland; at Reading.[3] ' Hec donationum concessio facta est a serenissimo rege Anglorum Henrico anno Dominice incarnationis M.CXI, indictione iiiiᵃ, anno vero regni sui xi.'[4] [20 March–4 Aug. 1111.]

288. Writ addressed to Hugh de Bocheland, the ministers of London, and Reiner the reeve, directing that Abbot Faritius shall have the addition to his lodging (in Westminster Street) which the king lately made by writ.[5] It is attested by Robert bishop of Lincoln and John of Bayeux the chaplain ; at Reading.[6]

289. Writ addressed to Robert and Alfred, ministers of the count of Meulan at Welgrave, in favour of the abbot of Abingdon. It is attested by Ranulf the chancellor and John of Bayeux, at Newbury.[7] [1107–16.]

21 May. ' At Whitsuntide the king did not wear his crown.'[8]

290. Writ, addressed by Thomas archbishop of York, Nigel de Aubigny, Robert de Heriz, sheriff of Nottingham, the barons and lieges of York and Nottinghamshire, directing that the monks of Durham shall hold in peace the lands and mills in Nottinghamshire, which they have by the king's concession, as his charter affirms,[9] which they have. It is attested by Robert bishop of Lincoln, Nigel de Aubigny, William de Tancarvill, and Ralph Basset ; at Westminster.[10] [c. 1110–Feb. 1114.]

290 A. Writ, addressed to Walter sheriff of Gloucester, Roger sheriff of Worcester, Hugh de Leicester, and the barons of England, directing that Thomas,[11] prior of Worcester, his monks, men, and land shall have the king's firm peace. It is attested by (Roger) bishop of Salisbury ; at Clarendon.[12] [1110–Aug. 1111 or July–Sept. 1113.]

291. c. July. Notification to Herbert bishop of Norwich, the barons and lieges of Norfolk and Suffolk, of the grant to Robert Fitz-Walter of the land late of Robert Fitz-Rabel in More [13] and Norwich. It is attested by Robert bishop of Lincoln, Reyner (*sic*) the chancellor, Walter archdeacon of Norwich, the masters, sons of John (*sic*),[14] William de Hocton,

---

[1] *Chron. of Abingdon*, ii. 119–20.

[2] Orderic, iv. 300.　　　　　　　　　　[3] *Chron. of Abingdon*, ii. 57.

[4] This precedes the testing clause.　　[5] No. 280 above.

[5] *Chron. of Abingdon*, ii. 76. See no. 280.　[7] *Chron. of Abingdon*, ii. 77.

[8] Chron.　　　　　　　　　　　　　　　[9] Cf. no. 15.

[10] *Hist. Dunelm. Script. Tres*, p. xxxi.

[11] Died 4 Oct. 1113; *Mon. Anglic.*, i. 580; *Annals of Worcester, s. a.*

[12] *Regist. Priorat. B. M. Wigorn.* (Camden Soc.), 30.

[13] Cf. *Domesday Book*, ii. 269 b.　　　　[14] ' magistris filiis Iohannis ' : MS.

Richard Fitz-Hermer, Ralph Fitz-Godric, Ralph Passelewe (?),[1] and Godric (?) ; at Winchester ' in transitu regis '.[2] [July 1108 ?–May 1116.]

8 Aug. The king and queen are at Bishop's Waltham awaiting a favourable passage to Normandy.

292. Confirmation in favour of the church of Bath and John the bishop. The signatories or witnesses are : the bishops, Roger of Salisbury, William of Exeter, William of Winchester, Richard of London, Robert of Lincoln, Reinhelm of Hereford, and Hervey of Ely ; Ranulf the chancellor, John of Bayeux, Evrard (the chaplain), Bernard the chaplain, Grimbald the physician, Simon earl (of Northampton), Stephen (count) of Aumâle, Hamon the sewer, Gilbert de Aquila, Geoffrey de Magnevill, T(homas) de St. John, and William Peverel of Dover. ' Hec cartula confirmata fuit apud Waltham Wintoniensis episcopi a rege et regina anno ab incarnatione Domini M.CXI., VI idus Augusti, in transitu regis in Normanniam, anno XII^{MO} regni sui.'[3]

In August the king went over sea to Normandy on account of the hostility that some had against him on the frontiers of France, and above all on account of the count of Anjou, who held Le Maine against him.[4]

4 Oct., or 5 Dec. Robert count of Flanders dies.[5]

293. Urse abbot of Rouen recovers a tenement in Rouen ' iudicio optimatum ', possibly in the king's court at Rouen. The king is not named as being present. The justices are : Geoffrey archbishop of Rouen, John bishop of Lisieux, Robert count of Meulan, William earl of Warenne, Gilbert de Aquila, William the chamberlain of Tancarvill, and William de Ferrers. The record supplies the date : ' pontificante papa Paschali, anno ab incarnatione Domini M.C.XI., sub rege Henrico,' &c.[6]

293 A. Notification to Richard bishop of Bayeux, the barons and lieges of Oismeis of the grant to the monks of St. Martin's, Troarn, of a certain marsh, touching which there had been a plea in the king's court. It is attested by Robert count of Meulan and Nigel de Aubigny ; at Rouen.[7]

1112.

293 B. Robert count of Meulan gives in the year 1112 for the support of the kitchen of the monks of Bec the manor of Chisenbury (' Chilingueberia ', Wiltshire). The same year Henry I confirms the gift.[8]

294. 2 Mar. A charter of confirmation is issued to the abbey of Holy Trinity, Savigny, of the gifts of Ralph de Fougères. It is attested by Baldric archbishop of Dol, Turgis bishop of Avranches, Ranulf the chancellor, William earl of Warenne, Richard earl of Chester, John of Bayeux,

---

[1] ' Passe-Godric ' : MS.   [2] Chartul. of St. Benet's, Holme, Galba E. ii, fo. 54.

[3] *Two Bath Chartul.* i, n. 43 ; *Mon. Anglic.* ii. 267, n. 12. Cf. *Cal. of Chart. Rolls,* iii. 471 ; *Dep. Keeper's Rep.* xxx, app. 6, p. 206.

[4] Chron. ; Hen. of Huntingdon, p. 237.

[5] Orderic, iv. 290, note by Le Prevost. In some chronicles the date is given as 4 October.

[6] Original in archives of the Seine-Inférieure ; Bibl. Nat., MS. Lat. 10055, fo. 84 ; *ante,* xxiv. 212 ; Haskins, *Norman Institutions,* p. 91.

[7] Archives of the Calvados ; Haskins, *Norman Institutions,* p. 90.

[8] Porée, *Histoire de l'abbaye du Bec,* i. 467 ; Bibl. Nat., MS. Lat. 13905, fo. 21 d ; 12884, fo. 156.

Grimbald the physician, William de Aubigny, Thomas de St. John, Roger Fitz-Richard, Humphrey de Bohun, Ingram de Abernone, Geoffrey de Magnevill, Hamon the sewer, Robert de Curci, William de Pirou, Jordan de Sai, Harscolf de St. James, Geoffrey de Dive chaplain, Humphrey Bigot (chaplain), Evrard de Calne, Robert Peche, William de Martinwast, William the almoner and Hugh the scribe. On the part of Ralph de Fougères many others also attested. ' Given and confirmed at Avranches, A.D. 1112, indiction 5, epact 20, 6 nones of March, in the 13th year of the king's reign, &c. It is also subscribed by the king, (Ranulf) the chancellor, William earl of Warenne, Eustace of Breteuil, Nigel de Aubigny, Richard ' sigilli custos ',[1] Hamon the sewer, William de Aubigny the butler, Humphrey de Bohun, Richard earl of Chester, Maugisius de Savigny and Robert his nephew and Johel brother of Robert, and Roger Fitz-Peter.[2]

c. Feb.–Mar. Henry sends William count of Evreux and Helewise the countess into exile for having destroyed the dongeon at Evreux.[3]

Henry fortifies Nonancourt and Illiers-L'Evêque, in Eure, against Gervase de Chateau-neuf, and takes from him Sorel Moussel, in Eure-et-Loire.[4]

5 May. Samson bishop of Worcester dies on Sunday, 3 nones of May.[5] Stephen, the first abbot of St. Mary's, York, dies about this time.[6]

295. Notification to Roger bishop of Salisbury, Aiulf the chamberlain,[7] and the barons and lieges of Dorset, of the grant to the abbey of Montebourg and Urse its abbot that the manor of Loders, given by Richard de Redvers, shall be assessed in gelds and other dues as 5 hides only. It is witnessed by Ranulf the chancellor, Roger de Magnevill, Nigel de Calna,[8] and Walcheline the canon ; at Sainte-Mère-Eglise [9] (' apud Sancte Marie ecclesiam ').[10] [1107–20.]

29 Aug. Gilbert bishop of Evreux dies on 4 kalends of September.[11]

Oct. King Louis sends Robert of Bellême on a mission to Henry,[12] who takes him prisoner at Cherbourg,[13] and later sends him to England and commits him to the castle of Wareham.[14]

4 Nov. At Bonneville-sur-Touque the king causes Robert of Bellême to be indicted of perjury in breaking his oath of fealty to him, and of aiding Fulk of Anjou ; and also for his neglect to render account as the king's sheriff and minister of the royal revenues of Argentan, Exmes, and Falaise.[15]

295 A. Mandate that the property of Vitalis the hermit of Savigny and his associates shall be quit of toll, custom, and passage. It is attested by Ranulf the chancellor and Nigel de Aubigny, at Varreville (' apud Warrevillam ').[16]

[1] Haskins, *Norman Institutions*, p. 311.

[2] *Gallia Christiana*, xi, instr., col. 111 ; Round, *Calendar*, no. 792. On the date of this confirmation see Haskins, l.c.

[3] Orderic, iv. 279.   [4] *Ibid.* p. 304.   [5] Florence of Worcester.

[6] *Mon. Anglic.* iii. 582 *b.*   [7] Of Ham Chamberlain, co. Dorset.

[8] Occ. c. 1123 ; *Regist. of St. Osmund*, i. 381.   [9] In La Manche.

[10] Round, *Cal. of Documents, France*, no. 876 ; *Mon. Anglic.* vi. 999.

[11] Orderic, iv. 301.   [12] *Ibid.* p. 376.

[13] Sym. of Durham, ii. 247.   [14] Chron.   [15] Orderic, iv. 305.

[16] *Mémoires de la Société des Antiquaires de la Normandie*, xx. 256, where the writ is assigned to the year 1112

Henry lays siege to Alençon. A few days later the town is surrendered.[1]

296. Queen Matilda, by charter addressed to Roger bishop of Salisbury, Walter Fitz-Eadward, the barons, Humphrey de Bohun and the king's ministers of Wiltshire and Malmesbury, grants to the monastery of Malmesbury an extension to 8 days of the fair of St. Aldhelm. It is attested by Richard bishop of London, Bernard (her) chancellor, William de Curci, and Aldhelm (her) chamberlain ;[2] at Westminster.[3] [1111–13.]

25 Dec. The king is in Normandy at Christmas.[4]

1113.

2–3 Feb. Henry and the court celebrate the feast of the Purification at St. Evroul.[5] He is attended by his nephews, Theobald and Stephen of Blois, and by Conan of Brittany and William bishop of Exeter.[6]

297. By the advice of Robert count of Meulan Henry directs that a charter of confirmation to the abbey of St. Evroul shall be prepared. This is done, and at a later date Prior Ernald and Gilbert of Les Essarts ('Sartensis') deliver the charter to the king at Rouen.[7]

The king gives certain comestibles to the monks of St. Evroul.[8]

297 A. 11 Feb. Hugh de Gournay II confirms certain gifts to the abbey of Bec and adds the gift of certain goods in England. Henry I confirms the gifts : 'Hec omnia concessit et sigillo suo firmavit Henricus rex Anglorum et dux Normannorum, iii idus Februarii supradicti anni [1113], apud Beccum.'[9]

Henry visits certain of the borders of his dominion and gives orders for the fortification of the vulnerable points.[10]

23 Feb.–1 Mar. In the first week of Lent Henry is at Pierre-Pecoulée, near Alençon. Thither comes Fulk, count of Anjou, and does fealty and homage for Maine, which he then receives from the king as a fief.[11] Fulk betrothes his daughter Matilda to William, the king's son.[12] At the same time the king restores the county of Evreux to Count William, and pardons Amaury de Montfort and William Crispin.[13]

25 Feb. William Peverel of Nottingham dies on 5 kalends of March.[14]

c. March. Foucher, abbot of Shrewsbury, dies.[15]

23–9 Mar. In the last week of March Henry and Louis meet in the field of Ormeteau-Ferré, near Gisors, and make peace. The terms, as recorded, are very favourable to Henry.[16]

6 April. The king is probably at Rouen at Easter.

298. The confirmation to St. Evroul, named above, is now issued. It is subscribed by the king, Geoffrey archbishop of Rouen, Robert count

---

[1] *Mémoires de la Société des Antiquaires de la Normandie*, xx. 256. The precise date of these events is uncertain.

[2] Cf. *Hist. MSS. Comm. Rep.* ix, pt. i, p. 66.

[3] *Regist. Malmesbur.* i. 329 ; Lansd. MS. 417, fo. 30 d.

[4] Chron.   [5] Orderic, iv. 301.   [6] *Ibid.*   [7] *Ibid.* p. 302.

[8] *Ibid.* p. 303 n. ; Chartul. of St. Evroul, Bibl. Nat. (Paris), i, fo. 4 d.

[9] Porée, *Histoire de l'abbaye du Bec*, i. 339 ; Bibl. Nat., MS. Lat. 13905, fo. 20.

[10] Orderic, iv. 303.   [11] *Ibid.* p. 306.   [12] *Ibid.*   [13] *Ibid.*

[14] Reg. of St. James's by Northampton ; Bridges' *Northamptonshire*, i. 501 n.

[15] Willis, *Mitred Abbeys*, i. 167.

[16] Orderic, iv. 307–8 ; Luchaire, *Louis VI*, n. 158.

of Meulan, Nigel de Aubigny, Richard earl of Chester, Goel ('Huell') de Ivry, William Peverel, William de Sai, Roger de Ticboudivill, William de la Lunde, Walter de Vernon, Robert Fitz-Anschetill and William his son, Patric de Chaources, Robert the king's son, and William Bigot. 'Hanc autem donationis cartulam ego Henricus rex scribi feci, anno quo comes Andegavensis mecum pacem fecit et Cenomannum de me, meus homo factus, recepit, et confirmavi atque confirmo in turre Rothomagensi, presentibus istis,' &c.[1]

299. Notification that Gerold, abbot of St. Wandrille, in the presence of the king and his barons, has demised Werelwast at farm to John bishop of Lisieux for the term of his life. It is attested by Geoffrey archbishop of Rouen, Ranulf the chancellor, Eustace count of Boulogne, Robert count of Meulan, the sewers Eudes and Hamon, Robert de Beauchamp, Geoffrey Fitz-Pain, Walter de Vernone, Alan de Alichervill, William Fitz-Ansger, William Fitz-Oine, William Fitz-Godfrey, and Atseline de Bois-Gerard, at Rouen.[2]

300. Notification to Ralph bishop of Rochester, Hamon the sewer, and the barons of Kent, of the grant to the abbey of St. Saviour, Bermondsey, of the church of Shorne (near Gravesend), to be held as Thurstan the king's chaplain used to hold it ('tenebat'). It is attested by the sewers Eudes and Hamon, William de Aubigny, and William Peverel; at Rouen.[3] [Aug. 1111–July 1113.]

301. Confirmation to the monks of Bec at Goldcliff of the possessions which Robert de Candos and Isabella his wife have given them. The signatories are : the king, Anselm the archdeacon, William de Viliers, chamberlain ('cubicularius'),[4] Eustace of Breteuil, and Richard earl of Chester.[5] [1113–18.]

1 May. On the kalends of May Henry lays siege to the castle of Bellême, then held by Aimeri de Vilerei and William son of Robert Talvace. With the king are Theobald count of Blois, Fulk count of Anjou, and Rotrou of Mortain, count of Perche.[6]

2 May. Nigel abbot of Burton dies on 6 nones of May.[7]

3 May. Henry orders the siege of the castle of Bellême to be suspended for the day of the feast of the Invention of the Holy Cross. Theobald of Blois and Rotrou of Mortain, in ignorance, or regardless, of the king's order, make an assault and take the place.[8]

25 May. Henry is in Normandy at Whitsuntide.[9]

July. After Midsummer Henry returns to England,[10] possibly by way of Portsmouth.

302. Notification to Robert bishop of Chester, Henry earl (of Warwick), the sheriff and barons of Warwickshire, of the grant to the wife of William (late) sheriff of Oxford and her son, of 30 solidates of land which William the sheriff, her husband, held of the crown in 'Chinton' (Kineton, co. Warw.),

1 Round, *Cal. of Documents, France*, no. 624; Orderic, iv. 302; v, app., p. 196. Professor Haskins dates this confirmation 'early March', 1113: *Norman Institutions*, p. 311.

2 Round, *Calendar*, no. 167.   3 *Mon. Anglic.* v. 100, n. 5.

4 Possibly William the chamberlain of Tancarville.

5 *Cal. of Chart. Rolls*, ii. 361.   6 Orderic, iv. 308.

7 *Chartul. of Burton* (Salt Arch. Soc.), 5, 32.   8 Orderic, iv. 308.

9 Chron.   10 Chron. ; 'in July' : Florence of Worcester.

particularly the land of ' Swinline ', in exchange for land in Bloxham (co. Oxon.). It is attested by Geoffrey de Clinton and Ralph Basset ; at Portsmouth.[1] [1109–16.]

303. Writ to Roger bishop of Salisbury and Walter sheriff of Wiltshire directing that the abbess and nuns of Romsey shall hold in peace certain tithes given to them by Stephen son of Arard.[2] It is attested by Gilbert de Aquila, at Portsmouth (' apud Porthesmudam ').[3] [1106–16.]

304. Mandate to Hugh de Bocheland to cause the county (court) of Bedfordshire to make a recognition on behalf of the abbot of Ramsey touching certain boundaries. It is attested by William de Aubigny, (and is issued) by Humphrey Bigot ; at Romsey.[4] [_c._ 1110–16.]

305. _c._ July. Notification to the justices, sheriffs, barons and ministers of Berkshire of the confirmation to the monastery of St. Mary of Hurley of the alms given by Geoffrey de Magnevill. It is attested by the Empress (_sic_) Matilda, Roger bishop of Salisbury, (and is issued) by Otuel son of Earl (Hugh) ; at the Tower of London.[5] [1110–16.]

306. Writ addressed to the justices, sheriffs, and ministers of England directing that the prior and monks of Hurley shall hold the tenements, which they have of the fee of Geoffrey de Magnevill in any county and especially in the manors of the honor of Geoffrey de Magnevill which are in the king's hands,[6] in as beneficial a manner as the same Geoffrey gave them to Hurley and William, the king's father, confirmed them. It is attested by Ranulf the chancellor, (and is issued) by Otuel son of Earl (Hugh) ; at the Tower of London.[7] [1110–16.]

307. Notification to the justices, sheriffs, and ministers of England and the seaports of the grant to the church of St. Peter, Westminster, of acquittance of toll throughout the realm. It is attested by Ranulf the chancellor, (and is issued) by Otuel son of Earl (Hugh) ; at the Tower of London.[8] [1110–16.]

17 July. Peter abbot of St. Peter's, Gloucester, dies on 16 kalends of August.[9]

15 Aug. Robert de Prunelai, a monk of St. Evroul, is nominated abbot of Thorney.[10]

308. Notification to Ranulf Meschin, Osbert the sheriff, Picot son of Colsuen, and the barons of Lincolnshire of the grant to Robert bishop of Lincoln of licence to make a door in the wall of the king's castle of Lincoln for the bishop's convenience in passing to his house, provided that the wall be not thereby weakened. It is attested by Alan of Lincoln and Osbert the sheriff ; at London.[11] [1101–15.]

---

[1] Chartul. of Kenilworth, Harl. MS. 3650, fo. 75.

[2] Cf. _Domesday Book_, p. 63 _b_. [3] _Cal. of Chart. Rolls_, ii. 103.

[4] _Chartul. of Ramsey_, no. 171.

[5] Madox, _Formulare Anglic._, p. 37 ; Robinson, _Gilbert Crispin_, p. 151 _f_.

[6] After the death of Geoffrey de Mandevill I and William his son, late constable of the Tower. Cf. nos. 292, 294.

[7] Westminster Abbey muniments, no. 3765 ; Robinson, _Gilbert Crispin_, p. 150.

[8] Chartul. of St. Peter's, Westminster, Faust. A. iii, fo. 130 ; Robinson, _Gilbert Crispin_, p. 150.

[9] _Chartul. of St. Peter's, Gloucester_, i. 14. [10] Orderic, iii. 382 n.

[11] Chartul. of St. Mary's, Linc., Vesp. E. xix, fo. 6, n. 5 ; _Mon. Anglic._ vi. 1272, n. 18.

309. Notification to Thomas archbishop of York and his clergy of the king's confirmation to the church of Bridlington of land given by Walter de Gaunt and his men. It is attested by William Peverel of Dover and William de Rullos ; at Rockingham.[1] [1109–13.]

310. Writ addressed to Adam de Port, W(illiam) son of Norman,[2] and the foresters (of Dean) directing them that Bishop Reinhelm shall have necessary materials in his forest beyond the Wye, as the king commanded by another writ. It is attested by Roger bishop of Salisbury, and Robert bishop of Lincoln ; at Waltham.[3] [1107–15.]

311. Mandate to Hugh de Legrecestria and his ministers to cause the monks of Northampton to hold in peace their land of Stutchbury, because the king wills that Earl David[4] and his monks shall hold it as beneficially as his ancestor held it. It is attested by Roger bishop of Salisbury ; at Waltham.[5] [1111–June 1123.]

312. Notification to the barons &c. of Essex, of the confirmation to St. Peter's, Westminster, of certain liberties in respect of the abbey at Feering in Essex. It is attested by William de Curci (the sewer) ; at Havering (' apud Haveringes ').[6] [1100–16.]

25 Dec. At Christmas Henry holds his court at Windsor.[7]

28 Dec. Theowulf, the king's chaplain, is nominated to the bishopric of Worcester on Sunday, the 5 kalends of January, at Windsor.[8]

1114.

6 Jan. On 8 ides of January Matilda the king's daughter is married to Henry, emperor of the Romans, and is crowned empress at Mayence.[9]

313. 2 Feb. Grant to Geoffrey archbishop of Rouen and his successors of the manor of Bentworth. It is attested by the bishops, Roger of Salisbury, Robert of Lincoln, and Ranulf of Durham ; Ranulf the chancellor, Robert count of Meulan, William earl of Warenne, Hugh de Gournay, William de Tancarvill the chamberlain, William de Aubigny the butler, and Nigel de Aubigny his brother, Hamon the sewer and Adam de Port ; at Windsor, on the Purification of St. Mary.[10]

314. Mandate to Walter Giffard and Agnes his mother to do right to Abbot Faritius in respect of land given to Abingdon by Ralph (de) Chaures-ham with Walter's consent. It is attested by Ranulf the chancellor ; at Windsor.[11] [1107–16.]

24 Feb. Thomas archbishop of York dies.[12]

315. Writ addressed to Hugh de Bocheland, Leo[f]stan,[13] W(illiam)

[1] Lancaster, *Chartul. of Bridlington*, p. 212.

[2] Of Kilpeck, co. Hereford. Cf. *Domesday Book*, p. 185 *b*.

[3] *Cal. of Pat. Rolls*, 1354–8, p. 195.

[4] This writ was issued after the death of Earl Simon, which occurred not later than 113, possibly in 1111–1112. Cf. no. 292.

[5] Chartul. of St. Andrew's, Northampton, Vesp. E. xvii, old fo. 14 *d*.

[6] Chartul. of St. Peter's, Westminster, Faust. A. iii, fo. 74.

[7] Chron.   [8] Florence of Worcester.

[9] Florence of Worcester.

[10] Round, *Calendar*, no. 5.

[11] *Chron. of Abingdon*, ii. 85. See no. 318.   [12] Florence of Worcester.

[13] Lofstan domesman ' died in 1115 : *Flores Histor.*

Cabus, Roger,[1] Otes, and the barons of London, directing that the church of the Holy Trinity shall have its pleas in the queen's court. It is attested by Roger bishop of Salisbury and (Ranulf ?) the chancellor; at Nuneham ('Niweham').[2] [1107–15.]

315 a. Notification to Roger bishop of Salisbury, Walter Hosate, and the lieges of Wiltshire of the grant to the monks of St. Martin's, Marmoutier, of the church of Coseham. It is attested by Harsculph Fitz-Eudes; at Nuneham ('Niweham').[3] [1100–16.]

11 Feb.–28 Mar. Possibly the king is at Woodstock during Lent.

316. Notification to (Robert) bishop of Lincoln, Thomas de St. John, and the lieges of Oxfordshire, of the confirmation to the church of Abingdon of land at Fencott, which Adelina de Ivry [4] has given. It is attested by Nigel de Oilli, Thomas de St. John, Hugh de Envremou, Geoffrey Fitz-Pain, Geoffrey de Magnevill, Roger de Oillei, Robert de Dunstanvill and Ralph de Angervill; at Woodstock, in Lent.[5]

317. Writ, addressed to Stephen (count) of Aumâle, Robert (de Ros) his sewer, and the ministers of Holderness, directing that Richard abbot of York shall hold freely the mere of Hornsea, as (count) Odo gave it to the abbey of York, and as William II confirmed it; and that Geoffrey de Spineto shall not fish there; 'et si aliquis quid reclamaverit inde ante me veniat placitare ex quo illum summonuero, excepto ipso sponte ad proprium opus suum.' It is attested by Nigel de Aubigny; at Woodstock.[6] [July 1113–May 1116.]

318. Mandate to Jordan de Saccevill to restore to Abingdon and to abbot Faritius the land which was given by Ralph de Caisnesham (*vel* Chauresham), otherwise Walter Giffard or Hugh de Bocheland shall cause it to be restored. It is attested by Geoffrey de Magnevill; at Woodstock.[7]

319. Notification to T(heowulf) bishop of Worcester, the barons, and lieges of Worcester that the king has commended to Walter de Beauchamp the shrievalty of Worcestershire, to be held as fully as it was held by former sheriffs; all men are to attend the pleas, hundreds, and shires as formerly. It is attested by Robert bishop of Lincoln, Roger bishop of Salisbury, Ranulf the chancellor, (Robert) count of Meulan, Hamon the sewer, Walter of Gloucester, and Thomas de St. John; at Woodstock.[8] [1114–May 1116.]

320. Confirmation, addressed generally, in favour of Abbot Geoffrey and the monks of Croyland. It is attested by Robert bishop of Lincoln, Hervey bishop of Ely, Warner de Lusours, Hugh de Essarts; at Oxford, A.D. 1114, and in the 14th year of the king's reign.[9]

321. Notification to Ranulf Meschin, Osbert the sheriff, and the lieges of Lincolnshire, of the grant to Robert bishop of Lincoln of the royal

---

[1] *Chartul. of Ramsey*, i. 130, 133.   [2] Cart. Antiq. roll N, no. 13 (10).

[3] *Cal. of Pat. Rolls*, 1334–8, p. 313.

[4] Died between May 1110 and May 1111; *Chron. of Abingdon*, ii. 72–3.

[5] *Ibid.* p. 73. An alternative date is Lent 1116.

[6] *Cal. of Pat. Rolls*, 1396–9, p. 75.

[7] *Chron. of Abingdon*, ii. 85. See no. 314.

[8] Add. MS. 28024, fo. 126 *d*. Cf. no. 335.   [9] *Mon. Anglic.* ii. 120.

warren of Lincoln, in so far as it lay in Newark and Stow. It is attested by Hugh de Evermue ; at Wallingford (' Warengefort ').[1] [1101–15.]

29 Mar. At Easter the king holds no court.[2]

April. A council is summoned to meet at Windsor. Faritius abbot of Abingdon is mentioned as likely to be appointed to the vacant see of Canterbury.[3]

26 April. Ralph bishop of Rochester is elected to the see of Canterbury on 6 kalends of May. He is enthroned on 17 kalends of June (16 May).[4]

322. Confirmation, addressed generally, to abbot (Geoffrey) and the monks of St. Peter's, Hyde, of the churches of Kingsclere and Alton,[5] given in exchange for the land on which William I built his hall in the town of Winchester, where the king's house now stands. It is attested by the bishops, Roger of Salisbury, Robert of Lincoln, and William of Exeter ; Robert count of Meulan and Henry de Porth ; at Windsor.[6] [1111–16.]

323. Easter or Michaelmas. The queen notifies the bishop of Lincoln, Thomas de St. John,[7] and the barons of Oxfordshire that in her lord's and her court at (the castle of) Winchester, in the treasury, before Roger bishop of Salisbury, Robert bishop of Lincoln, Richard bishop of London, William de Curci, Adam de Port, Thurstan the chaplain, Walter de Gloucester, Herbert the chamberlain, William de Oillei, Geoffrey Fitz-Herbert,[8] William de Enesi,[9] Ralph Basset, Geoffrey de Magnevill, Geoffrey Ridel, and Walter archdeacon of Oxford, Abbot Faritius of Abingdon, by the evidence of Domesday Book (' Liber de Thesauro '), deraigned that his manor of Lewknor owed no custom or due to be done in the hundred of Periton. This is attested by the bishop of Salisbury, William de Curci, and Adam de Port.[10] [Aug. 1111–July 1113.]

c. May–June. On 8 ides of April (*sic*) the king leads an army into Wales.[11] The English Chronicle states that ' at midsummer the king went with a force into Wales, and the Welsh came and made peace with the king ; and he caused castles to be built therein '.[12]

Alexander king of Scots and Richard earl of Chester lead a force into Wales from the north. Henry advancing on Powys occupies ' Mur Castell '.[13]

325. The king renews the grant of the bishopric of Ely to Hervey the bishop and announces that it is his will that the church of Ely shall enjoy the customs and franchises which it had enjoyed in the time of King Edward and as they had been deraigned before William I and his barons

[1] Chartul. of St. Mary's, Linc., Vesp. E. xvi, fo. 7, no. 10 ; *Mon. Anglic.* vi. 1273, no. 23.

[2] Chron. [3] Eadmer, p. 222.

[4] *Ibid.*, p. 223. [5] Cf. *Vict. County Hist., Hants*, i. 436.

[6] *Cal. of Chart. Rolls*, ii. 148. [7] Sheriff of Oxfordshire from c. 1110.

[8] Cf. Orderic, iv. 342, 359.

[9] Possibly one of the king's larderers. Cf. *Testa de Nevill*, pp. 147–8 ; *Red Book of the Exchequer*, p. 486.

[10] *Chron. of Abingdon*, ii. 116.

[11] *Flores Histor.* ii. 43 ; *Annales Camb. s. a.* 1114.

[12] *Op. cit., s. a.* 1114.

[13] *Brut y Tywysogion.* Archdeacon Thomas of St. Asaph suggests that ' Mur Castell ' was Tomen-y-Mur, at Trawsfynydd in Merionethshire.

at Kennetford (now Kentford, co. Camb.).　It is attested by Ranulf the chancellor, Gilbert de Aquila, Hamon the sewer, William de Aubigny, Pain Peverel, and William Peverel of Dover ; at Castle Holdgate in Shropshire ('apud castrum Helgoti in Salopescyra ').[1]　[1109–16.]

326. After the death of Richard de Meisnilhermer, the chaplain and a monk of Shrewsbury, Hubert his son claimed his father's late prebend in the church of St. Gregory (at Moreville, co. Salop).　A mandate was issued to Richard bishop of London to cause right to be done in the matter, whereupon Hubert relinquished his claim.　The witnesses of his release (in the king's court ?) were : the king, Richard bishop (of London), Alan Fitz-Flaald, Hamon Peverel, Roger Corbeth and Robert his brother, and Herbert Fitz-Helgot.[2]　[1108–16.]

327. Writ addressed to Herbert bishop of Norwich, Ralph de Belfou, Ralph Passelewe, and the lieges of Suffolk directing that Hervey bishop of Ely shall have his liberties in the 5½ hundreds of ' Wiclaua '.　It is attested by Ranulf the chancellor, Gilbert de Aquila, Hamon the sewer ; at Castle Helgot in ' Salopessyra '.[3]　[1109–16.]

328. Writ, addressed generally, directing that the monks of Ely shall have a fair share of the goods of the abbey of Ely, as they had before the abbey was made a bishopric.　It is attested by Ranulf the chancellor, Gilbert de Aquila, Hamon the sewer, William de Aubigny, Pain Peverel ; at Castle Helgot in ' Scalopescyra '.[4]　[1109–16.]

329. Writ addressed to Hugh Fitz-Thurstan[5] directing him to geld with Faritius abbot of Abingdon, as he was wont to geld, so that the abbot's land shall not be distrained by reason of Hugh's land, otherwise Aubrey (de Ver) of Berkshire shall constrain him to do so.　It is attested by Robert bishop of Lincoln ; at Wolverhampton ('apud Wlfruneham-tune ').[6]　[c. 1110–16.]

330. Mandate to Richard de Monte (sheriff of Oxfordshire) to cause the abbot of Westminster to have 10s. yearly of the king's alms ' sicut est in rotulis meis '.　It is attested by (Roger) bishop of Salisbury ; at Cannock (' apud Canot ').[7]　[1110–c. 1116.]

331. Notification to Robert bishop of Chester, Nicholas sheriff of Stafford-shire, and the barons of Staffordshire that Godwin (or Godric), the monk of St. Rémi of Rheims, has deraigned before the king and his barons at Tamworth against Robert of Rouen the king's chaplain, the church of Lapley.　It is attested by the bishops Robert of Lincoln, R(oger) of Salisbury, and William of Exeter ; Geoffrey Ridel and Alfred of Lincoln ; at Tamworth.[8]　[c. 1110–16.]

15 Aug.　On the feast of the Assumption of St. Mary, at Winchester,

---

[1] Cott. ch. x. 8 ; *Mon. Anglic.* i. 482, n. 16 ; Bentham, *Hist. of the Church of Ely,* app. 17*.

[2] Chartul. of Salop Abbey ; *Coll. Top. et Gen.* i. 25.

[3] Lib. Eliensis ; Bentham, *Hist. of the Church of Ely,* app. 19*.

[4] *Ibid.* 20*.

[5] Cf. Round, *The King's Serjeants,* p. 187 ; *Chron. of Abingdon,* ii. 90, 125–7.

[6] *Chron. of Abingdon,* ii. 91.

[7] Chartul. of St. Peter's, Westminster, Faust. A. iii, fo. 79 ; Robinson, *Gilbert Crispin,* p. 149.

[8] *Mon. Anglic.* vi. 1043, no. 6 ; 1099, no. 1 (c).

Thurstan the king's chaplain is preferred to the see of York.[1] At the same time Ernulf, abbot of Peterborough, is preferred to the see of Rochester.[2]

332. Writ addressed to R(ichard de Monte) sheriff of Oxford and Reiner de Bath in favour of Faritius abbot of Abingdon respecting a hide of land at Fencote, which was given by Adelina de Ivry. It is attested by Nigel de Aubigny ; at Winchester.[3] [1110-16.]

333. Mandate to Ranulf Meschin, Osbert the sheriff, Picot son of Colsuen, and Wigot of Lincoln to go and view the boundary between the king's manor of Torksey and that (of the bishop of Lincoln) of Stow. It is attested by Wigot of Lincoln ; at Winchester.[4] [1110-14.]

Thurstan, elect of York, who is a sub-deacon, is ordained in December (*sic*) by William bishop of Winchester. He is enthroned at York by Robert bishop of Chester and he then visits Durham and Hexham. At the former place he sees Turgot, bishop of St. Andrews, then lying on his death-bed.[5]

31 Aug. Turgot, bishop of St. Andrews dies.[6]

Nigel abbot of Burton dies during the year 1114 (*recte* 1113), to whom Abbot Geoffrey, prior of Winchester, succeeds the same year.[7]

Sept. The king is at Westbourne, co. Sussex, detained by unfavourable weather from crossing to Normandy.[8] A council of bishops and barons is held there which approves the king's appointment to the vacant see of Rochester.[9]

334. 13 Sept. Confirmation of an agreement made before the king and his barons between William bishop of Winchester and Geoffrey abbot of Newminster and Hyde. It is attested by the archbishops Ralph and Thurstan, the bishops Richard of London, Roger of Salisbury, Robert of Lincoln, John of Bath, William of Exeter, and Ranulf of Durham ; Robert count of Meulan, Henry earl of Warwick, Walter (de Gloucester) the constable, William the chamberlain of Tancardevill, Adam de Port, Nigel de Oillei, Henry de Port, Ralph de Limesi, and Nigel de Aubigny.[10] 'Hec conventio facta et confirmata est apud Burnam anno ab incarnatione domini M. centesimo XIIII, die iduum Septembrium.'[11]

335. Notification, addressed generally, of the grant to Walter de Beauchamp of all the land of Roger de Wygrecestra.[12] It is attested by Ralph [archbishop of Canterbury, Thurstan][13] archbishop of York, the bishops Roger of Salisbury, Robert of Lincoln, and Richard of London,

[1] Florence of Worcester.

[2] Sym. of Durham, ii. 248. Other chroniclers state that he was elected on 28 September following.

[3] *Chron. of Abingdon*, ii. 73.

[4] Chartul. of St. Mary's, Lincoln, Vesp. E. xvi, fo. 7, no. 13 ; *Mon. Anglic.* vi. 1273, n. 26.

[5] Hugh the Chantor : *Historians of York*, ii. 129-30.

[6] Eadmer, p. 236 ; *Durham Lib. Vitae*, p. 151.

[7] *Annals of Burton, s.a.* Cf. *Chartul. of Burton*, 32.

[8] Chron. ; cf. Eadmer, p. 224.   [9] Chron.

[10] *Cal. of Chart. Rolls*, iii. 346. The other part of the chirograph will be found in *Cal. of Chart. Rolls*, iv. 170. Cf. *Mon. Anglic.* ii. 444, no. 12.

[11] This clause precedes the testing clause.

[12] Roger son of Urse de Abetot. Cf. nn. 290 A, 319.

[13] Omission in manuscript.

Ranulf the chancellor, R(obert) count of Meulan ('Mellentz'), Henry earl
of Warwick, earl David, Robert the king's son, Richard the king's son,
Nigel de Aubigny, Hamon the sewer, Adam de Port, William de Pirou,
William de Tankardivilla, Brien Fitz-Count, Otuer son of Earl (Hugh),
William Peverel of Dover, Hamon Peverel, Richard Peverel, Simon de
Beauchamp, Ralph Basset, Edward of Salisbury, Robert Murdak, Walter
de Braci,[1] Walter of Gloucester (the constable), Robert de Brus, William
de Luisours ('de Lusoriis'); at Westbourne ('apud Burnam').[2]

336. Notification to William bishop of Exeter, Richard Fitz-Baldwin
(the sheriff), and the justiciary of Devon and Cornwall, of a grant to abbot
Osbert and the monks of Tavistock. It is attested by the archbishops
Ralph and Thurstan; the bishops William of Winchester, Robert of
Lincoln and Richard of London; Ranulf the chancellor, Robert count
of Meulan, and Nigel de Aubigny; at Westbourne 'in transitu'.[3]

337. Notification to Robert bishop of Chester, R(ichard) earl of Chester,
R(obert) de Ferrers, all sheriffs and ministers in whose bailiwicks the
monastery of Burton has land, of the grant of the abbey of Burton to
abbot Geoffrey. It is attested by the archbishops of Canterbury and
York, (William) bishop of Winchester, (Roger) bishop of Salisbury 'et
aliis episcopis', R(anulf) the chancellor, and (Robert) count of Meulan;
at Westbourne ('apud Burnam').[4]

338. Writ addressed to Ralph bishop of Chichester and the ministers
of Sussex notifying them that the abbot and monks of Battle have
deraigned before the king that they have not certain lands which the said
bishop alleged that they had, as belonging anciently to Alciston; and
mandate that they be henceforth quit thereof, and that their manor of
Alciston be quit of shires and hundreds, and particularly of work upon
London bridge and the castle of Pevensey. It is attested by William de
Pont de L'Arche; at Westbourne ('apud Burn''').[5] [1114–16.]

15 Sept. The king summons by writ Ernulf, abbot of Peterborough,
to come to Westbourne. He compels him to accept the bishopric of
Rochester.[6]

21 Sept. On 12 kalends of October the king and his court are at
Rowner. John, a monk of Sées, is appointed abbot of Peterborough.
On the same day the king goes on board ship at Portsmouth.[7]

339. Notification to Queen Matilda and the barons of Lincolnshire
of the confirmation to the church of Lincoln and Bishop Robert of (the
church of) St. Margaret (in Lincoln?) and the church of Haceby ('Bar-
sebi'), which (quas) Osbert the sheriff gave. It is attested by (Roger)
bishop of Salisbury; at Portsmouth ('apud Porc'es-muudam').[8]

340. Notification to archbishop T(hurstan), the sheriff, barons, and
lieges of Yorkshire, of the grant to Rainald Belet in fee farm of Hutton
(Bushell) and other lands (in the soc of Pickering). It is attested by

---

[1] Of Holdfast in Ripple, co. Worc.
[2] Add. MS. 28024, fo. 149.　　　　　[3] *Mon. Anglic.* ii. 501.
[4] *Chartul. of Burton* (Salt Arch. Soc.), v, pt. i, p. 11; *Mon. Anglic.* iii. 41.
[5] Harl. ch. 43, C. 12; *Journ. of the Arch. Assoc.* xxix. 257.
[6] Chron.　　　　　　　　　　　　　　[7] Chron.
[8] Chartul. of St. Mary's, Lincoln, Vesp. E. xvi, fo. 7; *Mon. Anglic.* vi. 1273, no. 22.

R(oger) bishop of Salisbury, Nigel de Aubigny, and Robert de Brus ; at Portsmouth.[1] [1114–27.]

341. Confirmation to the abbey of St. Georges de Bocherville of certain gifts made by Ralph de Tancarvill, William the chamberlain, his son, Geoffrey Fitz-Pain, and others. The signatories are the king, Geoffrey archbishop of Rouen, the bishops John of Lisieux and Roger of Coutances, William (de Tancarvill) the chamberlain, Rabel son of the (same) chamberlain, Geoffrey Fitz-Pain, and Edward of Salisbury. This is done in the year 1114, when, at William de Tancarvill's request, the king consented to the church of St. Georges being made an abbey.[2]

342. Notification to archbishop Thurstan, Hugh de Laval, the sheriff and barons of Yorkshire of the grant to the canons of St. Oswald of a fair at Nostell. It is attested by Ranulf the chancellor, Henry count of Eu, Roger Fitz-Richard, Humphrey de Bohun, Pain Fitz-John, Ralph de Todeney, and Ingram de Abernone ; at Rouen.[3] [1114–20.]

Before Christmas Archbishop Thurstan joins the king in Normandy and petitions to be allowed to go to Rome. The king refuses his permission.[4]

25 Dec. At Christmas the king is in Normandy.[5]

1115.

At Rouen, possibly early in the spring, Henry causes the magnates of Normandy to swear fealty to William his son.[6]

343. Notification to Geoffrey archbishop of Rouen, Henry count of Eu, Adam de Germunvill, and the lieges of Normandy, of a grant to the monks of the Holy Trinity, Tiron. It is attested by Robert bishop of Lincoln, Robert count of Meulan, Earl William de Warenne, William de Tancarvill the chamberlain, and Stephen of Aumâle ; at Rouen, ' on the day on which the barons of Normandy were made (*effecti*) the men of the king's son '.[7]

344. Confirmation, addressed generally for England, to the monks of St. Evroul, and restoration to them of the manor of Charlton (in Blunham, co. Beds), which Adelina de Ivri gave them. It is attested by Nigel de Aubigny, Fulk de Alnou, and Ralph de Pont Echanfré ; at Rouen.[8] [1111–20.]

345. Notification to Geoffrey archbishop of Rouen, (Richard) bishop of Bayeux, (   ) bishop of Evreux, and the ministers of Normandy, of the renewal of a grant to Rolland D'Oissel. It is attested by William de Aubigny, William Peverel of Dover, Ralph de Limesi, and Gilbert son of Reiner (' Rener.') ; at Caen.[9] [1111–28.]

18 April. Mary countess of Boulogne, sister of Queen Matilda, dies on 14 kalends of May.[10]

---

[1] *Cal. of Pat. Rolls*, 1374–7, p. 451 ; Farrer, *Early Yorkshire Charters*, no. 371.

[2] Round, *Calendar*, no. 196.

[3] Cart. Antiq., HH., no. 25 ; Farrer, *Early Yorkshire Charters*, no. 1433.

[4] Hugh the Chantor : *Historians of York*, ii. 131.   [5] Chron.

[6] *Flores Histor.* ii. 44 ; Chron. The place is not named. Professor Haskins assigns this event to the Christmas court at Rouen in 1114 ; *Norman Institutions*, p. 312.

[7] Round, *Calendar*, no. 994.   [8] *Mon. Anglic.* vi. 1079, no. 4.

[9] Round, *Calendar*, no. 1278.   [10] *Flores Histor.* ii. 44.

July. The king returns to England in the middle of July.[1]

346. Notification to Archbishop Thurstan, Nigel de Aubigny, Anscheti de Bolmere, and Odard sheriff of Northumberland, of the restoration to Ranulf bishop of Durham of all the lands of which the king had disseised him, 'et quas cepi in manu mea apud Sanctum Albanum, quando ibi coronatus fui in Pentecostes ', viz. Alverton, Houeden, Welleton, &c. It is attested by Ranulf the chancellor, Robert count of Meulan, and William de Tancarvill ; at Windsor.[2] [Mid. July 1115–2 April, 1116.]

Wilfred bishop of St. Davids dies during the year.[3]

16 Sept. The king summons the bishops and barons to his court at Westminster.[4] They discuss a letter from Pope Paschal,[5] which has been brought by Anselm, abbot of St. Saba, nephew of the late primate. The bishop of Exeter is chosen as envoy to the pope.[6]

18 Sept. Bernard the queen's chaplain and chancellor is elected bishop of St. Davids ' sabbato iciunii septimi mensis '.[7]

19 Sept. He is consecrated at Westminster Abbey by the primate in the presence of the bishops, William of Winchester, Robert of Lincoln, Roger of Salisbury, John of Bath, Urban of Glamorgan, and Gilbert of Limerick.[8]

The king, by the advice of the count of Meulan and Nigel de Aubigny, urges Archbishop Thurstan to seek consecration at the hands of the primate. Accompanied by Geoffrey archbishop of Rouen, John bishop of Lisieux, Ranulf bishop of Durham and others, he has an interview with the primate, but without result.[9]

347. 18 Sept. Grant to Bishop Bernard of the bishopric of St. Andrew the Apostle and St. David ' Menevensis ' in Wales, made in the presence of Queen Matilda, William their son, the archbishops of Canterbury and Rouen, Thurstan elect of York, the bishops, Richard of London, Roger of Salisbury, Robert of Lincoln, John of Lisieux, the other bishops of England, and Urban bishop of Glamorgan ; Ranulf the chancellor, John of Bayeux, Evrard son of Earl (Roger), Geoffrey the chaplain, Richard the chaplain and keeper of the king's seal, Robert count of Meulan and Earl Henry his brother, Richard earl of Chester, Robert the king's son, Gilbert Fitz-Richard, Walter de Gloucester, Adam de Port, Hamon the sewer, William de Aubigny and Nigel de Aubigny ; at Westminster in the council, A.D. 1115, on the 14 kalends of October, 8th indiction, 23rd epact, 4th concurrent, 15th (sic) year of the king's reign.[10]

348. Notification to Herbert bishop of Norwich, Hamon the sewer, the burgesses of Sudbury, and the ministers and lieges of Suffolk, of the confirmation to St. Peter's, Westminster, of the church of St. Bartholomew, Sudbury, which Wlfric the king's moneyer[11] has given. It is attested by Ralph archbishop of Canterbury, the bishops, Richard of London and Roger of Salisbury ; Ranulf the chancellor, and Nigel de Aubigny ; at Westminster.[12] [April 1114–2 April, 1116.]

---

[1] Florence of Worcester.   [2] *Mon. Anglic.* i. 242, n. 12.
[3] Florence of Worcester ; Sym. of Durham, ii. 249.   [4] Eadmer, p. 231.
[5] Dated at the Lateran on the kalends of April ; *ibid.* p. 233.
[6] *Ibid.* p. 234.   [7] *Ibid.* p. 235.   [8] *Ibid.* pp. 235–6.
[9] Hugh the Chantor: *Historians of York*, ii. 132.
[10] *Cal. of Pat. Rolls*, 1358–61, p. 7.   [11] Cf. *Domesday Book*, ii. 286 *b*.
[12] Chartul. of St. Peter's, Westminster, Faust. A. iii, fo. 79 ; *Mon. Anglic.* iii. 459.

349. Notification to Robert bishop of Lincoln, Hugh de Bocheland, and the lieges of Bedfordshire, of the confirmation to the church of Abingdon of land at Stratton, given by Henry de Aubigny.[1] It is attested by the bishops of Lincoln and Salisbury, Hamon the sewer, William de Aubigny, Nigel de Aubigny, and Grimbald the physician; at Westminster.[2] [1107–16.]

350. Notification to Roger bishop of Salisbury, William sheriff of Wiltshire, the barons, lieges, and ministers of Wiltshire, of the confirmation to Henry de Aubigny of the manor of (Great) Wishford, which Patric de Chaources has given to him with the king's consent with his daughter. It is attested by William de Aubigny and Nigel de Aubigny; at Westminster.[3] [1115–c. 1125.]

351. Writ addressed to Archbishop Ralph, Roger bishop of Salisbury, the sheriffs of London and Kent, the barons and ministers of London and Kent, directing that the abbot and monks of St. Peter's, Ghent, shall hold their manor of Lewesham and Greenwich as they held it in the time of the kings Edward and William I. It is attested by Robert count of Meulan, William earl of Warenne, William de Aubigny, Robert Fitz-Suen de Essex, and Simon de Molendinis; at Westminster.[4] [May 1114–April 1116.]

352. Notification, addressed to Herbert bishop of Norwich, R(alph) Basset and the justices, R(obert) Fitz-Walter and the barons of Norfolk and Suffolk, that Ralph Fitz-Godric has surrendered in the king's presence to Abbot Richer and the church of St. Benet's, Holme, land at Hardley which he held of the said church at farm. It is attested by Archbishop Ralph, and the bishops, Herbert of Norwich, Roger of Salisbury, Robert of Chester, and Hervey of Ely.[5] [Same as 351.]

353. Notification to the justice, sheriff, and barons of Berkshire, of the grant to Robert Achard, ' magistro meo ', of Aldermaston, Finchampstead, Coldrop (' Colsthorpe '), Sparsholt, and Challow (co. Berks.), to hold in fee and inheritance by the service of one knight. It is attested by Queen Matilda, Ranulf the chancellor, Richer de Aquila, Adam de Port, ' Henry ' de Port, ' et multis aliis ; apud West Munster '.[6] [Same as 351.]

353 A. A dispute between the monks of Colchester and those of Westminster touching the church of ' Niwechirche ' in London was arranged in the king's presence and that of Richard bishop of London and other bishops, earls, and barons in A. D. 1115, and the sixteenth year of Henry's reign.[7] [5 Aug.–31 Dec. 1115.]

354. Notification to Robert bishop of Lincoln, Walter de Gant, the sheriff and barons of Lincolnshire, of the grant to Ralph the monk, who was prior of Bardney, at the prayer of Walter de Gant and by the concession of Fulcard abbot of Chartres, ' cuius fuit monachus ', of the church and abbey of Bardney. It is attested by the bishops of Lincoln and

---

[1] On Easter Thursday, 1107 : *Chron. of Abingdon,* ii. 100.

[2] *Ibid.* 101.　　　　　　　　　　　　[3] *Cal. of Chart. Rolls,* ii. 94.

[4] Cart. Antiq. roll T, n. 19 (9) ; *Mon. Anglic.* vi. 987.

[5] Chartul. of St. Benet's, Holme, Cott. MS. Galba E. ii, fo. 31 ; *Mon. Anglic.* iii. 86, n. 8.　　　　　　　　[6] *Cal. of Chart. Rolls,* iii. 360.

[7] *Chartul. of Colchester,* 82. See *ibid.* 50.

Salisbury, Bernard of St. Davids and Ranulf of Durham ; Ranulf the chancellor, (Hugh) abbot of Selby, Walter de Gant, Alan de Percy, Ralph de Gant, Ralph de Alost, and Ralph de Nevill ; at Winchester in the sixteenth year after the king received the kingdom of England.[1] [18 Sept. 1115–May 1116.]

355. Confirmation, addressed generally, to the church of St. Georges de Bocherville of land and churches in England. It is attested by Bernard bishop of St. Davids, John bishop of Lisieux, William the chamberlain of Tancarvill, and Geoffrey Fitz-Pain ; at Winchester.[2] [Same as 354, or 1121–9.]

27 Oct. Reinhelm, bishop of Hereford, dies on the 6 kalends of November.[3]

356. Notification to Robert bishop of Lincoln, Thomas de St. John, Nigel de Oillei, and the barons of Oxford(shire), of the confirmation of an exchange of land near the church of St. Frideswide in Oxford, made between Roger bishop of Salisbury and Faritius abbot of Abingdon. It is attested by the bishops, Robert of Lincoln and Hervey of Ely ; Ranulf the chancellor, Robert the king's son, and Ranulf Meschin ; at Reading.[4] [1113–16.]

357. Notification to Ranulf Meschin, Wigot sheriff (of Lincolnshire), Robert de la Hay,[5] Ralph de Aincourt, and the lieges of Lincolnshire of the king's grant *in commendam* to the bishop of Lincoln of the church of All Saints (in Lincoln) and the church of Grimsby, to hold as beneficially as Osbert the sheriff held them on the day that he died. It is attested by Ranulf the chancellor ; at Headington ('apud Heddendonam').[6] [1114–April 1116.]

358. Notification to Herbert bishop of Norwich, the sheriffs of Essex and Suffolk, and the barons of those shires, of the confirmation to the church of Abingdon and Abbot Faritius of the church of Edwardstone, which Hubert de Montchenesy gave in alms. It is attested by Ranulf the chancellor, Grimbald the physician, Jurard the archdeacon, Walter the archdeacon, William de Aubigny, Roger Fitz-Richard, Nigel de Oillei, Ralph Basset, and Geoffrey Fitz-Pain ; at Woodstock. 'Descripta est autem huius concessionis carta anno ab incarnatione Dominica M.CXV.'[7]

359. Notification to Ralph archbishop of Canterbury, Hamon the sewer, and the barons of Kent, of the confirmation to St. Albans and Abbot Richard of a gift made by Nigel de Aubigny. It is attested by Robert count of Meulan, (and is issued) by Geoffrey Ridell ; at Woodstock.[8] [26 April, 1114–2 April, 1116.]

360. Writ, addressed to Robert bishop of Lincoln and Wigot the sheriff (of Lincoln), directing that the monks of Spalding shall have the wood of their manor as beneficially as they had it in the time of Ivo

---

[1] *Mon. Anglic.* i. 629 *b* ; from an *inspeximus* of 5 Edward III.

[2] *Cal. of Chart. Rolls*, i. 436.　　　　　　　[3] Florence of Worcester.

[4] *Chron. of Abingdon*, ii. 76.

[5] His appearance in the shire-moot of Lincoln suggests that Picot son of Colsuen was dead.

[6] Pat. Rolls, 2 Ric. II, pt. 1, m. 4 ; *Mon. Anglic.* vi. 1275, n. 45.

[7] *Chron. of Abingdon*, ii. 62.　　　　　　　[8] *Cal. of Chart. Rolls*, iii. 17.

(Taillebois) and Turald (the sheriff). It is attested by Nigel de Aubigny ; at Woodstock.[1]   [1114–2 April 1116.]

During the month of December Geoffrey de Clive, the king's chaplain, is nominated to the see of Hereford.[2]

25 Dec. In this year at the Nativity the king is at St. Albans, and there he caused the monastery to be hallowed.[3]

28 Dec. The ceremony is conducted on Tuesday, the 5 kalends of January, by Geoffrey archbishop of Rouen, who is assisted by the bishops, Richard of London, Ranulf of Durham, Robert of Lincoln, and Roger of Salisbury ; the king and queen being present with many earls and barons. A great number of those who are assembled there spend the days of the feast of the Nativity until the Epiphany (6 January) in feasting in the palace and attending services in the church.[4]

361. Notification issued at St. Albans on Holy Innocents' Day, A. D. 1116 (sic), indiction 9, that the king, at the prayer of Richard (de Aubigny) the abbot, has commanded that the church of St. Albans be dedicated and has appointed to that office Robert bishop of Lincoln together with Geoffrey archbishop of Rouen, the bishops, Roger of Salisbury, Richard of London and Ranulf of Durham ; the queen and William his son being present with the magnates of the realm, namely Robert count of Meulan, Stephen count of Mortain, Richard earl of Chester, William de Warenne, Earl David the queen's brother, Walter earl of Buckingham, Ranulf the chancellor, the sewers, Eudes, Hamon, and William Bigot, and William de Pirou another sewer ; William de Aubigny the king's butler, Walter (de Gloucester) the constable, Ranulf ' vicecomes ', Hugh de Bocheland, William Peverel, Pain his brother, Humphrey de Aubigny, Adam de Port, Thomas de St. John, William his brother, and Hugh de Gornai.[5]

26 Dec. On this day, at Canterbury cathedral, the primate Ralph consecrates Ernulf bishop of Rochester and Geoffrey bishop of Hereford. The bishops, William of Winchester, Herbert of Norwich, Ralph of Chichester, and Bernard of St. Davids are present.[6]

1116.

362. Notification to Robert bishop of Lincoln and generally, of the grant to Reinald, the monk, of the abbey of Ramsey. It is attested by the bishops, Roger of Salisbury and Herbert of Norwich ; Richard abbot of St. Albans, William de Aubigny, William de Tancarvill, Hamon the sewer, Gilbert Fitz-Richard, Walter Fitz-Richard, William Bigot, and William de Pirou ; at Thetford.[7]

Possibly the king visits Norwich at this time.

363. Confirmation to Holy Trinity, Norwich, of land given by Ralph Fitz-Godric. It is subscribed by the king, Queen Matilda, Roger bishop of Salisbury, William Bigot, and Ralph Fitz-Godric.[8] [1107–April 1116.]

---

[1] *Ibid.* iv. 162 ; Add. MS. 5844, p. 220.
[2] Sym. of Durham, ii. 249.   [3] Chron.
[4] *Gesta Abb. S. Albani*, i. 71.   [5] M. Paris, *Chron. Mai.* vi. 36.
[6] Eadmer, pp. 236–7.   [7] *Chartul. of Ramsey*, n. 163.
[8] Cott. ch. ii. 2 ; with seal ; Birch, *Brit. Arch. Instit.* xxix. 246–8 ; *Mon. Anglic.* iv. 18, n. 9.

364. Notification to Robert bishop of Lincoln, the barons and sheriffs in whose bailiwicks Robert, abbot of Thorney, has land, of the grant to the said abbot of various privileges. It is attested by the bishops, Roger of Salisbury, Robert of Lincoln, and Ranulf of Durham; William de Aubigny, Nigel de Aubigny, William de Tancarvill, Hamon the sewer, William Bigot, William de Pirou, and Geoffrey Fitz-Pain; at (Fen)-Ditton.[1] [15 Aug. 1113–April 1116.]

365. Writ, addressed to Richard de Monte (sheriff) and the barons of Oxfordshire, directing that Abbot Faritius and the church of Abingdon shall hold in peace the land of Garsington, which (Ralph de) Perchehai used to hold. It is attested by John bishop of Lisieux and Gilbert Fitz-Richard; at Windsor.[2] [1110–April 1116.]

366. Notification to Ralph bishop of Chichester and his barons of the confirmation to the monks of Battle of lands given, with the consent of Henry count of Eu, in the rape of Hastings. It is attested by Roger bishop of Salisbury, Eudes the sewer, and Robert de Ver; at Windsor.[3] [*Ante* May 1116.]

19 Mar. A council is held at Salisbury on Passion Sunday, being the 14 kalends of April. The king announces that it is his desire, before taking passage to Normandy, to make his son, William, heir to the kingdom. Thereupon the magnates of the realm are made William's men and do fealty. The primate and the bishops promise to do homage to William, when he becomes king, after his father's death.[4]

367. Confirmation to the monastery of Abingdon of fifteen specific gifts made whilst Faritius was abbot. The signatories are: the king and Queen Matilda, William their son, the archbishops Ralph and Thurstan, the bishops, William of Winchester, William of Exeter, and Theowulf of Worcester; Roger abbot of Fécamp and Ranulf the chancellor.[5] [1114–20.]

The dispute between the primate and Thurstan elect of York, touching the latter's subjection to Canterbury, has been in progress for nearly twelve months. Thurstan refuses to make profession of obedience and apparently renounces the see of York with the temporalities.[6]

368. Grant, addressed generally, in favour of the church and canons of Salisbury ('Sarum') of acquittance of toll in all markets and fairs throughout England. It is attested by R(anulf) the chancellor, and Walter de Gloucester; at Clarendon.[7] [1107–16, or 1121.]

369. Grant, addressed generally, in favour of St. Mary's, York, and Abbot Richard of various possessions and liberties. It is attested by Ranulf bishop of Durham, Nigel de Aubigny, William Peverel, and Ralph Basset; at Clarendon.[8] [1112–16, or 1121.]

370. During the first half of the year 1116 Ralph Basset holds pleas

---

[1] *Cal. of Chart. Rolls*, iii. 242.

[2] *Chron. of Abingdon*, ii. 89; *Mon. Anglic.* i. 521, n. 19.

[3] Chartul. of Battle, Lincoln's Inn Libr., n. 87, Hales, fo. 13 *d.*; *Mon. Anglic.* iii. 246, n. 14. (Probably spurious.)

[4] Eadmer, p. 237.

[5] No place named; *Chron. of Abingdon*, ii. 109; *Mon. Anglic.* i. 521, n. 21.

[6] Sym. of Durham, ii. 250.   [7] *Sarum Charters* (Rolls ser.), p. 4.

[8] Prescot, *Regist. of Wetherhal*, n. 7.

at Huntingdon. There are also present there Hervey bishop of Ely, Rainald abbot of Ramsey, and Robert abbot of Thorney. Bricstan of Chatteris is appealed by Robert Malarteis of concealing treasure trove. By Ralph Basset he is condemned to be at the king's mercy, and is committed to prison in London. After lying in chains there for five months he is set at liberty by command of Queen Matilda addressed to Ralph Basset.[1]

2 April. At Easter the king is at Odiham.[2]

371. Notification to William bishop of Exeter, Richard Fitz-Baldwin, sheriff, and the lieges of Devonshire and Cornwall of the grant of various privileges to the church of Tavistock. It is attested by Archbishop Ralph, William the king's son, and Robert count of Meulan ; at Odiham[3]

c. April–May. Immediately after Easter the king goes over seas to Normandy.[4] Whilst waiting for favourable weather the court is established at Westbourne.

372. Notification to Robert bishop of Lincoln, Richard bishop of London, Herbert bishop of Norwich, William Bigot, Earl David, Gilbert the sheriff, and the barons of Norfolk and Huntingdon of the confirmation to Rainald, abbot of Ramsey, of Wimbotsham (co. Norf.) and Bury (co. Hunt.), which William de Houcton held, quit of the same William, to whom the king has given an exchange for those lands by an order made before himself and his barons. It is attested by Thurstan (' Turi ') archbishop of York, the bishops, Robert of Lincoln and Richard of London ; (Robert) count of Meulan, Nigel de Aubigny, William de Aubigny, Walter de Gloucester, and Geoffrey Ridel ; at Westbourne (' Burna ').[5] [1114–16.]

373. Writ addressed to (Robert) bishop of Lincoln, Earl David, Gilbert the sheriff, and the barons of Huntingdon, authorizing (Rainald) abbot of Ramsey to take Girton into his demesne, which Abbot Aldwin gave to Hervey the monk, and other lands, unless the holders can rightly deraign the same in the court of St. Benet (of Ramsey). It is attested by Archbishop Thurstan, Robert bishop of Lincoln, and (Robert) count of Meulan ; at Westbourne.[6]

374. Notification to Albode, abbot of St. Edmunds William Bigot, and the ministers and barons of Suffolk of the confirmation to ' Reyner ', abbot of Ramsey, of warren in his manor of Lawshall. It is attested by Nigel de Aubigny ; at Westbourne.[7]

375. Notification to Ralph de Watnevill, Ralph de Boisrohard, and Hugh de Hottot of the confirmation to Robert bishop of Lincoln of the churches of Uffington and Barkston (co. Linc.), to hold the same as beneficially as Theodoric held them. It is attested by Matilda the queen, William de Tancarvill, and William de Aubigny ; at Hampton ' in transitu regis ' (' Hamtona ').[8] [1114–16.]

Thurstan elect of York crosses to Normandy with the king's court.[9]

c. Aug. Anselm, abbot of St. Saba, comes to the king in Normandy, bearing letters from Rome.[10]

[1] Orderic, iii. 125–31.   [2] Chron.   [3] Cott. ch. xvii. 7 ; *Mon. Anglic.* ii. 496.
[4] Chron.   [5] *Chartul. of Ramsey,* n. 168.   [6] *Ibid.* n. 169.   [7] *Ibid.* n. 181.
[8] *Cal. of Chart. Rolls,* iv. 138 ; Chartul. of St. Mary's, Lincoln, Vesp. E. xvi, fo. 3 *d* ; *Mon. Anglic.* vi. 1274, n. 36.
[9] Hugh the Chantor: *Historians of York,* ii. 140.   [10] Eadmer, p. 239.

Aug.–Sept. The bishops and barons meet in council at London, at which the queen is present. The primate, by the advice of the council, goes over to Normandy and seeks the king at Rouen.[1] He remains in Normandy until 4 January 1120.[2]

8 Sept. The primate, after being detained at La Ferté-Fresnel owing to a severe ulcer in his face, joins the king at Rouen[3] and, after consultation with Henry, pursues his journey to Rome, joining the legate Anselm at Lyons.[4]

1117.

23 Feb. Faritius, or Faritz, abbot of Abingdon, dies on 7 kalends of March, in the seventeenth year of his rule.[5]

376. Queen Matilda notifies Bishop Richard, the sheriff and barons of London, of her grant to St. Peter's and Gilbert abbot of Westminster of that which Hugh de Bocheland used to hold (*tenebat de me*) in London upon the abbot's wharf. It is attested by (Robert) bishop of Lincoln and Earl David;[6] at Westminster.[7] [1116–7.]

15–16 April. Richard abbot of St. Werburg's, Chester, dies.[8]

June–July (?). Henry being at Rouen is visited by the primate, Ralph, who has returned from Rome.[9]

377. Grant, addressed generally, in favour of St. Benet's, Holme, and Abbot Richer. It is attested by Ralph archbishop of Canterbury, Ranulf the chancellor, Robert count of Meulan, and William earl of Warenne ; at Westminster (*sic*). ' Facta est hec donatio anno ab incarnatione Domini M.CXVII.'[10]

30 Aug. or 1 Sept. Robert de Limesi, bishop of Chester, dies.[11]

378. Mandate of Matilda, queen of England, to Vitalis Engaine (' Inganius ') and William de Luisours to establish Malger the monk and his serjeants in Luffield, because the king has willed that he shall remain there. It is attested by (Roger) bishop of Salisbury ; at Oxford.[12] [1116–18.]

---

[1] Eadmer, p. 239.   [2] Orderic, iv. 430; Florence of Worcester, ii. 74.
[3] Eadmer, p. 239.   [4] *Ibid.* p. 240.
[5] *Chron. of Abingdon,* ii. 158 ; Chron., *s. a.* 1117. The length of his rule is incorrectly stated in the *Chron. of Abingdon,* ii. 286, 290.
[6] The queen and William her son attest two charters of Earl David to the monks of Durham about this time : Lawrie, *Early Scottish Charters,* nn. 29, 30.
[7] Chartul. of Westminster, fo. 516 *d* ; Robinson, *Gilbert Crispin,* p. 155.
[8] *Obits of St. Werburg's* (Lancs. and Chesh. Rec. Soc.), vol. 64, p. 94.
[9] Eadmer, p. 243.
[10] Chartul. of St. Benet's, Holme, Cott. MS. Galba E. ii, fo. 30 *d* ; *Mon. Anglic.* iii. 86 *b*.
[11] Le Neve, *Fasti Eccles. Anglic.*   [12] *Mon. Anglic.* iv. 378.

PART II

1118.

Feb. Thurstan, elect of York, having been reinstated in the temporalities of his see, returns to England in the month of February, in the second year after he had joined the king in Normandy.[1]

Henry seizes the castle of St. Clair-sur-Epte. Louis having fortified the priory of St. Ouen, Gani, Henry builds two forts, one at Malassis, the other at a place named Gête-à-Lièvres, to hold the French king in check.[2]

18 April. William, count of Evreux, dies on 14 kalends of May.[3]

1 May. Queen Matilda dies on the kalends of May and is buried in Westminster Abbey.[4]

5 June. Robert de Beaumont, count of Meulan and earl of Leicester, dies on the nones of June and is buried in the chapter-house at Préaux.[5]

By the king's advice Hugh, son of Gerard de Gournai, betroths his sister Gundreda to Nigel de Aubigny.[6]

Henry gives Sées, Alençon, and the domains of Robert of Bellême in that county to Theobald, count of Blois, who gives it, with the king's consent, to his brother Stephen of Blois, count of Mortain.[7]

379. Confirmation to the monks of the Holy Trinity, Tiron, of a gift made by Robert Fitz-Martin of his property in Wales. It is attested by Ranulf the chancellor, Geoffrey Fitz-Pain, William Peverel of Dover, Hugh de Montfort, and William de Rullos ; at Mortain.[8]

July–Aug. Henry besieges the castle of Saint-Claire sur-Epte and fortifies Malassis against Louis, who was then holding Gani.[9]

23–31 July. Henry hastens to Alençon to relieve the castle of La Motte-Gautier de Clerichamp, then besieged by the count of Anjou.[10]

1 Aug. The castle surrenders to Fulk, who razes it.[11]

7–8 Sept. Henry marches to Laigle, but arrives too late to relieve it, as Richer de L'Aigle had surrendered it to Louis four or five days earlier. Louis burned the town.[12] A few days afterwards Henry, being at Livet (in Ouche ?), is informed by William de Tancarvill that Rouen is being

---

[1] Eadmer, p. 244.   [2] Orderic, iv. 311.

[3] *Ibid.* p. 313.   [4] *Ibid.*   [5] *Ibid.*

[6] *Ibid.* p. 318.   [7] *Ibid.* pp. 323–4.

[8] ' Apud Moritonium ' : Round, *Calendar*, no. 995.

[9] Orderic, ii. 453 ; iv. 310.   [10] *Ibid.* iv. 322–3.

[11] *Ibid.* p. 323.   [12] *Ibid.* p. 325.

attacked by Hugh de Gournai and Stephen of Aumâle.[1] They are reported
to be making a castle in the monastery of the Holy Trinity on St. Catherine's
Mount at Rouen.[2] The king makes a forced march to Rouen, but on
arriving there finds that the report was untrue. He then leads forces to
harry Gournai's lands of Brai, and lays siege to his castle of La Ferté-en-
Brai.[3]

Later the king moves to Neubourg, where he makes an assault upon
the castle of Robert de Neubourg, which he takes and burns.[4]

While Henry is at Arques Count Baldwin burns the villages in the district of Talou.[5] Henry then fortifies Bures and places a garrison of Bretons
and English there. Count Baldwin is here wounded by Hugh Boterel,
and retiring to Aumâle, is received by Stephen and the Countess Hawise.[6]

380. 7 Oct. A council, held by Archbishop Geoffrey[7] on the nones
of October at Rouen, is attended by a great gathering of ecclesiastics, who
meet to discuss measures for the restoration of peace. Conrad, the legate
of the newly elected Pope Gelasius, and Archbishop Ralph are present
with the bishops Richard of Bayeux, John of Lisieux, Turgis of Avranches,
and Roger of Coutances ; the abbots Roger of Fécamp, Urse of Jumièges,
William of Bec, Odo of Caen, Richard of Préaux, Andrew of Troarn,
William of La Croix-Saint-Leufroy, and Osbern of Tréport. Serlo bishop
of Sées and Ouin bishop of Evreux are absent, being engaged in the
defence of their respective sees.[8]

381. A dispute is terminated before the king. It is between Eudes
abbot of Caen and Vitalis founder of the monastery of Savigny concerning
the alms in Mortain which was given by Count William to Vitalis. The
settlement is effected with the co-operation of the archbishops Ralph of
Canterbury and Geoffrey of Rouen ; the bishops Richard of Bayeux,
Turgis of Avranches, Roger of Coutances, William of Exeter, and Ildebert
of Le Mans ; and of many abbots and other religious men ; Pope Paschal
being recently dead and Gelasius having succeeded to the pontificate.
It is attested by Stephen count of Mortain, Earl Richard (of Chester),
Robert the king's son, Hameline of Mayenne, William de Aubigny, Nigel
(de Aubigny), Humphrey de Aubigny, William the chamberlain of Tancarvill, William Patricius, Thomas de St. John, William Peverel (' Piperellus ')
of Dover (' de Airam '), Geoffrey de Clinton, Robert de Hay (' de Haia
Putei '), Hugh de Guillei, Edward of Salisbury, Ranulf the chancellor,
John son of the bishop of Bayeux, Robert Peche (' Peccatum '), Geoffrey the
chaplain, Walter de Cullei, Ranulf de Dussei, the monks Wino de Allemania
and Nigel, Rotrou count of Le Perche, Roger Marmion, Richard the
chaplain, Simon de Molines, and Hamelin de Lesclusa.[9] ' Hec definitio fuit
definita et hec charta sigillata ante me apud Argenteium ' [i. e. Arganchy],[10]
John bishop of Lisieux and Eudes abbot of Caen being witnesses.[11]

---

[1] Orderic, iv. 327.   [2] *Neustria Pia*, p. 411.
[3] Orderic, iv. 327.   [4] *Ibid.*   [5] *Ibid.* p. 316.   [6] *Ibid.*
[7] *Gallia Christiana*, xi. 41.   [8] Orderic, iv. 329.
[9] The witnesses from William de Aubigny onwards have been added from Professor
Haskins's text of the original in the library of Rouen : *Norman Institutions*, p. 294.
[10] Professor Haskins assigns the visit to Arganchy to October 1118.
[11] Biblioth. de Rouen, MS. 3122, no. 2 ; *Gallia Christiana*, xi, instr. col. 111 ;
Haskins, *l c. cit.*

382. Eudes abbot of St. Stephen's, Caen, deraigns the mill of Crocy? ('Drocio'), near the Dive, against Robert Frelle, at Arganchy ('apud Argenteium') before King Henry and his court. The witnesses are the king and his barons, namely John bishop of Lisieux, Robert de Curci, William de Tancarvill, William Peverel, and Rainald de Arganchy ('de Argenteio').[1]

383. Notification, addressed generally, of the grant to the canons of St. Oswald's, Nostell, of the church of Bambrough, to hold *in manu propria* after the death of Algar the priest. It is attested by Archbishop Thurstan, Ranulf bishop of Durham, John bishop of Lisieux, Ranulf the chancellor, and Eustace Fitz-John; at Bonneville (-sur-Touques?).[2] [1116–19.]

384. Mandate to the justices (*iusticiariis*) of Normandy to cause the abbot of Fécamp to have land and meadow of the marshes of Aisi in as beneficial a manner as the count of Meulan held them in his time. It is attested by the chancellor; at Bonneville (-sur-Touques?).[3]

Oct.–Nov.? Archbishop Thurstan comes to the king at Rouen, but is detained there because he has not obtained the king's consent to visit Rome.[4]

Whilst at Rouen the king causes Henry count of Eu and Hugh de Gournai to be arrested as supporters of Amauri de Montfort.[5]

From Rouen Henry leads forces towards Evreux to oppose Amauri, who is laying claim to the county of Evreux. Later the king abandons his intention for the time being,[6] possibly because William Pointel has put Amauri in possession of the castle of Evreux.[7] The chief supporters of Amauri are: Hugh de Gournai, Stephen count of Aumâle, Eustace of Bréteuil, Richer de Aquila,[8] Robert of Neubourg, Baldwin of Flanders, and others to the number of eighteen barons.[9]

4–10 Nov. The king, accompanied by the counts and brothers, Theobald and Stephen, leads a force to Laigle. In an assault upon the castle he narrowly escapes being wounded.[10]

During the winter months Hugh de Gournai and his supporters ravage the country of the Talou and the district of Caux. William de Roumare, castellan of Neuf-Marché, opposes them on the king's behalf.[11]

Dec. Towards the end of the year Fulk count of Anjou is in possession of the town of Alençon. Theobald and Stephen go to the relief of the castle there, followed by Henry, who arrives too late to prevent its surrender to Fulk.[12]

384 A. Mandate of William, the king's son, to John bishop of Bath to put Modbert in seisin of land which Grenta of Stoca held. It is attested by (Roger) bishop of Salisbury.[13] [1116–19.]

---

[1] Original in Archives of the Calvados, H. 1834, nos. 13–15 *bis*; *ante*, xxiv. 215.

[2] Chartul. of Nostell, Vesp. E. xix, fo. 8; Farrer, *Early Yorkshire Charters*, no. 1424.

[3] Archives of the Seine-Inférieure, fonds de Fécamp, box A (Aisier); *ante*, xxiv. 213, note 14.

[4] Eadmer, p. 249. [5] Orderic, iv. 316.

[6] *Ibid.* pp. 313–14. [7] *Ibid.* [8] i.e. ' de L'Aigle '.

[9] Orderic, iv. 315. [10] *Ibid.* p. 331.

[11] *Ibia.* p. 322. [12] *Ibid.* p. 333.

[13] *Two Bath Abbey Chartul.* i. 49; Madox, *Hist. of the Exchequer*, i. 110 note.

385. Writ of William, the king's son, to William sheriff of Kent, commanding Hamon son of Vitalis and the true men of Sandwich (' Santwic '), whom Hamon shall nominate, to declare the truth concerning the ship of the abbot of St. Augustine's ; and, if that ship went to sea on the day when the king last went overseas, he shall let it go until the king returns to England and the abbot shall be again placed in possession thereof. It is attested by (Roger) bishop of Salisbury and (Ranulf ?) the chancellor ; at Woodstock.[1]

386. Mandate of William, the king's son, to W(illiam) the sheriff (of Kent) to place the abbot of St. Augustine's in possession of his ship, as he (William the king's son) commanded by his other writ, by reason that it was acknowledged by true men of the county that the abbot was seised thereof on the day when the king last passed overseas. It is attested by (Ranulf ?) the chancellor ; at Windsor.[2]

1119.

2 Feb. Geoffrey de Clive, bishop of Hereford, dies on 4 nones of February.[3]

16–22 Feb. While the king is leading an assault upon the castle of Bréteuil, his daughter Juliana, wife of Eustace of Bréteuil, makes an attempt on her father's life.[4]

Later the king is at Falaise and burns Rainald de Balliol's castle of Renouard.[5] The king's chief supporters at this time are : Richard earl of Chester and vicomte of Avranches, his cousin Ranulf Meschin or ' de Bricquessart ', vicomte of Bayeux, or the Bessin, William de Warenne, earl of Surrey, Walter Giffard, earl of Buckingham, Waleran de Beaumont, count of Meulan, Robert his brother, earl of Leicester, Ralph de Conches, William de Roumare, Nigel de Aubigny and William his brother, William de Tancarvill, the chamberlain of Normandy, and Ralph de St. Victor.[6]

1 Mar. Albold, formerly a monk of Bec and prior of St. Nicaise of Moulineaux, abbot of St. Edmund's since 1115, dies on the kalends of March.[7] He had some time previously enfeoffed Maurice de Windsor of the office of seneschal in fee with five knights' fees.[8]

During Lent the king fortifies Noyon, and places there 100 knights under the command of William Fitz-Thierri.[9]

16 May. Richard de Aubigny, abbot of St. Albans, dies on 17 kalends of June.[10]

After 17 May. Henry is at La Ferté-Fresnel.[11]

May. William the Ætheling joins his father in Normandy. Henry and Fulk of Anjou discuss terms of peace, which result in an agreement that the king's son shall marry Fulk's daughter Matilda. Fulk then surrenders Alençon[12] and Maine, which is nominally settled on the young pair.[13]

---

[1] Elmham, ed. Hardwick, p. 353.   [2] *Ibid.* p. 354.
[3] Sym. of Durham, ii. 254.
[4] Orderic, iv. 338.   [5] *Ibid.* p. 339.   [6] *Ibid.* p. 346.
[7] *Mon. Anglic.* iii. 155 b.   [8] *Ibid.*
[9] Orderic, iv. 342.   [10] *Gesta Abbat. S. Albani*, i. 72.
[11] Orderic, iv. 345.   [12] *Ibid.* p. 347.
[13] Henry had granted Maine to Fulk in 1113.

10 June. Petreius prior of Bermondsey dies on 4 ides of June.[1]

17 June. As the result of a wound received at Bures in September of the past year Baldwin count of Flanders dies at Roulers, near Bruges.[2]

20 June. Henry de Beaumont, earl of Warwick, dies on 12 kalends of July.[3]

June. The Ætheling and Matilda of Anjou are married at Lisieux in the month of June. At Fulk's request the king receives into favour William Talevas, son of Robert of Bellême, and restores to him his father's possessions of Alençon, Almanèches, and Vignats.[4]

At a council held at Lisieux Henry hears the news of the death of Baldwin of Flanders.[5] At the prayer of Count Fulk he pardons Robert de St. Ceneri for having lately joined the rebels, and restores to him Montreuil-l'Argillier and Echaufour.[6]

July. During the summer Henry leads an expedition to the country of those who are in arms against him. He burns Pont St. Pierre (in the valley of the Andelle) and other castles.[7]

Accompanied by his son Richard, his nephew Count Stephen, Ralph de Wader, and a large force, the king burns the city of Evreux. The castle is held by Philip and Fleury, sons of the late King Philip, by Bertrade, William Pointel, and Richard of Evreux, son of the provost Fulk.[8] The siege is continued apparently until October, when Amauri surrenders.[9]

22 July. Herbert bishop of Norwich dies on 11 kalends of August.[10]

20 Aug. At Noyon, between Lions-la-Forêt and Andelys, Henry wins a great victory in a chance encounter with Louis at Brémulé. With Henry are his sons Robert and Richard, Henry of Eu, William de Warenne, Walter Giffard, Roger Fitz-Richard, Walter of Aufai the king's cousin, William de Tancarvill, William de Roumare, Nigel de Aubigny, and many others.[11]

9 Sept. On 5 ides of September Pope Calixtus is at Angers.[12]

17–24 Sept. The king and his son Richard relieve Bréteuil.[13] Henry leads an army against the castles of Gloz and Lire, in Ouche, which surrender.[14]

End Sept. At the end of September Henry, victorious over his enemies, returns to Rouen.

387. A charter of confirmation is issued to the monastery of Colchester. The signatories are : William the king's son; the archbishops Ralph of Canterbury, Geoffrey of Rouen, and Thurstan elect of York ; the bishops William of Exeter, Bernard of St. David's, Ranulf of Durham, John of Lisieux, and Ouin of Evreux ; Ranulf the chancellor, Henry count of Eu, Walter Gifard, earl of ' Bucchingehamscyre ', William de Warenne, earl of Surrey, Robert the king's son and Richard his brother, Roger Fitz-Richard and Robert his brother, Nigel de Aubigny, Otuer son of Earl

[1] *Annals of Bermondsey*, p. 433.   [2] Orderic, iv. 316 n.

[3] ' On 20 June ': Dugdale, *Baronage*, p. 69 ; ' in 1119 ' : *Annals of Winchester*.

[4] Orderic, iv. 347.

[5] *Ibid*. p. 348. [6] *Ibid*. [7] *Ibid*.

[8] *Ibid*. pp. 350-2.   [9] *Ibid*. p. 393.

[10] Florence of Worcester. Cf. Sym. of Durham, ii. 254.

[11] Orderic, iv. 356-7.   [12] Round, *Calendar*, no. 794.

[13] Orderic, iv. 367-8.   [14] *Ibid*. p. 371.

Hugh, Thomas de St. John, William the chamberlain of Tancarvill, Michael de Hameslape ; the king's chaplains John of Bayeux, Nigel de Calne, and Robert Peche ; Richard the king's chaplain and keeper of his seal. ' Data Rothomagi, Deo gratias solemniter et feliciter, anno ab incarnatione Domini M.C.XIX., quo nimirum anno pretaxatus filius regis Henrici Willelmus et rex designatus puellam nobilissimam filiam Fulconis Andegavorum comitis, Mathildem nomine, Luxovii duxit uxorem.' [1]

388. Notification to Archbishop Ralph, Robert bishop of Lincoln, and generally, of the grant to Geoffrey, abbot of St. Albans, of the abbey of St. Albans, in succession to Abbot Richard. It is attested by the primate, Urban bishop of Glamorgan, Nigel de Aubigny, Roger Fitz-Richard, Geoffrey de Mandevill, Richard Fitz-Baldwin, Jordan de Sai, Henry de Aubigny, and Hugh de Laval ; at Rouen.[2]

October. Henry lays siege to Evreux. Stephen count of Aumâle surrenders himself to the king at Vieux-Rouen.[3]

389. Mandate to Geoffrey archbishop of Rouen and all the bishops, barons, &c., of Normandy that the monks of St. Mary's, Bec, are to hold in peace all lands, &c., of which they were in seisin on the day on which Normandy came into the king's hand ; they were not to be impleaded regarding the same except in the king's presence. It is attested by Ralph archbishop of Canterbury and Raimond the chanter ; at Rouen.[4] [1117–19.]

390. Writ to the sheriff of Vaudreuil directing that the nuns of Saint-Amand shall have their livery of the king's alms at Vaudreuil. It is attested by Ralph archbishop of Canterbury and Ranulf the chancellor ; at Rouen.[5] [1117–19.]

391. Accord made between Girard abbot of St. Wandrille and Hugh abbot of Cérisy, at Rouen, in the presence of Henry king of the English. It is attested by Ralph archbishop of Canterbury, Ranulf bishop of Durham, and Nigel de Aubigny.[6]

392. Robert earl of Leicester grants to the church of Notre-Dame of Bec and to the church of Saint-Nicaise of Meulan 10*li.* 5*s.* worth of land in the manor of Pimperne (' Pinpra '), in exchange for the land of Ralph Piquet (?) in Blandford (' Blinchefeld '), &c. This King Henry confirms with his seal. Witnesses : Waleran count of Meulan, Nigel de Aubigny, William de Tancarvill, Geoffrey de Magnavilla, William Fitz-Robert, Odard the sewer of Meulan, Ra(lph) the butler (?),[7] Geoffrey de Curvill ; in the king's bed-chamber at Rouen, in the year 1119.[8]

---

[1] *Chartul. of Colchester*, i. 6–10 ; *Cal. of Pat. Rolls, 1453*, p. 80.

[2] Matth. Paris, *Chron. Mai.* vi. 39 ; Cott. MS. Nero D. 1.

[3] Orderic, iv. 393, 395.

[4] *Neustria Pia*, p. 484, from an *inspeximus* by King Philip II, 1204. For ' Raimond the chanter ' one ought perhaps to read Ranulf the chancellor '.

[5] Archives of the Seine-Inférieure ; and Archives Nationales, JJ. 49, fo. 26 *d* ; Haskins, *Norman Institutions*, p. 295.

[6] Lot, *Études critiques sur l'Abbaye de Saint-Wandrille*, p. 115, no. 60 ; Cartul. de Rouen, fo. 297, no. 13 bis.

[7] ' Pinc.'

[8] Bibliothèque Nationale, Collection du Vexin, iii. 171, no. 246 ; Haskins, *Norman Institutions*, p. 295.

19–20 Oct. Pope Calixtus holds a general council at Rheims, where Archbishop Thurstan is consecrated by the pope on the day preceding the council.[1]

393. 17 Nov. The county court of Berkshire sits at Sutton, near Abingdon, William de Bocheland being sheriff of the county, on Monday next after the feast of St. Martin in the third year after the death of Abbot Faritius. A geld is being levied in each county. Seven score hides of land in the demesne of the abbot of Abingdon are affirmed to be geld-free. This recognition is made pursuant to a decree of the king's justiciary, namely Roger bishop of Salisbury, Robert bishop of Lincoln, Ranulf the chancellor, and Ralph Basset.[2]

20–7 Nov. Henry meets the newly-elected pope, Calixtus II, at Gisors.[3] He refuses to restore the see of York to Thurstan, unless the archbishop-elect will make profession of obedience and subjection to the archbishop of Canterbury. This Thurstan will not do, and therefore he remains in France.[4]

25 Dec. At Christmas Henry holds his court at Bayeux.

394. Notification to Ildebert bishop of the Mançeaux and the barons of Maine and Normandy of the grant to the church of the Holy Trinity of Savigny and Dom. Vitalis, its founder, of the church of St. Peter of Dompierre. It is attested by John of Bayeux, Geoffrey de Clinton, and Thomas de St. John; at Bayeux, at Christmas ' in anno quo rex Anglorum dimicavit et debellavit regem Francorum '.[5]

1120.

28 Feb. Eudes the sewer dies about the month of January at the castle of Préaux. His body is transported to England and buried at the monastery of St. John, Colchester, on the day before the kalends of March.[6]

395. Notification, addressed generally, of the grant to the monks of Tiron of 15 marks yearly at Winchester from the Treasury at Michaelmas. It is attested by Ranulf the chancellor, Geoffrey archbishop of Rouen, John bishop of Lisieux, Robert de la Hai, and Nigel de Aubigny; at Caen.[7] [1118–Nov. 1120.]

396. Confirmation, addressed generally, to Fulk the sewer of land which he held of Eudes the sewer by the service of two knights. It is attested by Nigel de Calne, Nigel de Aubigny, William de Pirou, Otuer son of Earl (Hugh), Hamon de St. Clare, and Roger nephew of Hubert; at Caen.[8]

397. Confirmation, addressed generally for England, to the monks of Colchester of the gift of the manor of Brightlingsea, made by Eudes the sewer, to be held in as beneficial a manner as the monks held it at the death of Eudes the sewer. It is attested by Nigel de Calne, Nigel de Aubigny, William de Pirou, and Otuer son of Earl (Hugh); at Caen.[9]

[1] Sym. of Durham, ii. 254; Orderic, iv. 373.
[2] *Chron. of Abingdon*, ii. 160.   [3] Orderic, iv. 398; Eadmer, p. 258.
[4] Sym. of Durham, ii. 257; *Historians of York*, ii. 168.
[5] Round, *Calendar*, no. 793.
[6] *Chartul. of Colchester*, p. xviii, from Nero D. viii; *Mon. Anglic.* iv. 607.
[7] Round, *Calendar*, no. 998.
[8] *Chartul. of Colchester*, i. 23.   [9] *Ibid.* p. 21.

398. In the castle of Caen in the presence of the justices ('tocius iusticie') Roger son of Peter de Fontenay surrenders to St. Stephen's, Caen, land which the church had from Godfrey, grandfather of the said Roger son of Peter. This is attested by the same justiciary, namely John bishop of Lisieux, Robert de la Hai, Hugh de Montfort, Geoffrey de Sublis, and Roger Marmion.[1]

11 Mar. Pope Calixtus, now at Gap, addresses letters to the king and Ralph archbishop of Canterbury threatening to place England under an interdict unless Archbishop Thurstan be promptly restored to his see.[2]

3 Mar.–17 April. Some time during Lent Henry is at Arganchy, near Bayeux.

399. Notification, addressed generally, of the restoration to Rohaise, late the wife of Eudes the sewer, of the land given to her by her late husband in dower. It is attested by William the king's son, Richard bishop of Bayeux, and Earl William de Warenne; 'apud Archenci iuxta Baiocas in quadragesima.'[3]

4 April. David the king's chaplain, having been nominated bishop of Bangor by Griffin, prince of Wales, and the clergy and people of the principality, is consecrated at Westminster by Ralph archbishop of Canterbury.[4]

400. Notification of the grant of certain liberties by the king, William his son, and Robert Fitz-Martin to the monastery of St. Mary, Kemeys, upon the foundation of the same by the said Robert as a cell of the monks of St. Sauveur, Tiron. It is attested by William de Aubigny the Breton and Othoer son of Earl (Hugh); at St. Vaubourg.[5] Done in the year 1120, 'regnante Ludovico Francorum rege et Henrico Angliam gubernante'.[6]

30 May. Henry and the papal legate, Conon, have an interview 'apud Vercionem' (? Vernon).[7]

401. June. Notification to Ralph, archbishop of Canterbury, of the king's consent to the investiture of (Eadmer), the monk (of Canterbury) in the bishopric of St. Andrew's. It is attested by Everard de Calne; at Rouen.[8]

402. Notification to Thurstan archbishop of York, Hugh de Laval ('de Valle'), and the sheriff and barons of Yorkshire of the grant to the canons of St. Oswald of a yearly fair at Nostell. It is attested by Ranulf the chancellor, Henry count of Eu, Roger Fitz-Richard, Humphrey de Bohun, Pain Fitz-John, Ralph de Todeney, and Engelram de Abernone; at Rouen.[9]

403. Writ to Nigel (de Aubigny), Anschetill de Bulemer, and the barons of Yorkshire commanding that Thurstan archbishop of York shall hold in peace the church of (South) Cave. It is attested by Ranulf the chancellor; at Rouen.[10]

---

[1] Original in Archives of the Calvados, H. 1834, nos. 13–15 *bis*; *ante*, xxiv. 215.
[2] *Historians of York*, ii. 192–4; Sym. of Durham, ii. 262.
[3] *Chartul. of Colchester*, i. 42.   [4] Le Neve, *Fasti*.
[5] Round, *Cal. of Docs., France*, nos. 996–7.   [6] *Ibid*. no. 997.
[7] *Historians of York*, ii. 186.
[8] Eadmer, p. 281. Cf. Lawrie, *Early Scottish Charters*, pp. 288–9.
[9] *Cartae Antiq.* HH.; Farrer, *Early Yorkshire Charters*, no. 1433.
[10] Regist. Mag. Album, pt. ii, fo. 83 *d*; Farrer, *Early Yorkshire Charters*, no. 1822.

404. Mandate to Hugh de Montfort to restore twenty acres of land to the abbot of Bec as belonging to the churches of St. Philibert (-sur-Risle) and St. Ouen (-de-Flancourt), the abbot having been in seisin when the honor of Montfort was restored to Hugh ; at Rouen[1]. [1106–20.]

405. Notification to Geoffrey archbishop of Rouen and the bishops, barons, &c., of Normandy, of the confirmation to the monks of St. Mary of Lire of the mill and forge of La Neuve-Lire (Eure) as Ralph de Witot had given the same. This is done at the petition of Earl Robert of Leicester and Guher de Moreville, and is attested by Ouin bishop of Evreux, John bishop of Lisieux, Ralph de Toeny, Ralph the butler, Robert de Neufbourg, and Ernald du Bois ; at Rouen.[2]

Some time during the year Henry and Louis meet. Prince William, at his father's command, does homage to Louis for Normandy.[3]

Oct. Henry meets the legate Conon at Gisors, shortly before crossing to England.[4]

2 Nov. Robert de Chandos, founder of Goldcliff Abbey, dies on 4 nones of November, leaving issue, Robert, Roger, and Godard.[5]

21 Nov. The king is at Barfleur waiting for a favourable wind for his passage to England.

406. Charter of confirmation to the monks of St. Vigor at Cerisy. The signatories are : the king ; Ranulf the chancellor ; Geoffrey archbishop of Rouen ; the bishops Richard of Bayeux, John of Lisieux, Roger of Coutances, and Turgis of Avranches ; Earl Robert, Earl Richard, Ranulf the viscount, Robert de la Hai, and Roger Fitz-Richard. ' Actum est hoc apud Barbefluvium, anno ab incarnatione Domini M.C.XX., indictione xiii, epacta xviii, xi kalendas Decembris, feria prima, luna v, regnante Ludovico rege in Gallia.' [6]

25 Nov. On the evening of 7 kalends of December the king embarks at Barfleur, having declined the invitation of Thomas, son of Stephen Fitz-Airard, to sail in his new ship ' La Blanche Nef '. To him, however, the king commits the charge of conveying his sons, William and Richard.[7] Two monks of Tiron, Count Stephen, William de Roumare, Rabel [son of] the chamberlain, Edward of Salisbury, William de Pirou the sewer,[8] and some others go on board the ' White Ship ', but leave it before it sets sail, being alarmed at the overcrowding of the vessel with passengers, rowers, and guards, many of whom are seen to be more or less intoxicated.[9] Not long after leaving port the vessel strikes a rock and founders. Among those on board who perish by drowning are : William the Ætheling, the king's son and daughter, Richard and Matilda, Richard earl of Chester and his wife Matilda, sister of Theobald count of Blois, Otuer, brother of Earl Richard and governor and tutor of the king's sons, Theodoric (or Dietrich),

---

[1] MS. Lat. 13905, fo. 83 ; Haskins, *Norman Institutions*, p. 296.

[2] Copied from a lost chartulary in the Jesuit college at Paris : Haskins, *Norman Institutions*, p. 297.

[3] Luchaire, *Louis VI*, no. 298 ; Sym. of Durham, ii. 258.

[4] *Historians of York*, ii. 189.   [5] *Mon. Anglic.* ii. 60 *b*.

[6] *Neustria Pia*, p. 432 ; *Mon. Anglic.* vi. 1075.

[7] Orderic, iv. 411.

[8] Orderic wrongly includes him among those who were lost.

[9] *Ibid.* p. 412.

nephew of the Emperor Henry, Geoffrey, son of Gilbert de Aquila and younger brother of Richer, the two sons of Ives de Grentemesnil and their cousin William of Rhuddlan, son of Robert of Rhuddlan, William Bigod the sewer, Geoffrey Ridel, Hugh de Molines, Gilbert de Exmes, Ralph le Roux of Pont-Echanfré, Robert Mauduit, Gisulf the king's scribe,[1] and many of the king's court, sewers, chamberlains, butlers, and other officers.[2]

John of Worcester adds the names of Walter de Everci and Geoffrey archdeacon of Hereford.[3]

Ranulf Meschin, viscount of Bayeux, resigns Cumberland to the king on succeeding to the earldom of Chester.[4]

25 Dec. Henry keeps Christmas at Brampton (near Huntingdon) with Theobald, count of Blois.[5]

1121.

6 Jan. On the feast of the Epiphany, at a council of the prelates and barons held in London, the king announces his intention to wed Adheliza, daughter of Godfrey, duke of Louvain.[6] A deputation is sent to Dover to meet the future queen with her retinue, and to conduct her to the court.[7]

7 Jan. Richard de Capella, the king's chaplain and keeper of his seal under the chancellor, is appointed to the see of Hereford;[8] Robert (Peche), steward of the meat and drink in the king's household, is appointed to that of Chester; and Herbert the almoner, a monk of Westminster, is made abbot of St. Peter's, Westminster.[9]

Possibly at this council, and in any case during this year, Anselm the legate, abbot of St. Saba and nephew of Archbishop Anselm, is appointed abbot of St. Edmund's.[10]

407. Notification to Adam de Port, the barons and lieges of the shires of Hereford, Gloucester, and Salop, of the grant to Richard de Capella of the bishopric of Hereford. It is attested by Archbishop Ralph; the bishops Richard of London, William of Winchester, Roger of Salisbury, Robert of Lincoln, Ranulf of Durham, Theowulf of Worcester, William of Exeter, John of Bath, Ernulf of Rochester, Ralph of Chichester, Bernard of St. David's, Urban of Llandaff, and David of Bangor; Ranulf the chancellor, Stephen count of Mortain, Ranulf earl of Chester, Robert the king's son, Nigel de Aubigny, William de Tancarvill, William de Aubigny, Walter de Gloucester, Adam de Port, William de Pirou, Walter de Gant, and Richard Fitz-Baldwin; at Westminster.[11]

408. Notification, addressed generally, of the grant of the abbey of Barking ('Berchingis') to Agnes the abbess. It is attested by Ralph

---

[1] Orderic, iv. 411-19.　　　　　[2] Rob. of Torigny, p. 104.

[3] Weaver, *op. cit.*, p. 15.

[4] ' M.C.XXI. Ranulphus Miscinus factus comes ': *Annales Cestr.* p. 18.

[5] Hen. of Huntingdon, p. 243.　　　[6] John of Worcester, p. 15.

[7] Eadmer, p. 290.　　　　　　　[8] *Ibid.* p. 291.

[9] John of Worcester, p. 15; Sym. of Durham, ii. 259.

[10] Orderic, iv. 429; *Mon. Anglic.* iii. 155 *b*.

[11] Harl. Ch. iii. B, 46; *Brit. Mus. Facsimiles of Charters*, no. 3; *Cal. of Pat. Rolls*, *1355-8*, p. 196.

archbishop of Canterbury; the bishops Richard of London, Roger of Salisbury, and Robert of Lincoln; Ranulf the chancellor, Nigel de Aubigny, William de Tancarvill, and Geoffrey de Clinton ; at Westminster.[1]

29 Jan. Before the Purification a council of all England assembles at Windsor for the ceremony of the king's marriage to Adheliza of Louvain. The ceremony is performed by the bishop of Winchester.[2]

30 Jan. The queen is consecrated and crowned by the primate, who was absent on the previous day through sickness.[3]

Thurstan, archbishop of York, having received at Rouen three days before the Purification the king's mandate recalling him, embarks and comes to the king at Windsor. Shortly afterwards he is reinstated in his see.[4]

409. Notification to the burgesses of London, and generally, of the confirmation to the church of Westminster and Abbot Herbert of certain lands in London. It is attested by the archbishops Ralph of Canterbury and Geoffrey of Rouen ; the bishops Richard of London, William of Winchester, Roger of Salisbury, and Robert of Lincoln; Ranulf the chancellor, John of Bayeux,[5] Theobald count of Blois, Earl David, Robert the king's son, William de Tancarvill, William de Aubigny, Nigel de Aubigny, Geoffrey de Clinton, and Ralph Basset ; at Windsor.[6]

410. General charter of confirmation in favour of St. Peter's, Westminster. It is attested by eleven of the above witnesses.[7]

411. Several writs are issued in favour of the same monastery. They are attested by Ranulf the chancellor, Geoffrey de Clinton, and Ralph Basset ; at Windsor.[8]

412. Writ directing that certain manors which have been alienated with the consent of the chapter shall be restored to the church of St. Peter, Westminster, and Abbot Herbert. It is attested by Ranulf the chancellor, Geoffrey de Clinton, and R(alph) Basset ; at Windsor.[9]

A deputation from the monastery of Abingdon attends the king at Windsor and petitions for the appointment of an abbot to their house, vacant for the past four years. They are summoned to be at Winchester in five days' time with their prior.[10]

Feb. The king visits Winchester a few days after leaving Windsor. The appointment of Vincent to be abbot of Abingdon is made in 'the presence of the bishops and barons, and by their advice.[11]

413. Possibly whilst at Winchester the king notifies Theold bishop of Worcester, Walter of Gloucester, and the barons of Gloucestershire of his confirmation to the abbot and monks of Gloucester of land which Roger of Bayeux held (' tenuit ') of Thomas, archbishop of York, as of the

---

[1] *Cal. of Chart. Rolls*, v. 284.   [2] Sym. of Durham, ii. 259.

[3] Eadmer, p. 293 ; John of Worcester, p. 16.

[4] Hugh the Chantor, pp. 190–1 ; Sym. of Durham, ii. 262.

[5] Chartul. of St. Peter's, Westm., Faust. A. iii, fo. 129.

[6] Madox, *Formulare Anglic.*, no. 75, p. 39 ; *Mon. Anglic.*, i. 307, no. 51 ; Robinson, *Gilbert Crispin*, p. 163.

[7] *Mon. Anglic.* i. 307, no. 52 ; Madox, *op. cit.*, no. 496, p. 291.

[8] Chartul. of St. Peter's, Westm., Faust. A. iii, ff. 75–8.

[9] *Ibid.* fo. 75 d.

[10] *Chron. of Abingdon*, ii. 161, 166.   [11] *Ibid.* p. 161.

manor of St. Peter, at Standish. It is attested by Ralph archbishop of Canterbury and Bernard bishop of St. David's.[1]

13 Mar. The primate accompanies the king to Abingdon and on 3 ides of March there consecrates Robert Peche, bishop of Chester. He is assisted by the bishops William of Winchester, William of Exeter, Urban of Llandaff, and Bernard of St. David's.[2]

414. March. Notification, addressed generally, of the grant to Abbot Vincent of the abbey of Abingdon. It is attested by Roger bishop of Salisbury, Ranulf the chancellor, John of Bayeux, and William de Pont de l'Arche ; at Woodstock.[3]

415. Notification to the bishop of Lincoln, Gilbert the sheriff, and the barons of Huntingdon(shire) of the restoration to Rainald abbot of Ramsey of land in Adlington and Wardboys, which Hugh de Wirec(estre) used to hold. It is attested by the bishops (Roger) of Salisbury, (Robert) of Lincoln, and (William) of Winchester ; Ranulf the chancellor, Nigel de Aubigny, Walter de Gloucester, Ralph Basset, Vitalis Engaine, Eurewin, Durand, and Herbert ; at Woodstock.[4] [1121–2.]

416. Writ, addressed to Nigel de Aubigny, Anschetil de Bulemer, and the barons of Yorkshire, directing that the land of the canons of St. Peter's, York, St. John's, Beverley, St. Mary's, Southwell, St. Wilfrid's, Ripon, and of Hexham shall be quit of service in the army (*expeditio*) and castle-work, as in the time of the king's father and brother. It is attested by Ranulf the chancellor ; at Woodstock.[5]

417. Notification to Richard bishop of London, Aubrey de Ver, the sheriff, &c., of Essex, of the confirmation to the church of Salisbury ('Sarum') of two hides in Leyton ('Linton') which Simon de Mol(ines) and Adela his wife gave. It is attested by the bishops Roger of Salisbury, William of Exeter, and Bernard of St. David's ; John of Bayeux, Geoffrey the chaplain, Adam de Port, Walter de Gloucester, Geoffrey de Clinton, William de Pont de L'Arche, and Pain Fitz-John ; at Woodstock.[6] [1121–6.]

418. Notification to William bishop of Winchester, William de Pont de l'Arche, and the barons of Wiltshire, of the grant to Roger bishop of Salisbury and the church there of the church of Hurstbourn and whatever Thurstan son of Vitalis holds of the king. It is attested by Ranulf the chancellor ; at Cricklade ('apud Grecheladam').[7]

6 Apr. In the chapter of St. Peter, York, on Wednesday before Easter,[8] before Archbishop Thurstan and the bishops Ranulf of Durham and Ouen of Evreux, the monks of Durham claim the church of Tynemouth. On Wednesday in Easter week (13 April) the claim is renewed at Durham before a large gathering of northern magnates, namely Robert de Brus,

---

[1] *Chartul. of St. Peter's, Gloucester*, ii. 108. Dated 1121: *ibid.* i. 100 note. A charter of confirmation, similarly addressed, was probably issued at the same time : *ibid.* ii. 97.

[2] John of Worcester, p. 16 ; Eadmer, p. 293.

[3] *Chron. of Abingdon*, ii. 162.   [4] *Chartul. of Ramsey*, no. 178.

[5] Reg. Mag. Album, i. 65 ; Farrer, *Early Yorkshire Charters*, no. 130 ; *Mon. Anglic.* vi. 1179, no. 22.

[6] Cart. Antiq. roll N, no. 13 (6).   [7] *Sarum Charters* (Rolls Series), no. 4.

[8] 'Media fermo Quadragesima.'

Alan de Percy, Walter Espec, Forne son of Sigulf, Robert de Witvill, Odard the sheriff of the Northumbrians, and Arnold de Percy.[1]

Fulk of Anjou reclaims his daughter, late the wife of William the king's son. Accordingly she is sent home by Henry.[2]

10 April. The king keeps Easter at Berkeley.[3]

419. Notification to Adam de Port, Walter de Gloucester, and the lieges of Herefordshire, of the grant to the church of St. Mary and St. Ethelbert (of Hereford) and Bishop Richard of a three days' fair at Hereford. It is attested by Geoffrey archbishop of Rouen, the bishops Roger of Salisbury and Theulf of Worcester; Ranulf the chancellor, William de Tancarvill, Adam de Port, Walter de Gloucester, Pain Fitz-John, Geoffrey de Clinton, and Roger de Candos; at Berkeley (' Berchelai '), at Easter.[4]

420. Notification, addressed generally, of the grant to Richard bishop of Hereford of a park at Hereford. It is attested by Roger bishop of Salisbury, Ranulf the chancellor, William de Tancarvill, and Geoffrey de Clinton; at Alveston (' apud Alewestan ').[5] [1121–2.]

421. Notification to Archbishop Thurstan, Anschetill de Bulemer, and the barons of Yorkshire of the confirmation, for the souls of the king's late wife and son, to the canons of St. Oswald's, (Nostell), of various gifts made to them by Hugh de Muscamp, Alan de Creon, and others; and of the agreement which Archbishop Thomas II made between the canons of St. Oswald and of Featherston and the monks of La Charité (-sur-Loire).[6] It is attested by Archbishop Thurstan, Ranulf bishop of Durham, Ranulf the chancellor, Nigel de Aubigny, and Pain Fitz-John; at Clarendon.[7] [1121–2.]

422. Mandate to E(rnulf) bishop of Rochester to cause the abbess and nuns of Malling to have their tithes of Cuxton and ' Burcstall ' as Bishop Gundulf gave them and as they held them in the time of Bishop Gundulf and Ralph, his predecessors. It is attested by John of Bayeux; at Clarendon.[8] [December 1120–June 1123.]

423. Notification, addressed generally, of the grant to Miles of Gloucester of Sibil, daughter of Bernard de Neuf-Marché, with the lands of her said father and of her mother after their deaths, or during their lives if they are willing. It is attested by the bishops Roger of Salisbury and Robert of Lincoln, Ranulf the chancellor, Robert the king's son, William de Tancarvill, Nigel de Aubigny, Pain Fitz-John, Geoffrey Fitz-Pain, Geoffrey de Clinton, Ralph Basset, William de Aubigny the Breton; at Winchester, between Easter and Whitsuntide in the year in which the king married the daughter of the duke of Louvain.[9]

424. Charter of confirmation to the church of St. Mary, Rouen. It is attested by G(eoffrey) archbishop of Rouen, W(illiam) bishop of Winchester,

---

[1] Sym. of Durham, ii. 260–2.   [2] *Ibid.* p. 263.   [3] Chron.

[4] Duncumb, *Hist. of Herefordshire*, i. 296.

[5] *Cal. of Pat. Rolls, 1354–8*, p. 106.

[6] Established in the priory of St. John the Evangelist at Pontefract.

[7] Chartul. of Nostell, Vesp. E. xix, fo. 7 *d*; Farrer, *Early Yorkshire Charters*, no. 1430. The record of a plea in 1285 states that Henry I in 1121 gave 12*d*. a day to Nostell: *Abbrev. Placit.* p. 207 *b*. Cf. *R. Mag. Pipae*, p. 24.

[8] *Cal. of Chart. Rolls*, v. 56.

[9] *Ancient Charters* (Pipe Roll Soc.), no. 6.

R(oger) bishop of Salisbury, R (*sic*) count of Meulan, G(eoffrey) de Clinton, N(igel) de Aubigny, R(alph) Basset, R(anulf) the chancellor, and A(ubrey) de Ver ; at Winchester, ' anno incarnationis Dominice millesimo centesimo vicesimo secundo (*sic*), regni vero mei vicesimo primo '.[1]

425. Notification, addressed generally, of the grant to the church of Rouen and Archbishop Geoffrey of the manor of King's Clere. It is attested by the bishops William of Winchester, Roger of Salisbury, Robert of Lincoln, and Bernard of St. David's ; Ranulf the chancellor, William de Warenne (*sic*), Robert the king's son, Nigel de Aubigny, William de Aubigny, William de Tancarvill, Geoffrey de Clinton, Geoffrey Fitz-Pain, and Ralph Basset ; at Winchester.[2] [1120–2.]

426. Notification, addressed generally, of the grant to the canons of St. Oswald of liberty to build their church above the vivary (at Nostell), where they previously commenced to build it. It is attested by Ranulf the chancellor, Ranulf earl of Chester, Earl David, Walter Giffard, Nigel de Aubigny, William Peverel of Nottingham, Humphrey de Bohun, William Maltravers, and Peverel de Beauchamp ; at Winchester.[3] [1120–2.]

427. Notification to Archbishop Thurstan, Hugh de Laval, A(nschetil) de Bulemer the sheriff, the barons and lieges of Yorkshire, of the confirmation to the canons of St. Oswald of St. Oswald's wood, which Robert de Lascy gave. It is attested by Ranulf the chancellor and Nigel de Aubigny ; at Winchester.[4] [1120–2.]

428. Notification, addressed generally, of the confirmation to Pontius abbot of Cluny of the monastery of the Holy Trinity of Lenton, which William Peverel gave with the vill of Lenton, the church of St. Mary of Nottingham, &c., tithes of hides in the Peak, &c. ; also of the church of Wigston (' Wichingest ') given by Robert count of Meulan ; of two parts of the tithes of the demesne of Boney (co. Nott.), the church of Barton and a mediety of the church of Attenborough (co. Nott.), given by Odo de Bonai ; also of the king's grant of a fair and liberties. It is attested by Ranulf the chancellor, Geoffrey de Clinton, Aubrey de Veer, and William de Aubigny ; at Winchester.[5] [1114–22.]

429. Notification to William (de Pont de l'Arche) the sheriff and the barons of Wiltshire of the grant to the church of St. Mary, Salisbury (' Sarum ') and Bishop Roger of certain churches in Wiltshire. It is attested by William bishop of Winchester, Ranulf the chancellor, Herbert the chamberlain, and Humphrey de Boun ; at Winchester.[6] [1110–22.]

430. These are the men who were present when King Henry confirmed to Bernard the scribe the lands which he has in Cornwall, &c., namely Roger bishop of Salisbury, Ranulf the chancellor and Geoffrey his chaplain, Robert de Sigillo, Nigel de Aubigny, Geoffrey de Clinton, Edward of Salisbury, William de St. Clare, and Grimbald the physician.[7] [1121–2.]

[1] *Cal. of Chart. Rolls*, iii. 60.   [2] *Ibid.* p. 462.
[3] Chartul. of Nostell, Vesp. E. xix, fo. 7 ; Farrer, *Early Yorkshire Charters*, no. 1427.
[4] Chartul. of Nostell, Vesp. E. xix, fo. 8 ; Farrer, *Early Yorkshire Charters*, no. 1425.
[5] *Cal. of Chart. Rolls*, v. 149.   [6] *Reg. of St. Osmund*, i. 208.
[7] Chartul. of Merton, Cleop. C. vii, fo. 76 ; *ante*, xiv. 418.

Evrard, ' one of the king's chapel ' and archdeacon of Salisbury, is elected to the see of Norwich.[1]

29 May. At Whitsuntide the king holds a great court at Westminster, at which he and the queen are again crowned.[2]

431. Notification to Archbishop Thurstan, the ministers and lieges of Cumberland and Westmorland of the confirmation to St. Mary's, York, and Abbot Richard of certain churches and tithes in Westmorland which have been given by Ranulf Meschin ; and of the king's grant of fuel in the forest of Carlisle. It is attested by Eustace Fitz-John and Jordan Paynel ; at Reading.[3]

18 June. The abbey of Reading is founded on 14 kalends of July.[4]

June. In June the king leads an expedition against the Welsh.[5] The sons of the Welsh king (Cadwgan), after hearing of the drowning of Richard, earl of Chester, reduced two of his castles to ashes, slew many of his people, and laid waste a number of places in that province.[6]

432. Notification to Robert bishop of Lincoln, the canons of St. Mary's, Lincoln, the barons of Lincolnshire and Oxfordshire and those of the bishopric of Lincoln of the gift to the church of Lincoln and Bishop Robert of the prebend in the church of Long Sutton, co. Linc., and in the land of Horley, co. Oxon., which Bishop Ranulf and Ellis his son have for their lives, in augmentation of the prebend in the church of Lincoln. It is attested by Geoffrey archbishop of Rouen and Ranulf the chancellor ; at Hereford.[7] [1110–16, 1121–2.]

433. Notification to Richard bishop of Hereford, the sheriff, and lieges of Herefordshire of the confirmation to the monks of Tiron of land at Kington and Beverton, co. Hereford, given by Adam de Port. It is attested by Geoffrey archbishop of Rouen, the bishops Roger of Salisbury and Richard of Hereford, Ranulf the chancellor, and Reginald Fitz-John ; at Hereford.[8] [1121–2.]

434. Ranulf, physician to King Henry, grants to the monks of Montacute, with the consent of Robert de la Hai, then lord of Wentloog, land at Mendelgif. It is attested by King Henry, Robert de la Hai, Ranulf the king's chancellor, Winebald de Balun, William then sheriff of Kaerdiff, Robert Sor, Roger de Sumeri, Robert Fitz-Joce, Herbert de St. Quintin, Landomar Ace, Aldred (*sic*) de Nichole and Robert his son.[9]

435. Confirmation to the monks of Tiron of the gifts made by Robert Fitz-Martin (whose charter, dated 4 ides of September and attested by Bernard bishop of St. David's, W(illiam) abbot of Tiron, Richard Fitz-Gilbert, and others, is recited). The signatories are : King Henry and

---

[1] John of Worcester, p. 16. [2] Hen. of Huntingdon, p. 243.

[3] Prescott, *Chartul. of Wetherhal*, no. 9.

[4] *Annals of Waverley*, p. 218. A writ in the Reading chartulary (Harl. MS. 1708, fo. 17 d) proves that the abbey was founded before 23 April 1124, when Earl David succeeded to the Scottish crown, for it is addressed to him as earl, in conjunction with the bishop of Salisbury.

[5] ' In aestate ' : Chron. [6] Sym. of Durham, ii. 263.

[7] Chartul. of St. Mary's, Linc., Vesp. E. xvi, fo. 7 d, no. 17 ; *Mon. Anglic.* vi. 1273, no. 30.

[8] Round, *Calendar*, no. 1005.

[9] *Chartul. of Montacute* (Somerset Rec. Soc.), no. 164.

Queen Adelaide, Robert (Fitz-Martin), Bernard bishop (of St. David's), Matilda (wife of Robert Fitz-Martin), Richard Fitz-Gilbert, Stephen (the sewer of Richard Fitz-Gilbert), Alvered (de Bennevill), and Humphrey (Fitz-Gosmer).[1] [1121–33.]

436. Notification to Robert bishop of Coventry, Richard bishop of London, and the barons of Shropshire of the grant to the monks of St. Peter's, Shrewsbury, of the multure of that city. It is attested by Bernard bishop of St. David's, Grimbald[2] the physician, and Hamon Peverel; at Bridgenorth ('apud Brugiam').[3] [1121–3.]

437. Notification to Robert bishop of Lincoln, Robert bishop of Coventry, Richard bishop of London, Gilbert the sheriff, and the barons, &c., of Huntingdonshire and Shropshire of the confirmation to Thurstan, the sewer of William Peverel of Dover, of a grant made by the same William Peverel of the land of 'Goduig' (in Huntingdonshire ?). It is attested by William Fitz-Odo and Geoffrey Fitz-Pain; at Bridgenorth ('apud Bruges').[4] [1121–2.]

438. Writ, addressed to Richard bishop of London, and all sheriffs in whose bailiwicks the abbot of Shrewsbury has lands, in favour of Godfrey abbot of Shrewsbury. It is attested by the bishops Richard of London, Bernard of St. David's, and Robert of Chester; and Hamon Peverel; at Condover ('apud Conedoveram').[5] [June–July 1121.]

439. A charter of confirmation is issued in favour of the abbey of Shrewsbury. The signatories are : the king; Ralph archbishop of Canterbury; the bishops Richard of London, William of Winchester, Robert of Lincoln, Roger of Salisbury, Robert of Chester, Richard of Hereford, Theowulf of Worcester, Ralph of Chichester, John of Bath, Bernard of St. David's, and David of Bangor; Robert the king's son, Stephen count of Mortain, Ranulf the chancellor, William de Tancarvill, Geoffrey de Clinton, Walter de Gloucester, Grimbald the physician, Robert de Stotesberi, Evrard son of Earl Roger, William Peverel, Hamon his brother, Roger Fitz-Corbet, and Robert his brother, Fulcoin the sheriff, Herbert Fitz-Helgot, Baldwin de Bollers, Ulger the huntsman, and Ralph de Conedovre.[6] [1121–2.]

440. Notification to Robert bishop of Coventry, Richard bishop of London, the barons and lieges of Shropshire, of the grant to the abbot and monks of Shrewsbury of the mill of Shrewsbury. It is attested by Richard bishop of London, Grimbald the physician, William the almoner and king's chaplain, Hamon Peverel, and Fulcoin ('Fulcoius') the sheriff; at Shrewsbury ('apud Salopesberiam').[7] [1121–6.]

441. 30 June. On the morrow of the feast of St. Peter and St. Paul, 1121, John bishop of Bath is alleged to have held a court, in the presence of his friends and barons, to adjudicate in a cause concerning which he had received a writ issued by William the king's son, 'cum sigillo regio'. There

---

[1] *Mon. Anglic.* iv. 130.　　　　　　　　　　[2] 'Cunbert' in Chart. Roll.

[3] *Cal. of Chart. Rolls,* ii. 81.

[4] Cart. Antiq. roll P, no. 15 (34) ; Cur. Regis R., Mich. 9 Hen. III, m. 12 ; Eyton, *Hist. of Shropshire,* i. 246.

[5] Chartul. of Salop Abbey (MS. *penes* W. Farrer), no. 43 C.

[6] Chartul. of Salop Abbey ; *Coll. Topog. et Geneal.* i. 191–6.

[7] Chartul. of Salop Abbey, no. 47 B.

were present, besides the bishop himself, an Irish bishop named Maurice, the three archdeacons Johel of Salisbury, Girbert of Bath, and Arald, with others, and these witnesses : Patrick de Chaources, Hubert de Saint Susanna, Winibald de Baalun, Alexander de Aunou (' Alnoth '), Reinald de Dunstanvill, and others.[1]

The king leads an army as far as ' Snawedun ',[2] apparently without meeting much opposition. Maredudd son of Bleddyn and his nephews, the sons of Cadwgan, come and make submission and undertake to pay a fine of 10,000 head of cattle and sheep.[3]

442. Notification to William bishop of Exeter, the sheriff of Devonshire, the barons and lieges of Devonshire of the acquittance of certain specified lands of St. Martin des Champs and the monks of Barnstaple from gelds, aids, and other exactions ' a proximo Pentecoste postquam duxi uxorem Adelizam reginam in antea semper et imperpetuum '. It is attested by Walter de Gloucester and Henry de Pomereda ; at Westminster.[4] [May–Sept. 1121.]

443. *c.* 3 Dec. ? At the prayer of Gilbert the sheriff the king expedites a charter of confirmation in favour of Merton priory, ' anno ab incarnatione Domini M.C.XXI., regni autem mei vicesimo secundo '. The signatories are : the king and queen; the archbishops Ralph and Thurstan ; Ranulf the chancellor; the bishops William of Winchester, William (*sic*) of London, Roger of Salisbury, Robert of Lincoln, Ranulf of Durham, William of Exeter, Evrard of Norwich, Theowulf of Worcester, Ernulf of Rochester, Ralph of Chichester, Robert of Chester, Richard of Hereford, Bernard of St. David's, Hervey of Ely, and John of Bath ; Herbert abbot of Westminster, Hugh abbot of St. Augustine's, William de Warenne, earl of Surrey, David earl of Lowthian, Waleran count of Meulan, Earl Ralph (*sic*), Robert earl of Gloucester, Stephen archdeacon (of Surrey), Simon dean of Leu . . ., Alexander archdeacon (of Salisbury).[5]

444. Notification, addressed generally, of the confirmation to the monks of Tewkesbury of their possessions. It is attested by Roger bishop of Salisbury, Robert bishop of Lincoln, Robert (*sic*) count of Meulan, Robert earl of Gloucester,[6] Brien Fitz-Count, Hamon the sewer, and Walter de Gloucester ; at Winchester.[7] [1120–2.]

445. Confirmation of a gift made in 1121 by William Malet to St. Mary's, Bec. The signatories are the king, Queen Adeliza, the bishops William of Winchester and Roger of Salisbury, Ranulf the chancellor, Drew de Muncei, Walter Fitz-Richard, Hugh de Gornai, Waleran count of Meulan, and Robert earl of Leicester.[8] [1120–2.]

446. Notification to Archbishop Thurstan, the justices, barons, and ministers of Yorkshire, of the confirmation of a gift made by Osbert the

---

[1] *Two Bath Abbey Chartularies*, n. 49.   [2] Sym. of Durham, ii. 264.

[3] *Annales Cambr.*, *s. a.* ; *Brut-y-Tywysogion*, *s. a.* 1118 (= 1121).

[4] *Cal. of Chart. Rolls*, iii. 331 ; Round, *Calendar*, no. 1269.

[5] *Mon. Anglic.* vi. 247.

[6] See Mr. Round in *The Genealogist*, N.S. iv. 129 ff.

[7] Probably spurious : *Cal. of Pat. Rolls, 1494–1509*, p. 103 ; Cart. Antiq. roll T, no. 23 ; *Mon. Anglic.* ii. 66 *b*. See Mr. Round's remarks on this charter in *Geoffrey de Mandeville*, p. 431 ; *The Genealogist*, N.S., vii. 92–4.

[8] Round, *Calendar*, no. 372.

sheriff to St. German's, Selby, of land in Acaster. It is attested by the bishops Robert of Lincoln and Bernard of St. David's, and Earl Robert the king's son ; at [*blank*].[1] [1115–16, 1121–2.]

447. Mandate to Robert bishop of Lincoln and Gilbert the sheriff that neither man nor house shall remain in the holme (*insula*) of the abbot of Ramsey, save by the abbot's permission. It is attested by Nigel de Aubigny ; at Brigstock.[2] [*c.* 1110–22.]

William Fitz-Ansger dies before the year 1122.[3]

25 Dec. The king celebrates the feast of the Nativity at Norwich.[4]

31 Dec. Richard abbot of St. Mary's, York, dies on the day before the kalends of January.[5]

1122.

448. Notification to the bishop of Norwich and the lieges of Norfolk of the confirmation to the monks of St. Alban's at Binham, of land which Robert (Godchild) [6] holds in the vill of Wells (co. Norfolk), to be held after the death of the said Robert as it was given by Peter de Valoignes, Roger his son, and the said Robert. It is attested by Nigel de Aubigny ; at (King's) Cliff (' apud Clivam ').[7] [1110–29.]

449. Writ, addressed to all sheriffs in whose bailiwicks the abbess of Barking has lands, directing that Adelica [8] the abbess shall hold her lands, &c., freely as heretofore. It is attested by W(illiam) de Aubigny the Breton ; at (King's) Cliff.[9] [1107–33.]

450. Mandate to Richard bishop of Hereford, and all bishops in whose dioceses the abbot of Shrewsbury has churches, lands, and tithes, in favour of the abbot of Shrewsbury. It is attested by Bernard bishop of St. David's ; at (Green's ?) Norton.[10] [1121–7.]

26 Mar. The king celebrates Easter at Northampton.[11]

451. Notification, addressed generally, that the monks of St. Martin's, Battle, shall hold in peace, with certain liberties, their lands, including Appledram, which they have received in exchange for Reading. It is attested by Roger bishop of Salisbury, Ranulf the chancellor, and Nigel de Aubigny ; at Northampton.[12] [1121–2.]

452. Notification to Richard bishop of London, Aubrey de Ver, the sheriffs, barons and lieges of London of the grant to Norman the prior and the canons of the Holy Trinity (Christchurch), London, that they may enclose with walls the road between their church and the wall of the city ; and that the said road shall now be before their church on the other side. It is attested by Ranulf the chancellor, Geoffrey de Clinton, and Ralph Basset ; at Northampton.[13] [1121–2.]

---

[1] *Chartul. of Selby*, n. 30. [2] *Chartul. of Ramsey*, ii. 81.
[3] Delisle, *Rouleaux des Morts*, p. 293. [4] Chron.
[5] Chron. of St. Mary's, York, Bodl. Libr. 8 W. 46, fo. 94 ; *Mon. Anglic.* iii. 569.
[6] *Mon. Anglic.* iii. 346.
[7] Chartul. of Binham, Claud. D. xiii, fo. 40 *d.*
[8] ? *Lege* Agnes. [9] *Cal. of Chart. Rolls*, v. 285.
[10] Chartul. of Salop Abbey, no. 47 C. [11] Chron.
[12] *Cal. of Pat. Rolls, 1429–36*, p. 174. A similar notification was attested by Roger bishop of Salisbury at Winchester : *Mon. Anglic.* iii. 247, no. 16.
[13] *Mon. Anglic.* vi. 155, note 5 ; from Stevens's *Continuation.*

453. Grant to the canons regular of the Holy Trinity, London, for the soul of Queen Matilda, late the king's wife, of £25 *blanche* yearly from the issues of the same Queen Matilda at Exeter, which she gave them during her life ; and that whosoever be sheriff of Devon shall pay them to the canons at Easter and Michaelmas, in London ; also grant of the gate of Al(d)gate with the soc belonging to the same, and that the canons shall have the soc of the English Cnihtengild, with the lands and liberties belonging to the same. It is attested by Ranulf the chancellor, G(eoffrey) de Clinton, and Ralph Basset ; at Northampton.[1] [1121–2.]

454. Notification to Robert bishop of Lincoln, Earl David, and generally, of the confirmation to the priory of St. Andrew, Northampton, of their possessions. It is attested by the bishops Robert of Chester and Hervey of Ely, Ranulf the chancellor, Geoffrey de Glinton, Ralph Basset, and Hugh de Legrecestria ; at Northampton.[2] [1121–2.]

455. Notification, addressed generally, of the confirmation to the church of St. Oswald, Nostell, and Prior Adelwald of the church of Tickhill, which Roger de Bulli gave to the prior and canons. It is attested by Waleran count of Meulan, Ranulf the chancellor, Nigel de Aubigny, Robert de Brus, Roger Fitz-Richard, and Pain Fitz-John ; at Northampton.[3] [1121–2.]

456. Writ, addressed to Evrard bishop of Norwich, Robert Fitz-Walter (the sheriff), and the lieges of Norfolk, directing that the monks of Binham shall make certain roads as they please. It is attested by Nigel de Aubigny ; at Hertford.[4] [1121–9.]

457. Notification to William bishop of Winchester, Gilbert the sheriff, and the barons of Surrey of the grant to the monks of Bermondsey of the manor of Waddon (in Croydon). It is attested by Ranulf the chancellor and Nigel de Aubigny ; at Waltham.[5] [*c.* 1110–22.]

458. Writ, addressed to the justices, sheriffs, barons, foresters, officials, and lieges of Cumberland, directing that the canons of Carlisle shall have the bounds of their forest as the king gave them to them in alms, and as he ordered them to be determined. It is attested by Nigel de Aubigny ; at Waltham.[6] [1121–9.]

2 May ? Gwymund the king's chaplain reads the lesson on one of the Rogation days, when the king is hearing mass,[7] possibly at Oxford.

459. Notification to the sheriff and citizens of Oxford of the grant to the canons regular of St. Frideswide's of the monastery of St. Frideswide. It is attested by Ranulf the chancellor ; at Oxford.[8] [1111–22.]

14 May. At Whitsuntide the king is at Windsor [9] for two days and at Westminster for the remainder of Whit-week.[10]

460. Notification to William bishop of Winchester, Gilbert the sheriff,

---

[1] *Ibid.* p. 157, note 11.   [2] Add. Ch. 57166 ; *Mon. Anglic.* v. 192.
[3] Chartul. of Nostell, Vesp. E. xix, fo. 8.
[4] Chartul. of Binham, Claud. D. xiii, fo. 41 *d.*
[5] *Cal. of Chart. Rolls*, iv. 182.
[6] *Ibid.* iii. 82. Possibly issued after the king's visit to Carlisle later in the year.
[7] *Chartul. of St. Frideswide's, Oxon.,* i. 9.
[8] *Ibid.* i. 11. See *ibid.* note 1, p. 10.
[9] Hen. of Huntingdon, p. 244.
[0] Rob. of Torigny, p. 105.

the barons and lieges of Surrey of the grant to the abbey of Chertsey, and Abbot Hugh of the manor of Ham (near Kingston-on-Thames). It is attested by Ranulf bishop of Durham, Evrard bishop of Norwich, and Maurice of Windlesore ; at (Windsor ?).[1] [1121–3.]

461. Notification to Evrard bishop of Norwich, Robert Fitz-Walter the sheriff, the barons and lieges of Suffolk of the grant to the monks of St. Edmund's of land which Berard has surrendered to them, which the king gave him of the demesne of their church. It is attested by Ranulf the chancellor, Nigel de Aubigny, and Maurice of Windlesore ;[2] (at Windsor ?). [1121–3.]

462. Confirmation to the canons regular of St. Oswald's, Nostell, of various gifts made to them by Ilbert de Lascy (*sic*), Robert de Lascy, Archbishop Thurstan, and others. The signatories are : the king; Archbishop Thurstan; the bishops Richard of Hereford, William of Winchester, and Evrard of Norwich ; Eustace Fitz-John, Pain Fitz-John, and Walter Espec.[3] [1121–7.]

463. Robert the king's son notifies W(illiam) de Ainesford and his wife H(   ) that he has rendered to William Mauduit the land (of Fyfield) which Robert Mauduit his brother held of him (the king's son), and directs him to be answerable therefor to the said William, as he used to be to Robert (Mauduit), William's brother. It is attested by Richard the constable ; at London.[4] [1121–3.]

On Whit-Tuesday the king goes to London, and after Whit-week he proceeds into Kent,[5] in the expectation of meeting his daughter, the queen of Germany, who has sent word that she wishes to come to England. She is hindered from coming—so folks said—by the count of Flanders, who forbade her to pass through his land.

464. Notification to Ranulf earl of Chester, Hugh de Leicester (' Legrecestria '), and the barons of Lincolnshire of the restoration to Robert bishop of Lincoln of 6 bovates in Brough (-on-Bain), and 6 carucates in Willingham, which Ralph Basset has deraigned to be in the royal demesne. It is attested by Ranulf the chancellor, Nigel de Aubigny, William de Tancarvill, and Geoffrey de Clinton; at Guildford (' apud Geldefordam ').[6]

465. Writ addressed to the sheriffs, ministers, and barons of England and Wales notifying them of the grant of acquittance of toll to the men of the monks of Battle. It is attested by Richard the chaplain ; at Rochester.[7] [1100–33.]

466. Notification to William bishop of Winchester, the sheriff of Hampshire, the reeve of Winchester, the barons and lieges of ' Hamscira ' and Winchester of the restoration to William Mauduit (' Maledoctus ') of the whole dower of his mother, which his father (William) gave her, after her

[1] *Mon. Anglic.* i. 432, no. 15.

[2] Chartul. of St. Edmund's, Camb. Univ. Libr., fo. 25 (45).

[3] Chartul. of Nostell, Vesp. E. xix, fo. 150 ; Farrer, *Early Yorkshire Charters*, no. 1428. A doubtful charter.

[4] Add. MS. 28024, fo. 28 *d*. See no. 466.

[5] Rob. of Torigny, p. 105; Hen. of Huntingdon, p. 244 ; Twysden, *Decem Scriptt.*, col. 1014.

[6] Chartul. of St. Mary's, Linc., Vesp. E. xvi, fo. 8 *d ; ante*, xxiii. 725 ; *Mon. Anglic.* vi. 1274, no. 38.   [7] *Cal. of Pat. Rolls, 1429–36*, p. 174.

decease; until which time William de Pont de l'Arche shall pay him £10 a year. Grant also of the land of Fyfield ('Fihida'), which his father held of Robert Fitz-Hamon, and Robert, the king's son, has granted to him. It is attested by R(obert) bishop of Lincoln, Ranulf bishop of Durham, Nigel de Aubigny, Geoffrey Fitz-Pain, Edward de Saresberia, Robert de Crevecor, Robert de Ver, Robert de Ollei, and Hamon de Amando; at Perry Court ('apud Peri').[1] [May or June 1122.]

467. Grant, addressed generally, to the church of St. John, Beverley, and Archbishop Thurstan, of an increase of three days to the two days' fair at Beverley. It is attested by Robert bishop of Lincoln and Nigel de Aubigny; at Perry (Court).[2]

10 June. Girmund, abbot of Winchcomb, dies on 4 ides of June.[3]

468. Notification to the bishop of Lincoln, the sheriff, barons, and lieges of Lincolnshire of the confirmation of a gift of land and property made by Ralph de Limesi to the church of St. Mary of Hertford. This the king does 'pro meipso et pro uxore mea Matilda regina et pro pueris nostris et pro Willelmo filio nostro et uxore sua et filiis suis' (sic). It is attested by Roger bishop of Salisbury, R(obert) bishop of Lincoln, Geoffrey abbot of Winchester, Ranulf the chancellor, and Nigel de Aubigny; at Westminster.[4] [1120–2.]

469. Notification, addressed generally, of the king's consent to an exchange of lands made between Roger bishop of Salisbury and Hugh prior of Lewes.[5] It is attested by Robert bishop of Lincoln, Ranulf the chancellor, Walter de [Gloucester], Ralph Basset, and Geoffrey de Clinton; at Westminster.[6] [1120–2.]

470. Mandate to William the chamberlain and Aubrey de Ver, all the chamberlains their successors, and the sheriffs of London to pay from the farm of London to the sacristan of St. Peter's, Westminster, one half-penny daily to purchase a light to burn before the tomb of Queen Matilda from Michaelmas past for evermore. It is attested by Roger bishop of Salisbury, Robert bishop of Lincoln, Ranulf the chancellor, and Ralph Basset; at Westminster.[7] [1120–2.]

471. Notification to Ralph archbishop of Canterbury, William de Hammesford the sheriff, the barons and lieges of Kent, of the grant to St. Augustine's, Canterbury, and Abbot Hugh of a market in the isle of Thanet. It is attested by Roger bishop of Salisbury, Ralph (sic) the chancellor, and Nigel de Aubigny; at Westminster.[8] [1114–22.]

472. Notification to Robert de (sic) Bercherol and the barons of the honor late of Otuer son of Earl (Hugh) of the grant to the monks of St. Peter's, Westminster, of the church of Sawbridgeworth. It is attested by the chancellor and Geoffrey de Clinton.[9] [1120–32.]

[1] Add. MS. 28024, fo. 28; also on fo. 28 d. See no. 463.
[2] Harl. MS. 560, fo. 25; Farrer, *Early Yorkshire Charters*, no. 94.
[3] *Mon. Anglic.* ii. 298.   [4] *Cal. of Pat. Rolls, 1361–4*, p. 322.
[5] First abbot of Reading; said to have been appointed in 1123.
[6] Chartul. of Lewes, Vesp. F. xv, fo. 80 d.
[7] Chartul. of St. Peter's, Westm., fo. 363 d; Robinson, *Gilbert Crispin*, p. 156.
[8] *Hist. Mon. S. Augustini*, p. 365.
[9] Chartul. of St. Peter's, Westm., Faust. A. iii, fo. 75; Robinson, *Gilbert Crispin*, p. 156.

473. Mandate to Robert bishop of Lincoln to keep with Abbot Herbert and the monks of Westminster the agreement, made in the time of William II, between the same Robert and Gilbert abbot of Westminster concerning the manor of Leosne (Lesnes), which the bishop holds of them. It is attested by Roger Fitz-Richard ; at Woodstock.[1]　[1121–3.]

June–Sept. Robert the king's son is created earl of Gloucester.[2]

474. Notification to William bishop of Exeter and the archdeacons of Devon of the confirmation of an agreement made before the king between Roger bishop of Salisbury and Serlo the king's collector of Devonshire. It is attested by the bishops William of Winchester and Robert of Lincoln, Robert earl of Gloucester, and Robert earl of Leicester ; at Westminster.[3]

Oct. After Michaelmas the king enters the parts of Northumbria from York,[4] and visits Durham.[5]

475. Notification to the sheriffs and ministers of Northumberland that the king retains the church and monks of Tynemouth in his own hands and wills that neither the abbot of St. Albans nor the prior of Durham shall interfere with them. It is attested by Nigel de Aubigny ; at Durham.[6]

20 Oct. Ralph of Escures, archbishop of Canterbury, dies on 13 kalends of November.[7]

From Durham the king moves towards the western sea to inspect the city of Carlisle, which he commands to be strengthened with a castle and keep, for which object he makes a provision.[8]

He returns to York, where he hears some important complaints made by the citizens and people of the county.[9]

6 Dec. Two monks of St. Evroul find the king at York on the feast of St. Nicholas the bishop of Myra.[10]

476. Notification to John bishop of Lisieux, Stephen count of Mortain, Robert de la Haye, and the barons and lieges of Normandy, of the confirmation of the election of Warin des Essarts to be abbot of St. Evroul. It is attested by Archbishop Thurstan, William de Tancarvill, and William de Aubigny ; at York.[11]

477. Notification, addressed generally, of the confirmation to the monks of Noion of the gifts which William count of Evreux gave them in England. It is attested by Thurstan archbishop of York, John bishop of Lisieux, Stephen count of Mortain, Robert de Hai, William de Tancarvill, William de Aubigny, and Hamon de Falaise ; at York.[12]

478. Letters of protection, addressed generally, are issued in favour of the prior and convent of the Holy Trinity, Kirkham. They are attested

---

[1] Chartul. of St. Peter's, Westm., Faust. A. iii, fo. 67 *d* ; Robinson, *Gilbert Crispin*, p. 157.

[2] See Round, *The Genealogist*, N.S., iv. 139–40. Cf. *ante*, nos. 443 and 466, and no. 474.　　　　[3] *Reg. of St. Osmund's*, i. 381.

[4] Sym. of Durham, ii. 267 ; Rob. of Torigny, p. 105.

[5] Hen. of Huntingdon, p. 244.

[6] Craster, *Hist. of Northumb.* viii. 55, note 17 ; *Mon. Anglic.* iii. 317 *b*.

[7] Eadmer, p. 302. On 14 Kal. Nov., feria v : John of Worcester, p. 17.

[8] Sym. of Durham, ii. 267 ; *Chron. de Mailros, s. a.*

[9] Sym. of Durham, ii. 267.　　　　[10] Orderic, iv. 435.

[11] *Ibid.* pp. 434–6.　　　　[12] *Cal. of Pat. Rolls, 1330–4*, p. 333.

by Archbishop Thurstan, Adelulf prior of St. Oswald's, Earl David, and Nigel de Aubigny ; at York.[1]

479. Writ, addressed to Anschetil (de Bulemer) the sheriff, the reeves and ministers of Driffield, Pocklington, Kilham, Pickering, and Aldborough, directing that Hugh dean (of York) shall have the due tithes of the royal desmesne. It is attested by Walter Espec ; at York.[2]

480. Writ addressed to Ralph de Belfou and Hubert de Montchenesy (' de Monte Canesi ') directing that the monks of Eye shall hold their lands, &c., as beneficially as they held them in the time of Robert Malet. It is attested by William de Hocton ; at York.[3]

481. Confirmation, addressed generally, to the canons of Bridlington of the carucate of land (in Bridlington) which Gertrude, wife of Jordan (Paynel), and Stephen (de Meinill) her son, gave, and Stephen of Albemarle confirmed. It is attested by William de Tancarvill and Walter Espec ; at York.[4]

482. Grant to William son of Ulf (de Grimthorpe) of land in Grimthorpe and other places in Yorkshire. It is attested by Robert de Ferrers, Walter Espec, Roger de Valoignes, and Forne son of Sigulf ; at Nottingham.[5] [1120-9.]

483. Mandate to Robert bishop of Chester and Godfrey the archdeacon (of Derby) to cause the king's church of Darley, co. Derby, to have the tithes which belong to it. It is attested by Roger bishop of Salisbury ; at Nottingham.[6] [1121-6.]

484. Notification to the justices, sheriffs, and foresters of Yorkshire of the grant to the hospital of St. Peter, York, of materials in the royal forest in Yorkshire for building and burning. It is attested by Archbishop Thurstan, Geoffrey Fitz-Pain, and Eustace Fitz-John ; at Nottingham.[7] [1120-33.]

485. Writ, addressed to Archbishop Thurstan, Nigel de Aubigny, and Rainald Bucell, directing that the church of Pickering shall have its parish, as in King Edward's days. It is attested by William de Warenne (*sic*) ; at (East) Bridgeford (' apud Bruggeford ').[8] [1114-16 or 1120-30.]

25 Dec. The king celebrates Christmas at Dunstable, where he is accompanied by Ranulf the chancellor.[9] Here envoys from the count of Anjou find him.[10]

486. Notification to Odard the sheriff and the justices of Northumberland of the grant to the abbot of St. Albans and monks of Tynemouth of warren in their lands in Northumberland. It is attested by William de Pirou and Henry de Pomerey ; at Dunstable.[11]

29 Dec. John bishop of Bath dies on 4 kalends of January.[12]

---

[1] *Cal. of Pat. Rolls, 1461-7*, p. 311.
[2] Reg. Mag. Album, i. 64 ; Farrer, *Early Yorkshire Charters*, no. 429.
[3] *Cal. of Chart. Rolls*, v. 362. [4] Lancaster, *Chartul. of Bridlington*, p. 212.
[5] *Archaeologia*, vi. 49. [6] *Cal. of Chart. Rolls*, iv. 138.
[7] *Cal. of Chart. Rolls*, ii. 438 ; *Early Yorkshire Charters*, no. 167.
[8] Reg. Mag. Album, pt. ii, fo. 11 ; *Early Yorkshire Charters*, no. 399.
[9] Hen. of Huntingdon, p. 244. [10] Chron.
[11] Craster, *Hist. of Northumb.* viii. 55, note 16.
[12] John of Worcester, p. 17. ' The day after the Nativity ' : Sym. of Durham, ii. 268.

1123.

c. 1 Jan. From Dunstable the king rides to Berkhampstead, to be the guest of Ranulf the chancellor at his castle there. On the way, when the royal party are in sight of the castle, Ranulf falls from his horse and is ridden over by a monk, receiving injuries from which he dies in the course of a few days.[1]

10 Jan. From Berkhampstead the king moves to Woodstock. Here, on 4 ides of January, he is riding in the deer-park, between Roger bishop of Salisbury and Robert bishop of Lincoln, towards a remarkable place where he has caused lodges to be constructed for the housing of wild animals and their keepers.[2] Suddenly the bishop of Lincoln sinks down and dies ere he can be removed to his lodgings.[3]

2 Feb. In response to the royal summons the bishops, abbots, and thegns throughout England attend a council at Gloucester on Candlemas Day, at which the king bids them elect an archbishop of Canterbury.[4]

4 Feb. After two days' debate between those who were of the order of monks and those of the clerical orders William of Corbeil, canon of St. Osyth (Chiche), is elected, and to him the king grants the archbishopric.[5]

At this time, if not during the past month, the king appoints Geoffrey Rufus, the chaplain (of the late chancellor ?), to be his chancellor.

487. Writ, addressed to Walter de Gloucester, Warin sheriff of Somerset, and the ministers of Somerset, directing that the monks of Bath shall be free of all pleas, &c., except of murders and highway robberies, ' dum fuerint in manu mea '. It is attested by Nigel de Aubigny ; at Gloucester.[6]

488. Writ, addressed to Walter de Beauchamp and the ministers of Worcestershire, directing that the property of the monks of Gloucester and of their men shall be quit of toll and customs. It is attested by Walter de Gloucester ; at Gloucester.[7] [1121–33.]

25 Mar. On the day of the Annunciation of St. Mary the king is at Woodstock.[8] He gives the bishopric of Bath to Godfrey of Louvain, the queen's chaplain and chancellor.[9] At the same time[10] (' ipso quadragesimali tempore ') the bishopric of Lincoln is given to Alexander archdeacon of Salisbury,[11] nephew of Roger bishop of Salisbury and chief justice of England.[12]

The king has an interview with the primate and Archbishop Thurstan at Woodstock.[13]

The envoys of Fulk, count of Anjou, who was angered because the king retained the dower of his late son's wife,[14] return with hostile intent to their own country.[15]

---

[1] Hen. of Huntingdon, p. 244 ; Rob. of Torigny, p. 105.

[2] William of Malmesbury, *G. R.* ii. 485 ; Hen. of Huntingdon, p. 244.

[3] Chron. ; Roger of Howden, i. 180.

[4] Chron.   [5] Chron. ; Rob. of Torigny, p. 105.

[6] *Two Bath Chartularies*, no. 48.   [7] *Chartul. of St. Peter's, Glouc.*, no. 644.

[8] Hugh the Chantor, p. 200.   [9] Chron.

[10] ' At Easter at Winchester ', in respect of both appointments : Rob. of Torigny, p. 105.   [11] John of Worcester, p. 17 ; Sym. of Durham, ii. 269.

[12] Chron., where the date of appointment is said to be at Easter.

[13] Hugh the Chantor, p. 200.

[14] William of Malmesbury, *Gesta Regum*, ii. 498.   [15] Chron.

The king, having learnt of the giving of a daughter of Fulk of Anjou to his nephew William with a promise that he should be the count's heir in every part of his inheritance, takes counsel with his court at Woodstock and (after Easter) sends his son Robert and Ranulf earl of Chester to Normandy with a numerous company of knights to guard certain places.[1]

489. The king notifies Ralph de Aencurt, William de Luvetot, and the lieges of Nottinghamshire that he wills that the monks of Durham shall hold two carucates of land which they deraigned in his court against Fulk de Luisours, according to the verdict of the county (court). It is attested by Nigel de Aubigny ; at Woodstock.[2] [1120–9.]

15 April. At Easter the king is at Winchester, where he remains during all Easter-tide.[3]

15 April. Hugh de Amiens, prior of St. Pancras, Lewes, is appointed abbot of the new abbey which the king has founded at Reading, on 17 kalends of May.[4]

490. Notification, addressed generally, that the *canonicatus* of St. Mary's, Southwark (' Sudewerca '), shall be established and shall have all its liberties. It is attested by the bishops William of Winchester, William of Exeter, and Bernard of St. David's ; Siefrid abbot of Glastonbury, William earl of Warenne, William de Aubigny, Robert de Ferrers, R(oger) nephew of Hubert, and William de Pont de l'Arche ; at Winchester.[5] [1120–5.]

491. A confirmation is issued in favour of the monastery of St. Peter, Exeter. The signatories are : the king; Queen Adeliza; the archbishops William of Canterbury and Thurstan of York ; the bishops Richard of London, William of Winchester, Roger of Salisbury, Alexander (elect) of Lincoln, Evrard of Norwich, Hervey of Ely, Ralph of Chichester, Ranulf of Durham, Robert of Coventry, Theold of Worcester, Bernard of St. David's, Richard of Hereford, and Godfrey (elect) of Bath ; Geoffrey the chancellor ; the abbots Geoffrey of St. Peter's, Winchester, Osbert of Tavistock, Thurstan of Sherbourne, Vincent of Abingdon, and Siefrid of Glastonbury ;[6] the earls Robert of Gloucester, William (de Warenne) of Surrey, David of Huntingdon, Ranulf of Chester, Roger (de Beaumont) of Warwick, and Robert of Leicester ; the sewers Hugh Bigot and William de Pirou ; William de Aubigny, Nigel de Aubigny, Richard Fitz-Baldwin, Baldwin de Redvers, Johel de Berdestapul, Guy de Toteneis, Robert de Badenton, William Fitz-Odo, Goislin de Pomerey (' de Pomereda '), Rainald de Vautort (' de Valle Torta '), William Fitz-Richard, Herbert de Aunou (' de Alneto '), Humphrey de Bohun, and Walter Fitz-Turstin.[7]

During Lent[8] (or after Easter ?) the two archbishops, William of Canterbury and Thurstan of York, with Bernard bishop of St. David's,

---

[1] Sym. of Durham, ii. 267.

[2] Original in Durham Treasury, 2. 1. Regalium, G. i, n. 7 ; *Journ. of Brit. Arch. Assoc.* xxix. 240 ; *Hist. Dunelm. Script.* p. xxxi.

[3] Chron.

[4] *Flores Histor.* ii. 49 ; *Mon. Anglic.* iv. 30, n.

[5] Add. Ch. 44694 (inspeximus of Henry VI) ; *Cal. of Chart. Rolls,* v. 34.

[6] ' William abbot of Cerne ' added in *Mon. Anglic.* ii. 539 *b*.

[7] *Dep. Keeper's Rep.* xxx, app., p. 207. See Round, *Feudal England,* p. 482.

[8] In Lent : Chron.

Siefrid abbot of Glastonbury, Anselm abbot of St. Edmund's, John archdeacon of Canterbury, and Giffard the king's domestic chaplain, go to Rome; the primate to obtain the pall.[1] The primate returns before 22 July following.

19 May. The city of Lincoln is almost totally destroyed by fire on 14 kalends of June.[2]

492. Writ, addressed to Theowulf bishop of Worcester, Robert bishop of Chester, Earl Roger (de Beaumont), Geoffrey de Clinton, and the barons of Warwickshire, in favour of the church of All Saints, Warwick. It is attested by (Alexander ?) bishop of Lincoln; at Woodstock.[3]

493. Notification to the bishop of Bath, the sheriffs, barons, and lieges of Somerset of the confirmation to the monks of Montacute of the manor of Tintihull, as Ranulf the chancellor gave it, and so that the church of Cluny shall have 100s. yearly for the anniversary of the chancellor. It is attested by Roger bishop of Salisbury, Geoffrey the chancellor, William de Tancarvill, William de Aubigny, and Nigel de Aubigny; at Woodstock.[4] [1123–27.]

494. Notification to the bishop of Lincoln, Earl David, (Robert) earl of Leicester, Ranulf earl of Chester, the lords of whom Geoffrey Ridel held lands, and the sheriffs of counties in whose bailiwicks the said Geoffrey held lands, of the gift of Geoffrey's daughter to Richard Basset to wife with the custody of Geoffrey's land until Robert Ridel can be a knight (subject to other provisions). This is done at the prayer of Ranulf (earl) of Chester, William (de Roumare) his brother, Nigel de Aubigny, and others his kinsmen, Geva his mother, Geoffrey chancellor of Earl Ranulf, Simon dean of Lincoln, William (Meschin) son of Ranulf, Thomas de St. John, Geoffrey de Clinton, Pain Fitz-John, William de Aubigny, William de Bowhun, Robert Musard, Robert Basset, Osmund Basset, Thurstan Basset, William the constable of Ranulf earl of Chester, Ralph Fitz-Norman, and Hugh Maubanck; at Windsor.[5] [1120–3.]

3–10 June. During Whit-week the king is at Portsmouth, waiting for a fair wind.[6]

495. Confirmation by Hugh de Laval to the monastery of St. Mary de La Charité, to the use of the Benedictine monks in the monastery of St. John the Evangelist of the castle of Kirkby (Pontefract), of the gifts made by Robert de Lascy and the grantor, and others. The signatories are: the king, Richard de Brus, the bishops Roger of Salisbury and Robert of Chester, Geoffrey the chancellor, Geoffrey de Clinton, Robert de Oilli, Thomas de St. John, Robert de Sigillo, Hugh Bigot the sewer, Baldwin Fitz-Gilbert, William de Munfichet, Earl David, Ellis abbot of the Mount ('de Monte'), Hugh de Brietel, and Richard bishop of Hereford.[7] [1123–4.]

496. Notification, addressed generally, of the confirmation to the monks of St. John's, Pontefract, of various possessions. It is attested by

---

[1] John of Worcester, p. 17; Hugh the Chantor, pp. 201–6.
[2] Chron.   [3] *Mon. Anglic.* vi. 1327.   [4] *Ibid.* v. 167, no. 5.
[5] Rot. Sloan, xxxi. 4, no. 47.   [6] Chron.
[7] Chartul. of Pontefract at Woolley Hall, fo. 1 *d* (Yorkshire Rec. Soc., vol. xxv, pt. i, p. 21).

[Thurstan] archbishop of York and the bishops Roger of Salisbury, Robert of Chester, and Richard of Hereford ; Richard de Brus, Geoffrey the chancellor, Geoffrey de Clinton, Robert de Oilli, Thomas de St. John, Hugh Bigot, William de Munfichet, Hugh de Bretoil, and Robert de Sigillo.[1] [1123-6.]

497. Notification to T(heoulf) bishop of Worcester, R(obert) earl of Gloucester, the barons and lieges of Gloucestershire, of the confirmation to Walter de Gloucester of the land of Edric son of Chetel. It is attested by Pain Fitz-John, William de Pirou, Hugh Bigot, and Walter de Beauchamp ; at Portsmouth, ' in transfretatione mea '.[2]

498. Notification to William bishop of Exeter, Richard Fitz-Baldwin the sheriff, the reeve, barons, and lieges of Devonshire, and the burgesses and ministers of Exeter, of the confirmation to the canons of the Holy Trinity (Christchurch), London, of £25 yearly by weight of the rents of the late Queen Matilda in Exeter, which she gave to them. It is attested by Geoffrey the chancellor, Nigel de Aubigny, and Geoffrey de Clinton ; at Portsmouth.[3] [1123 or 1127.]

499. Notification to Ralph bishop of Chichester, William Fitz-Auger, and the barons of Sussex of the grant to the monks of Battle of the manor of Appledram, in exchange for their possessions in Reading, with 40s. of yearly rent in Appledram which the king had previously retained. It is attested by Roger bishop of Salisbury and Adam de Port ; at Portsmouth.[4]

500. Notification to the bishop of Norwich, and generally, of the confirmation to the monastery of Binham of two carucates of land in Walsingham and a mediety of the church there, given by Roger de Valoignes. It is attested by Nigel de Aubigny ; at Portsmouth.[5] [1120-9.]

501. Mandate to W(illiam) archbishop of Canterbury to preserve the lands and men of the abbess of Malling from injury. It is attested by Earl David ; at Portsmouth.[6]

11 June. On Monday in the week next after Whit-week the king sails from Portsmouth.[7]

The king causes the keep of the castle of Caen to be strengthened.[8]

Aug.-Sept. Amaury de Montfort count of Evreux, William de Roumare, Waleran count of Meulan, Hugh de Montfort (sic), Hugh de Châteauneuf, and William Louvel of Ivry rebel against Henry.[9]

Beginning Oct. The king is at Rouen, where he causes the keep to be strengthened and surrounded by a curtain wall.[10] He takes steps to suppress the rising of Amaury count of Evreux and his colleagues.[11]

20 Oct. Theowulf bishop of Worcester dies on 13 kalends of November.[12]

27 Oct. Serlo bishop of Sées dies on Friday, 6 kalends of November.[13]

[1] Chartul. of Pontefract, fo. 21 *d* (Yorkshire Rec. Soc. xxv, no. 72).

[2] Duchy of Lanc., Royal Charters, no. 5 ; *Ancient Charters* (Pipe Roll Soc.), no. 10.

[3] Cott. Ch. vii, no. 2 ; *Brit. Mus. Facsimiles of Charters*, no. 7.

[4] Campbell Ch. xvi. 13 ; *Mon. Anglic.* iii. 247.

[5] Chartul. of Binham, Claud. D. xiii, fo. 40 *d*.

[6] *Cal. of Chart. Rolls*, v. 56.   [7] Sym. of Durham, ii. 273.

[8] *Flores Histor.* ii. 50.

[9] Orderic, iv. 441.   [10] *Flores Histor.* ii. 50.

[11] Orderic, iv. 448.   [12] John of Worcester, p. 18.

[13] Orderic, iv. 444-7.

On the following day the king sends John bishop of Lisieux from the siege of Pont-Audemer to the bishop's funeral.[1]

Oct.–Nov. The king proceeds to Waleran count of Meulan's castle of Pont-Audemer, which he takes after a siege which has lasted six weeks.[2] With the assistance of troops collected from Coutances and other districts by Robert earl of Gloucester and Nigel de Aubigny, the king takes the castle of Montfort.[3]

Possibly the king moves to Gisors. Theobald Pain de Gisors is deprived of his patrimony and Henry gives it to Hugh, second son of Theobald Pain.[4] Possibly at this time Henry grants Burton Latimer, co. Northampton, to Alan de Dinan, 'who fought against the champion (*pugilis*) of the king of France between Gysorz and Trie '.[5]

502. Grant, addressed generally for England, to the monastery of Mont St. Michel of land in Devonshire, in exchange for the monastery's churches of Wargrave and Cholsey, which the king has given to the abbey of Reading in alms. It is attested by John bishop of Lisieux, Geoffrey the chancellor, William earl of Warenne, William de Tancarvill, Geoffrey de Clinton, William de Pont de l'Arche, and Thomas de St. John ; at Perriers-sur-Andelle (' apud Pirarios super Andelam ').[6] [1123–9.]

503. Notification to the bishop of Norwich (' Tetford '), the barons, sheriff, ministers, and lieges of Suffolk and Norfolk of the confirmation to the nuns of Redlingfield of the endowments which have been given by Emma countess of Guisnes (' Gennes '), with the consent of Stephen count of Mortain. It is attested by William earl of Warenne and William de Tanei ; at Aumâle (' apud Albam Marlam ').[7] [1123–35.]

8 Dec. Robert abbot of Tewkesbury dies on 6 ides of December.[8]

14 Dec. ? Ralph bishop of Chichester dies.[9]

1124.

504. A release of certain land by Thomas de St. John to the monks of Mont St. Michel in the time of Abbot Richard, and after the grantor's return from captivity at Gorron in Mayenne, is made before King Henry at Argentan. It is attested by Geoffrey archbishop of Rouen, the bishops John of Lisieux and Richard of Bayeux, Robert de la Hai the sewer, William de Tancarvill, William de Aubigny the butler, and William (de Aubigny) the Breton.[10] [1123–8.]

505. Writ to the justices, &c., of Norfolk and Suffolk directing that St. Edmund's and Abbot Anselm shall have the market with the toll in the town of (Bury) St. Edmund's, as Abbot Baldwin or any of his predecessors held them. It is attested by Aubrey de Ver ; at Falaise.[11] [1123–9.]

15 Mar. Ernulf bishop of Rochester dies on the ides of March.[12]

[1] Orderic, iv. 447.   [2] *Ibid.* pp. 448–52 ; Chron. ; *Flores Histor.* ii. 50.
[3] Orderic, iv. 443.   [4] *Ibid.* p. 453.
[5] *Testa de Nevill* (Rec. Comm.), p. 25 b.   [6] Round, *Calendar*, no. 723.
[7] *Cal. of Chart. Rolls*, ii. 308.   [8] John of Worcester, p. 18.
[9] Le Neve, *Fasti*.
[10] Round, *Cal. of Docs., France*, p. 262. The document contains a confusion of dates: The year 1121, indiction 2 (i.e. 1124), concurrent 6 (1122).
[11] Chartul. of St. Edmund's, Harl. MS. 743, fo. 60 *d* ; Cart. Antiq. roll P., no. 15 (9).
[12] Chron.

25 Mar. In an engagement near La Bourg-téroude, between Belmont and Wattevill, Ranulf earl of Chester and William the chamberlain of Tancarvill take prisoners Waleran count of Meulan, Hugh Fitz-Gervase, and Hugh de Montfort.[1] The king was then at Caen.[2]

After Easter Henry puts the captured rebels on trial at Rouen.[3] Some of them are sent to England, where Fitz-Gervase and Montfort lay in prison for several years.[4]

15–16 April. After Low Sunday Henry comes to Bec. Learning that Abbot William, whom he greatly loved, lies dying, he goes to see him. The abbot dies during the night (16 kal. May), and John bishop of Lisieux performs the funeral rites.[5]

25 April. Alexander king of Scots dies on 9 kalends of May.[6] David earl of Huntingdon, his brother, succeeds.

506. A charter of confirmation is issued in favour of the abbey of St. Pierre-sur-Dive. The signatories are : the king and queen, Geoffrey archbishop of Rouen, the bishops John of Lisieux and Bernard of St. David's, Humphrey de Bohon, Robert earl of Leicester, Nigel de (Aubigny), Juhel de Mayenne, Robert de la Hay, Roger the sheriff, Geoffrey Fitz-Pain.[7] [1123–6, 1127–8.]

507. A charter of confirmation is issued in favour of Abbot Warin and the monks of St. Evroul. It is attested by Geoffrey archbishop of Rouen, William count of Penthieu, Nigel de Aubigny, Robert de Grentemesnil, Robert Giroie, Patric de Chaources, Goel de Ivri, and William de Saci ; at Rouen.[8] [1123–8.]

508. Notification to T(hurstan) archbishop of York, the bishop of Durham, the barons and lieges of Northumberland, Yorkshire, and Haliwerfolk of the confirmation of the gift by Nigel de Aubigny to the church of Durham of (the vill of) Barmton. It is attested by Geoffrey de Clinton ; at Rouen.[9] [1123–32.]

509. Mandate to Richard de Angerville and W(illiam) de Saint-Germain, ordering that the abbot of Montebourg shall have the eighth part of the church just as he has the eighth part of the land of Helleville (Manche). The monks of Héauville 'had failed to appear in the plea concerning it. It is attested by Robert de Hai, through Thomas de Pont-l'Évêque ; at Rouen.[10] [1114–35.]

510. Mandate to Richard bishop of Coutances and William de Albini, ordering that Humphrey de Albini shall hold his land in peace together

---

[1] *Ibid.* ; Orderic, iv. 455–8.

[2] Rob. of Torigny, *s. a.*   [3] Orderic, iv. 459.

[4] *Ibid.* p. 463. Waleran and Fitz-Gervase were with Henry when he returned to England in September 1126.

[5] Life of Abbot William, in Migne, *P. L.* cl, col. 722.

[6] 23 April: Chron. ' On 6 Kalends of May ' (26 April) : Sym. of Durham, ii. 275. ' On 7 Kalends of May ' (25 April) : *Chron. de Mailros*, 67. His anniversary was kept on 7 kalends of May : *Durham Lib. Vitae*, p. 150.

[7] *Gallia Christ.* xi. instr., col. 157.

[8] Orderic, v. 202 ; Round, *Cal. of Documents, France,* no. 623.

[9] Original in the Treasury, Durham, 2. 1. Regalium, n. 9 ; *Feod. Priorat. Dunelm.* (Surtees Soc.), p. 152 *b.*

[10] MS. Lat. 10087, no. 14 ; Haskins, *Norman Institutions,* p. 102.

with the tithe and mill of Morsalines (Manche), with reversion to the church of Montebourg after his death. It is attested by Robert de Hai ; at Rouen.[1] [1124–31.]

In April Henry besieges and takes Brionne.[2]

18 May. Henry, at Rouen, on the Sunday after the Rogations, approves the election of Boso the prior as abbot of Bec, though he had previously rejected him.[3]

4 July. Stephen count of Mortain founds a monastery of Cistercian monks at Tulketh, in Amounderness, co. Lanc.[4]

21 or 29 Aug. Ralph abbot of Battle dies on 4 (or 12) kalends of September.[5]

After 30 Nov. After St. Andrew's mass Ralph Basset and the king's thegns (i.e. barons) hold a court at Huncot, co. Leicester, and hang many thieves.[6]

25 Dec. Roger bishop of Salisbury causes all false moneyers to be brought to Winchester, and, during the twelve days of the feast of the Nativity, he causes each to be deprived of his right hand and to be emasculated.[7]

1125.

Jan. 19. Richer abbot of St. Bennet's, Holme, dies on 14 kalends of February.[8]

c. Mar. Henry nominates Siegfrid, abbot of Glastonbury, to the see of Chichester.[9]

During Lent John of Crema, the newly-appointed legate, comes to England[10] accompanied by the primate, Archbishop Thurstan, and the two bishops elect, Simon and Siegfrid.[11]

Mar. 21. Hugh archdeacon of Worcester dies on 12 kalends of April.[12]

April 13. Honorius, by letter dated at the Lateran on the ides of April, summons the archbishops William and Thurstan to be in Rome on the feast of the Purification next to come.[13]

May 7. Henry nominates Simon, the queen's chancellor, to the see of Worcester.[14]

John archdeacon of Canterbury is preferred by the primate to the see of Rochester.[15]

Eustace count of Boulogne bestows his inheritance in marriage with Matilda his daughter on Stephen of Blois, count of Mortain, and takes the habit at Cluny.[16]

July 26. Gilbert the Norman, sheriff of the counties of Surrey, Cambridge, and Huntingdon, and founder of Merton priory, dies on 7 kalends of August.[17]

---

[1] MS. Lat. 10087, no. 12 ; Haskins, *Norman Institutions*, p. 102.

[2] Orderic, iv. 462.   [3] Life of Abbot William, in Migne, *P. L.* cl, col. 723.

[4] *Mon. Anglic.* v. 246.   [5] *Ibid.* iii. 234 *b.*   [6] Chron.

[7] *Ibid.*   [8] *Mon. Anglic.* iii. 63.

[9] John of Worcester, p. 18.   [10] Hugh the Chantor.

[11] ' After Easter ' : John of Worcester, pp. 18–19.   [12] *Ibid.* p. 18.

[13] Hugh the Chantor, pp. 209–10.

[14] Ralph de Diceto ; John of Worcester, p. 18 ; Rob. of Torigny, p. 110.

[15] Consecrated on 24 May.   [16] Round, *Cal. of Documents, France*, no. 1385.

[17] Arundel MS., Coll. of Arms, 28, fo. 11 *d.*

Sept. 8. During the summer the newly-appointed legate travels through England and into Scotland. On the Nativity of St. Mary he holds a council in London, and afterwards crosses to Normandy.[1]

Oct. The archbishops cross to Normandy on their journey to Rome. They are accompanied by the bishops Alexander of Lincoln and John of Glasgow, and the abbots Geoffrey of St. Albans and Thurstan of Sherburne.[2] They have speech with Henry. The primate, departing first, arrives in Rome three weeks sooner than Thurstan, who is accompanied by his brother, Audin bishop of Evreux, and John of Crema, the legate.[3]

511. Grant, addressed generally, to Ralph Mauduit (abbot of Athelney) of the abbey of Athelney. It is attested by John of Crema, cardinal and legate in England, William archbishop of Canterbury, the bishops Alexander of Lincoln and Siefrid of Chichester, the abbots Anselm of St. Edmund's and William (*sic*, for Geoffrey) of St. Albans, Robert earl of Gloucester, William earl of Warenne, William de Tancarvill the chamberlain, Gilbert (*sic*, for Geoffrey) de Clinton, and Hugh de Gornay ; at Rouen.[4]

512. Notification, addressed generally, of the foundation of, and gifts to, the monastery of Reading. The signatories are : the king and Queen Adelaide ; John (of Crema) cardinal and legate ; the archbishops William of Canterbury, Thurstan of York, and Geoffrey of Rouen ; the bishops William of Winchester, William of Exeter, Bernard of St. David's, Siegfrid of Chichester, Simon of Worcester, John of Lisieux, Ouin (or Audin) of Evreux, and Turgis of Avranches ; the abbots Anselm of St. Edmund's, Warner of St. Martin's, Battle, Boson of Bec, Gilbert of Sées, and Richard of Mont St. Michel ; Robert earl of Gloucester, William earl of Surrey, Roger earl of Warwick, Stephen count of Aumâle, William the chamberlain of Tancarvill, Brien Fitz-Count of Wallingford, Humphrey de Buhun, Robert de la Hai, William Fitz-Odo, and Hugh Bigot. ' Actum anno verbi incarnati M.C.XXV, papa Ro(mano) Henrico (*sic*, for Honorio) II°, Romanorum imperatore augusto Henrico [x]IIII^to.' [5]

513. Notification, addressed generally, of the grant to Geoffrey de Clinton, the king's treasurer and chamberlain, that he may found the church of St. Mary in the land of Kenilworth, which the king gave him for his demesne. The signatories are : the king and Queen Adelaide ; the archbishops William of Canterbury, Thurstan of York, and Geoffrey of Rouen ; the bishops William of Winchester, Roger of Salisbury, Robert of Chester, Richard of Hereford, Henry of Ely, Audin of Evreux, John of Lisieux, John of Sées, and Bernard of St. David's ; Robert earl of Gloucester, Roger earl of Warwick, Ranulf earl of Chester, William earl of Warenne, Robert earl of Leicester, William de Tancarvill the chamberlain, Geoffrey de Clinton, Robert de Warwyc, Nicholas de Stafort, and Hugh Fitz-Richard.[6]

514. Notification to Robert bishop of Chester, the earl of Warwick,

---

[1] Chron. ; Hugh the Chantor, p. 210.

[2] *Ibid.* ; Chron.   [3] Hugh the Chantor, pp. 212-13.

[4] *Chartul. of Athelney* (Somerset Rec. Soc.), p. 133.

[5] *Mon. Anglic.* iv. 40.

[6] *Cal. of Chart. Rolls*, iii. 275 ; *Mon. Anglic.* vi. 223. The charter is of doubtful authenticity. The three last names may have been added later.

the barons and lieges of Warwickshire, of the grant to the canons of Kenilworth of the church of Stoneleigh, made at the prayer of Thurstan archbishop of York, who held the church of the king. It is attested by Geoffrey
the chancellor, Robert de la Hai, and Geoffrey de Clinton ; at Rouen.[1]
[1123–6.]

515. Notification to Robert bishop of Chester, Roger earl of Warwick,
Geoffrey de Glinton, and the barons, &c., of Warwickshire, of the release
to Miles and the other sons of William de Oxineford of the rent of 30*s.*
which William the sheriff held of the king in Chinton. It is attested by
William de Tancarvill, William Peverel of Dover, Geoffrey Fitz-Pain,
Edward of Saresberi, and William Maltravers ; at Rouen.[2]

516. Confirmation to the church of St. Gervase and St. Protase of
Vire of the possessions in Normandy and England which were given by
Ranulf de Vire and his brothers and kinsfolk ; and of the gift of the church
with its endowments to Holy Trinity of Savigny. The signatories are
the king and queen ; the bishops John of Lisieux, Richard of Bayeux,
and John of Sées ; William de Aubigny, Henry de Fougères, John of
Bayeux, Ranulf de Vire, Geoffrey the chancellor, Stephen count of Mortain, Richard Fitz-Gilbert, Robert earl of Gloucester, Geoffrey de Clinton,
Turgis bishop (of Avranches), Fulcher the archdeacon, and Henry the
treasurer.[3] [1124–31.]

14 Oct. John de Sais, abbot of Peterborough, dies on 2 ides of
October.[4]

517. Confirmation, addressed generally for Yorkshire, in favour of
St. Peter's hospital, York. It is attested by Archbishop Thurstan, Alexander bishop of Lincoln, and Robert de Oilli ; at Evreux.[5] [1123–35.]

518. Notification to Richard bishop of Bayeux and the barons and
men of the Bessin of the confirmation to Savigny of land in Escures
which Robert de Tôtes had given in alms. It is attested by Thurstan
archbishop of York, Audin his brother, bishop of Evreux, and John of
Bayeux ; at Evreux.[6]

1126.

519. During this year an agreement is made in a plea which is heard
before the king at St. Vaubourg, near Rouen, between the monks of
Marmoutier and John bishop of Sées, in the presence of Geoffrey archbishop of Rouen, Ouin bishop of Evreux, Bernard bishop of St. David's,
Geoffrey the king's chancellor, Waleran the archdeacon, Robert de Sigillo ;
and the following laymen : Robert de la Hai, Grimbald the physician,
Robert de Dangu, Robert de Chandos, Roger his brother, Hugh de Braitell ;
and of Marmoutier : Abbot Odo, Prior Geoffrey, William prior of Belesme,
William prior of Perrières, and seventeen others (named).[7]

520. 28 Feb.–6 Mar. Notification to the archbishops, &c., and sheriffs

[1] Chartul. of Kenilworth, Harl. MS. 3650, fo. 72 *d.*
[2] *Ibid.* fo. 73.
[3] Round, *Cal. of Documents, France,* no. 795.   [4] Chron.
[5] *Mon. Anglic.* vi. 612 ; Charter Roll, 22 Edw. I, m. 9.
[6] Original charter in the Archives of the Manche ; Haskins, *Norman Institutions,*
p. 296.
[7] Round, *Cal. of Documents, France,* no. 1191.

in whose counties Robert Fitz-Richard has lands, and to all ministers, of the grant to the same Robert of free customs through his lands with sac and soc, &c., as any of his brothers or others of the king's barons have. It is attested by Richard the chaplain, Evrard de Calne, Robert de Limesi, Robert de Crievecwer, William de Clinton, William de Pirou the sewer, Robert de Candos, Robert de Oilli, Edward of Salisbury, Oine sheriff of Rouen, William de Thurbertevill, and Baldwin son of Gilbert Fitz-Richard ; at St. Vaubourg, in the first week of Lent.[1]

23 Mar. Henry with all his nobles is present at the dedication of Sées by the archbishop of Rouen, and gives £15 a year of the money of Rouen to the church.[2]

28 Mar. Hugh abbot of St. Augustine's, Canterbury, dies on Passion Sunday.[3]

Honorius appoints Lent in the ensuing year for the hearing of the dispute between Archbishop Thurstan and John bishop of Glasgow. The primate, having received the legation, prepares to return home.[4] Thurstan follows shortly after, and they break their journey at Rouen, where Henry and his court are established.[5]

521. Notification, addressed generally, of the grant to Abbot Osbern of the abbey of St. Peter's, Winchester (Hyde). It is attested by the archbishops William of Canterbury and Thurstan of York ; the bishops William of Winchester, William of Exeter, Bernard of St. David's, and Siefrid of Chichester ; Warner abbot of Battle, William earl of Warenne, Brien Fitz-Count, and William Fitz-Odo ; at Rouen.[6] [1125 or 1126.]

29 June. Archbishop Thurstan reaches York on the feast of the Apostles (Peter and Paul ?).[7]

Henry sends to the abbey of Reading the hand of St. James the Apostle, which his daughter, Matilda the empress, in returning to him from Germany, has brought with her.[8]

522. Notification, addressed generally, of the confirmation to the abbey of the Holy Trinity, L'Essay, of the gifts made by Robert de la Hai and Muriel his wife [9] of lands and churches in Lincolnshire, which he had received with his said wife, and by Roger de Aubigny and Amicia his wife ; made with the consent of their sons, William and Nigel. The signatories are : the king ; Robert earl of Gloucester ; the bishops (John of Lisieux), John of Sées, and Audin of Evreux ; (William earl of Warenne, Robert de la Hai), Jordan de Sai, (William Truseb[ut]), Hamon de Falaise, Hugh de Aurea Valle, and William Fitz-Odo. 'Anno ab incarnatione Domini M.C.XXVI peracta feliciter.' [10]

---

[1] Cart. Antiq. roll F, no. 6 (4).

[2] Orderic, iv. 471 ; Haskins, *Norman Institutions*, p. 301.

[3] John of Worcester, p. 23.

[4] Hugh the Chantor, pp. 215, 217.   [5] *Ibid.* p. 216.

[6] *Mon. Anglic.* ii. 445, no. 13.

[7] ' In Natali Apostolorum ' (*sic*) : Hugh the Chantor, p. 217.

[8] *Mon. Anglic.* iv. 41, no. 3 ; Roger of Howden, i. 181.

[9] Mr. Round has suggested that Muriel was sister and heir of Picot son of Colsuein. This is confirmed by Richard de la Hai (son of Robert) describing himself as nephew of Picot : Transcript of Spalding Chartul. (Cole), Add. MS. 5844, fo. 450.

[10] Round, *Cal. of Documents, France*, nos. 923 and 924.

22 Aug. Robert Peche, bishop of Chester, dies on 11 kalends of September.[1]

523. Writ addressed to the archbishop of Canterbury, the bishop of Norwich, the barons of Norfolk and Suffolk, the justices and sheriffs, directing that Abbot Anselm and the monks of St. Edmund's shall have the church of Beccles freely. It is attested by A(ubrey) de Ver; at Dieppe.[2]

11 Sept. Henry, accompanied by his daughter, the Empress Matilda, whose husband Henry, emperor of the Romans, died at Utrecht on 23 May, 1125, returns to England on 3 ides of September.[3] Waleran count of Meulan and Hugh Fitz-Gervase cross to England as prisoners at the same time.[4]

After Michaelmas David, king of Scots, comes on a visit to Henry's court. 'He abode all that year in this land.'[5]

524. Notification, addressed generally, of the confirmation to the monks of St. Mary's, Malvern, of their possessions. It is attested by the bishops Richard of Hereford, Bernard of St. David's, and Simon of Worcester; William the chamberlain of Tancarvill, Brien Fitz-Count, William de Aubigny the butler, Miles of Gloucester, Adam de Port, Pain Fitz-John, Geoffrey Fitz-Pain, Roger de Candos, and Walter de Beauchamp; at Hereford.[6] [1126-7.]

525. Notification to the archbishop of York, the barons, ministers, and lieges of Cumberland and Westmorland, of the gift to the canons of St. Mary's, Carlisle, of the churches and land late of Walter the priest. It is attested by Nigel de Aubigny, Walter Espec, and Pain Fitz-John; at Worcester.[7] [1126-9.]

526. Notification, addressed generally for England, Yorkshire, and Northumberland, of the confirmation to the monastery of Austin canons lately founded at Kirkham, co. York, by Walter Espec, of their possessions. It is attested by Archbishop Thurstan, the bishops Roger of Salisbury and Alexander of Lincoln, Geoffrey the chancellor, (Adelwold) prior of St. Oswald's, (Nostell), Robert de Sigillo, Nigel nephew of the bishop of Salisbury, Robert earl of Gloucester, William de Tancarvill, Brien Fitz-Count, Eustace Fitz-John, Alan de Percy, Anschetill de Bulemer, and John de St. John; at Rockingham.[8] [1126-9.]

527. Writ addressed to Adelica, the wife of Roger Bigot, directing her to cause the monks of Belvoir to have their lands, tithes, and property as given by her father, Robert de Todenei, especially at Bradley, (co. Suffolk); otherwise Robert Fitz-Walter shall cause this to be done. It is attested by Richard Basset; at Rocking(ham).[9] [1126-9.]

528. Notification, addressed generally, of the grant to the monks of Tewkesbury of acquittance of toll. It is attested by Geoffrey the chan-

---

[1] *Annals of Waverley*; John of Worcester.

[2] Chartul. of St. Edmund's, Camb. Univ. Libr., Ff. ii. 33, fo. 24 *d*, no. 35. Another writ in favour of the abbot, touching his customs at Thetford, was also attested by A. de Ver at Dieppe: *ibid.* fo. 29, n. 108.

[3] Sym. of Durham, ii. 281. 'Between the Nativity of St. Mary (8 September) and Michaelmas': Chron.; 'circa festum S. Michaelis': Rob. of Torigny, p. 111.

[4] Chron.   [5] Chron.   [6] *Mon. Anglic.* iii. 447 *b*.

[7] *Cal. of Chart. Rolls*, iii. 81.   [8] *Ibid.* iv. 360.

[9] *Belvoir MSS.* (Hist MSS. Comm.), iv. 158.

cellor, Roger bishop of Salisbury, and Robert de Sigillo ; 'apud Wolest' [-onam ?] (Wollaston, co. Northampton ?).[1]

529. Mandate to Evrard bishop of Norwich that Roger de Valoignes and the monks of Binham shall hold their part of the church of Walsingham, which Wakin (?) the priest withholds, as Robert his ancestor held it, and as the said Roger has deraigned it against G(eoffrey) de Favarch. It is attested by the chancellor ; at Silverstone ('apud Silvestr.').[2] [1121–30.]

530. Notification to Richard bishop of London, the sheriff, reeve, and barons of London and Middlesex, of the confirmation to the canons of the Holy Trinity (Christchurch), London, of the soc of the English Cnihtengild and the church of St. Botulph. It is attested by Queen Adelaide, Geoffrey the chancellor, Geoffrey de Clinton, and William de Clinton ; at Woodstock.[3]

531. Writ addressed to the bishop of Lincoln, Earl Ranulf of Chester, the justices, barons, and lieges of Lincolnshire in favour of Hugh Fitz-Pinchon. It is attested by Henry de Pomerey ; at Woodstock.[4] [1121–33.]

532. Confirmation, addressed to Richard Fitz-Baldwin and the barons of Devonshire, in favour of St. Nicholas's priory, Exeter. It is attested by William Fitz-Odo ; at Woodstock.[5] [Before Aug. 1127.]

25 Dec. Henry holds his court at Christmas at Windsor. It is attended by David king of Scots and the chief ecclesiastics and barons of the realm,[6] including Conan (*sic*, for Stephen) count of Brittany, and Archbishop Thurstan, who is on his way to Rome to hear the pope's decision in the dispute with John bishop of Glasgow.[7]

30 Dec. Henry comes to London, accompanied by David of Scotland, to discuss with Thurstan the question of the Scottish bishops.[8]

1127.

The court having moved to London, at Henry's command the two archbishops, the English bishops and abbots, David king of Scots, Stephen of Blois, now count of Boulogne and Mortain, Robert earl of Gloucester, and the other earls and the barons of the realm swear fealty to the king's daughter, Matilda the empress, as the king's successor in England and Normandy.[9]

533. Notification to the bishop of Salisbury and all of Berkshire of the confirmation to St. Mary's, Abingdon, and Abbot Vincent of the hundred of Hormer. It is attested by the bishops Roger of Salisbury and Alexander of Lincoln, Geoffrey the chancellor, Robert de Sigillo, Nigel nephew of the bishop (of Salisbury), William de Aubigny, Robert de Oilli, Ralph Basset, Geoffrey de Clinton, William de Pont (de l'Arche), Miles of Gloucester, Aubrey de Ver, William de Aubigny the Breton, and Richard Basset ; at London.[10] [1126–8.]

[1] *Cal. of Pat. Rolls, 1494–1509*, p. 102.
[2] Chartul. of Binham, Claud. D. xiii, fo. 41.
[3] Cott. MS. xiii. 18, n. 27 ; *Mon. Anglic.* vi. 153.
[4] *Cal. of Pat. Rolls, 1409–13*, p. 300.
[5] *Collect. Topog. et Geneal.* i. 250.   [6] Chron. ; Chron. Petroburg. 1.
[7] Hugh the Chantor, p. 217.   [8] *Ibid.*
[9] Chron. ; John of Worcester, p. 22 ; Sym. of Durham, ii. 281.
[10] *Chron. of Abingdon*, ii. 164–5.

533A. Notification, addressed generally, of the confirmation to the monks of St. Walery of their possessions in England. It is attested by Alexander bishop of Lincoln, Geoffrey the chancellor, and Miles of Gloucester ; at London.[1] [1123–31.]

Jan. Between Christmas and Candlemas [2] Henry gives the abbey of Peterborough to his kinsman, Henry of Poitou, abbot of St. Jean d'Angely. Later the abbot accompanies Henry to Winchester.[3]

534. Notification to the men of Kent that the king has committed the castle of Rochester to Archbishop William and his successors, to be constables thereof; at Winchester.[4]

Richard de Belmeis, bishop of London, dies during the spring and prior to the holding of the council at Westminster.[5]

17 Feb. Conrad abbot of St. Bennet's, Holme, dies on 13 kalends of March.[6]

535. Notification, addressed generally, that the king has built a new abbey at Reading. It is attested by the archbishops William of Canterbury, Thurstan of York, and Geoffrey of Rouen ; the bishops William of Winchester and Siefrid of Chichester ; Robert earl of Gloucester and William earl of Surrey ; at Winchester.[7] [1126–7.]

16 Feb.–9 April. During Lent and at Easter Henry is at Woodstock, where messengers bring news of the assassination of Charles of Flanders (on the kalends of March), and of the bestowal by Louis of the comté on his nephew, William of Normandy.[8]

536. Mandate to the abbot of Peterborough to permit (Rainald) abbot of Ramsey to take stone for the use of his buildings and to have his customs, as Abbot Aldwin his predecessor had ; in default Hugh de Leicester shall cause this to be done. It is attested by Ralph Basset ; at Woodstock.[9] [1120–9.]

537. Writ to Ranulf earl (of Chester) notifying him of the grant to Robert de Glanvill (*rectius* Grainvill) of the land of Asgherbi, which the earl has deraigned against Walter de Gant and given to the said Robert in alms. It is attested by Geoffrey the chancellor, Nigel nephew of the bishop (of Salisbury), and William de Tancarvill ; at Woodstock (' Odestoca ').[10] [1126–9.]

538. Charter, addressed generally, in favour of the Cluniac monks of Thetford. It is attested by the bishops Roger of Salisbury and Siefrid of Chichester, Aubrey de Ver, Ralph Basset, and Pain Fitz-John, ' per precatum abbatis Cluniacensis ' ; at Reading.[11] [1126–9.]

9–11 May. The king holds a council in London at Rogationtide.[12]

---

[1] Original charter at New College, Oxford ; kindly supplied by the Rev. H. E. Salter.

[2] But ' on 10 kalends of May, 1128 ' : Soc. of Antiq., London, MS. 60, fo. 67.

[3] Chron. Shortly afterwards the abbot resigns : *ibid.*

[4] John of Worcester, p. 23 ; also under date ' 3 kalends of May ' (29 April) : Stowe MS. 927, fo. 3 ; Add. MS. 6037.   [5] John of Worcester, p. 23.

[6] *Mon. Anglic.* iii. 63.   [7] Add. Ch. 19571.

[8] Hen. of Huntingdon, p. 247 ; Rob. of Torigny, p. 112.

[9] *Chartul. of Ramsey,* ii. 102.

[10] Vesp. E. xvi, fo. 11, no. 39. Roger FitzGerald had given Asgarby for a prebend for Robert de Grainvill, one of the canons of Lincoln : *ibid.* fo. 10 *d*, nos. 38, 53.

[11] *Cal. of Chart. Rolls,* iii. 376.   [12] Hen. of Huntingdon, p. 247.

13–16 May. The primate holds a council at Westminster at which the king is present and the bishops of Winchester, Salisbury, Exeter, Ely, Lincoln, Norwich, Chichester, Hereford, Bath, Rochester, St. David's, Llandaff, and Bangor. As yet no appointments have been made to the vacant sees of London and Chester.[1] Thurstan excuses himself from attendance ; Ranulf of Durham has been taken ill on the way ; Simon of Worcester is on a visit to relatives beyond seas.[2]

539. Notification to Siefrid bishop of Chichester, Anselm de Rouen, the sheriff, barons, and lieges of Sussex, of the grant to the abbot and monks of Battle of 40s. of yearly rent which the king has retained in the manor of Appledram with the farm of Bosham, for part of the exchange for their land of Carmarthen, which he has given to Bishop Bernard and the church of St. David. It is attested by William archbishop of Canterbury, Roger bishop of Salisbury, Geoffrey the chancellor, Robert de Ver, and William de Pont de l'Arche ; at Westminster.[3] [1126–33.]

540. Writ addressed to the bishop of Norwich, the justice, sheriff, and barons of Suffolk and Norfolk, in favour of the nuns of Redlingfield. It is attested by G(eoffrey) de Cancellis, Robert de Sigillo, Hugh Bigod, Humphrey de Boun, Robert de Curcy, Robert de Ver, Aubrey de Ver, and R(alph) Basset ; at Westminster.[4] [1123–7.]

541. Notification to Alexander bishop of Lincoln, the sheriff, barons, and ministers of Buckinghamshire, of the grant to St. Mary's, Kenilworth, of the land of Hughenden (' Hichedena '), which Geoffrey de St. Roeri held of the king, the said Geoffrey conceding it ; for which gift Geoffrey de Clinton, the founder, to whom the king had previously given that land in fee, gave the king 60 ounces of gold and 40 marks of silver. It is attested by Geoffrey the chancellor, Ralph Basset,[5] and Pain Fitz-John ; at Westminster.[6] [1123–7.]

541 A. Writ to Osbert de Abetot and the foresters of Fetcham directing that Walter de Beauchamp shall have the foxes in the forest of Fetcham (co. Worcester). It is attested by Robert de Essex ; at Woodstock.[7] [1114–33.]

22 May. At Whitsuntide Henry is at Winchester.[8] Soon afterwards he sends his daughter Matilda in charge of her brother, Robert earl of Gloucester, and Brien son of Count Alan Fergant, to Rouen to be betrothed to Geoffrey Martel, son of Fulk count of Anjou.[9]

542. General notification that the monks of Gloucester and Gilbert de Miners came before the king in his court touching the plea of the manor of Coln (' Culna '), which Gilbert claims, and Adam de Port and William Fitz-Odo have testified before the king that they were present at the place where Roger de Gloecestra had given that manor in alms to the church of

---

[1] John of Worcester, p. 23.　　　　　　　　　　　　　　　　[2] *Ibid.*

[3] *Ancient Charters* (Pipe Roll Soc.), no. 15.

[4] *Cal. of Chart. Rolls*, ii. 309.

[5] Ralph Basset does not attest official documents issued in England after the king's passage to Normandy in 1127. He died at Northampton during the period 1127–9, whilst Vincent was abbot of Abingdon : *Chron. of Abingdon*, ii. 170.

[6] Chartul. of Kenilworth, Harl. MS. 3650, fo. 75.

[7] Add. MS. 28024, fo. 127 d.　　　　　　　[8] Hen. of Huntingdon, p. 247.

[9] Chron. See Le Prevost's note in Orderic, iv. 498.

St. Peter, where also the king at the request of the same Roger confirmed the gift to the monks, and whereof the same Gilbert has renounced judgement. Witnesses: William archbishop of Canterbury; the bishops Roger of Salisbury, William of Winchester, Bernard of St. David's, William of Exeter, and Urban of Glamorgan; Geoffrey the chancellor, Robert de Sigillo, Miles de Gloecestra, Henry de Port, Walter de Amfrevill, William de Folia, and Roger and William sons of Adam de Port; at Winchester, A.D. 1127.[1]

543. Confirmation charter to the church of Malvern. The signatories are: the king and queen, Roger bishop of Salisbury, Bernard bishop of St. David's, Geoffrey the chancellor, William de Tancarvill, Pain Fitz-John, and Miles of Gloucester; at Winchester, A.D. 1127, indiction 5.[2]

12 June. Hugh, of the diocese of Rochester, is instituted abbot of St. Augustine's, Canterbury.[3]

544. Writ addressed to the barons and vavasours who owe ward at Rockingham castle, commanding them to reside in the said castle at the summons of Michael de Hamsslape, who has the custody thereof, as they rightly ought to do, otherwise he or the sheriffs shall compel (*iustificare*) them by their property (*pecunia*). It is attested by [Miles ?] of Gloucester; at Gillingham.[4] [1121–9.]

545. Writ to Roger bishop of Salisbury and Robert Fitz-Walter directing that the abbot and monks of St. Edmund's shall have the ' werpeny ' of 8½ hundreds as beneficially as in the time of William I and William II and during the king's reign; anything that has been withdrawn ' postquam novissime mare transivi ' is to be promptly restored. ' Per breve regis '; at Wilton.[5] [1121–33.]

546. Writ in favour of the monks of Beaubec. It is attested by Bernard bishop of St. David's, William de Tancarvill the chamberlain, and R(oger ?) Fitz-Richard; at Clarendon.[6] [1115–27.]

547. Writ addressed to Pain Fitz-John and the barons of Herefordshire directing that Richard bishop of Hereford shall hold ½ hide in Wellington (-Heath, co. Hereford), and that he shall not be impleaded by Roger de Chandos or his heir. It is attested by Geoffrey the chancellor, Geoffrey Fitz-Pain, and William de Pont de l'Arche; at Winchester.[7] [1123–7.]

548. Confirmation, addressed generally, in favour of the monks of Holy Trinity, Canterbury. It is attested by Geoffrey the chancellor and William de Tancarvill; at Winchester.[8] [1123–9.]

549. Writ to Serlo de Burgh to cause the canons of St. Peter's, York, to have the tithes and rights of the church of St. Andrew, Aldborough (co. York), otherwise Walter Espec, Forne (son of Sigulf) and Anschetill de Bulmer are enjoined to see that this is done. It is attested by Nigel de Aubigny; at Winchester.[9] [1123–9.]

---

[1] W. of Malmesbury, *Gesta Regum*, ii. 521.

[2] *Mon. Anglic.* iii. 448.   [3] John of Worcester, p. 25.

[4] ' Ryllyngham ' (*sic*); Add. MS. 28024, fo. 53 *d*.

[5] Chartul. of St. Edmund's, Harl. MS. 743, fo. 148.

[6] Archives Nationales, JJ. 46, fo. 37 *d*; *ante*, xxiv. 214 n.

[7] *Cal. of Pat. Rolls, 1354–8*, p. 197.   [8] *Ibid. 1429–33*, p. 417.

[9] Farrer, *Early Yorkshire Charters*, no. 500; *Mon. Anglic.* vi. 1180, no. 26.

550. These are the men who were present when King Henry gave to Bernard the scribe void land in the castle of Launceston, between the pit and the chapel, for his lodging ; namely, William de Tancarvill, William de Aubigny the butler, William de Aubigny the Breton, Pain Fitz-John, and Drew de Monci.[1] [1121–9.]

4 July. Stephen count of Mortain removes the Cistercian monks from Tulketh and places them in Furness, co. Lanc., of which region he gives them a half part.[2]

Aug. Henry moves to Eling[3] in Hampshire, where he is detained some time, possibly by judicial business, and possibly by weather unfavourable for the passage to Normandy.

551. Notification to William bishop of Winchester, William de Pont de l'Arche the sheriff, Warin de Hamton, the burgesses of Southampton, and the lieges of Hampshire of the grant to the canons of St. Denis by Southampton of land between Portswood and the River Itchen. It is attested by William archbishop of Canterbury ; the bishops Roger of Salisbury, Alexander of Lincoln, Bernard of St. David's, Godfrey of Bath, and Siefrid of Chichester ; Geoffrey the chancellor, Robert de Sigillo, Geoffrey de Clinton, William de Pont de l'Arche, Hugh de Laval, and William Mauduit ; at Eling (' apud Eilingas ').[4]

552. Grant, addressed generally, restoring to the church of the bishopric of Winchester the manor of Chilbolton, which William Esturmi[5] has recently lost by the judgement of the king's court. It is attested by Roger bishop of Salisbury, Geoffrey the chancellor, Robert de Sigillo, Geoffrey de Clinton, and William de Pont de l'Arche ; at Eling.[6]

553. Notification to Samson bishop of Worcester, Miles of Gloucester, and the barons of Gloucestershire that Roger de Berchley may give ' Acheolt ' in alms to monks or canons. It is attested by William the chamberlain of Tancarvill, Miles of Gloucester, and Pain Fitz-John ; at Eling.[7]

554. Writ to William sheriff of Kent to permit Hugh abbot of St. Augustine's, Canterbury, to have the tithes of Middleton, as Hugh his predecessor had them. It is attested by the chancellor ; at Eling.[8]

555. Grant, addressed generally, to the church of St. Etheldreda, Ely,[9] at the prayer of Bishop Hervey, pardoning £40 of the £100 which the church used to give for scutage when a scutage ran. It is attested by Roger bishop of Salisbury, Geoffrey the chancellor, Robert de Sigillo, William de Tancarvill, William de Aubigny the butler, Ralph Basset, Geoffrey de Clinton, and William de Pont de l'Arche ; at Eling, ' in transitu meo '.[10]

---

[1] Chartul. of Merton, Cleop. C. vii, fo. 76 ; *ante*, xiv. 420.

[2] *Mon. Anglic.* v. 246.

[3] Judicial business transacted in the court at Eling is reflected in the Pipe Roll of 1130, pp. 17, 37–9.

[4] *Cal. of Chart. Rolls*, iii. 336. See also another charter similarly addressed and attested ; *ibid.*

[5] Cf. *Rot. Mag. Pipae*, 31 Hen. I, p. 38.   [6] *Cal. of Chart. Rolls*, iii. 345.

[7] *Mon. Anglic.* v. 427, no. 8.   [8] *Dep. Keeper's Rep.* xxx. app. 6, p. 198.

[9] Cf. *Rot. Mag. Pipae*, 31 Hen. I, p. 44.

[10] Lib. Eliensis, iii, no. 21   Round, *Feudal England*, p. 268

555 A. Notification, addressed generally for England, that the barons and vavassours who in the time of William I held land which was sworn to be of the fee of the church of Ely shall hold their lands from the bishop of Ely by the same service. It is attested by Roger bishop of Salisbury, G(eoffrey) the chancellor, Robert de Sigillo, William de Tancardivilla, William de Aubigny the butler, Ralph Basset, Geoffrey de Glinton, William de Pont de l'Arche ; at Eling, ' in transitu meo '.[1]

556. Grant, addressed generally, to the church of St. Mary of Chatteris (' Catriz '),[2] at the request of Bishop Hervey, releasing 6s. 8d. of wardpenny which the church used to pay. It is attested by Roger bishop of Salisbury, Geoffrey the chancellor, Robert de Sigillo, William de Tancarvill, William de Aubigny the butler, Ralph Basset, Geoffrey de Clinton, William de Pont de l'Arche ; at Eling, ' in transitu meo '.[3]

557. Writ to Adelica Bigot directing her to permit the monks of Belvoir to hold their tithe of Bradley (co. Suffolk), &c., as in the time of her father ; unless she does this Robert Fitz-Walter shall cause it to be done, and unless he does this Ralph Basset shall do it. It is attested by Miles of Gloucester and William de Aubigny the Breton ; at Southampton (' apud Hamtonam ').[4]

15 Aug. Richard bishop of Hereford dies on 18 kalends of September.[5]

26 Aug. Henry sets sail for Normandy,[6] possibly from Portsmouth.

558. Confirmation, addressed to the bishop of Chester, the barons and lieges of Shropshire, in favour of Richard de Belmeis, nephew of Richard bishop of London, of the churches and property which the said bishop held of the king and were late of Godebald and Robert his son, to hold as beneficially as Bishop Richard held them. It is attested by Geoffrey the chancellor, Nigel de Aubigny, Walter de Gloucester, Pain Fitz-John, and William Peverel ; at Portsmouth.[7]

559. Notification to Thurstan archbishop of York, the barons and lieges of Yorkshire, of the confirmation to St. Oswald's, (Nostell), of churches and lands given by Hugh de Laval. It is attested by Nigel de Aubigny, Jordan de Sai, Walter Espec, and Forne son of Siwulf ; at Portsmouth, ' in transfretatione '.[8]

560. Notification of John bishop of Sées to Odo abbot of Marmoutier of the settlement by the advice of King Henry and Geoffrey archbishop of Rouen of an old dispute. It is attested by King Henry at Sées and is dated in 1127, indiction 6, and ends ' quando (rex) dedit filiam suam Gaufrido comiti Andegavensi iuniori '.[9]

561. Confirmation, addressed generally, to the monks of St. Evroul

---

[1] Original charter in the Treasury at Ely (abstract supplied by the Rev. H. E. Salter). See Bentham's *Hist. of Ely*, app. no. 19.

[2] Cf. *Rot. Mag Pipae*, 31 Hen. I, p. 44.

[3] Orig. ch. in the Treasury at Ely, Cole's MS. viii, Add. MS. 5809, fo. 100 *d*.

[4] Round's *Cal. of Belvoir Castle MSS.* (Hist. MSS. Comm.), iv. 157. Cf. *Rot. Mag. Pipae*, 31 Hen. I, p. 17.

[5] John of Worcester, p. 25.   [6] Hen. of Huntingdon, p. 247.

[7] *Mon. Anglic.* vi. 262, no. 2.

[8] Farrer, *Early Yorkshire Charters*, iii, no. 1435.

[9] Round, *Cal. of Documents, France*, no. 1192.

of a messuage in Falaise given by a tenant of Gervase Cornet. It is attested
by John bishop of Sées and Nigel de Aubigny ; at Falaise.[1] [1124–9.]

562. Writ in favour of Anselm abbot of St. Edmund's touching his
market and toll of (Bury) St. Edmund's. It is attested by Aubrey de Ver ;
at Falaise.[2] [1123–35.]

563. Notification, addressed generally, of the grant to Bishop Hervey[3]
and the church of Ely of the abbey of Chatteris. It is attested by Geoffrey
the chancellor, William de Aubigny the butler, Geoffrey de Clinton, and
Pain Fitz-John ; at St. Pierre-sur-Dive.[4] [Sept. 1127–July 1129.]

29 Oct. Roger de Berkeley dies on 4 kalends of November.[5]

564. Confirmation, at the prayer of Hervey bishop of Ely, to the church
of Ely of a weekly market at Hadstock. It is attested by Roger bishop of
Salisbury, Geoffrey the chancellor, Robert de Sigillo, William de Tancarvill, Ralph Basset, Geoffrey de Clinton, and William de Pont de
l'Arche ; at Rouen.[6] [1123–9.]

565. Notification to Geoffrey archbishop of Rouen, Turgis bishop of
Avranches, and the lieges of Normandy of the confirmation made in the
presence of King Henry by Stephen count of Mortain to the monks of
Bec of certain possessions, which are now the grantor's, given by William
Peverel of Dover with the consent of his brothers, Pain and Hamon.
It is attested by Thurstan archbishop of York, Audin bishop of Evreux,
Bernard bishop of St. David's, Geoffrey the chancellor, Earl Walter
Giffard, Robert earl of Leicester, William de Tancarvill, William de
Aubigny, Nigel de Aubigny, William Fitz-Odo, Geoffrey de Clinton,
Ranulf of Bayeux, and Pain Fitz-John ; at Rouen. 'Fuit facta hec
concessio in presentia domini et avunculi mei Henrici regis Anglorum,' &c.[7]

566. Confirmation, dated 1127, of gifts made by Jordan de Sai and
Lucy his wife and their sons Ingram, Gilbert, and Peter, with the permis-
sion of Stephen count of Mortain and the authority of Richard bishop of
Bayeux, to Vivian the abbot and monks of Holy Trinity, Aunay.[8]

566 A. Writ to the bishop of Worcester, the sheriff, &c., of Worcestershire, directing that no one shall take the 'fesandes' which Walter de
Beauchamp has placed in his manor of Elmley ('Almega'), co. Worcester,
under pain of forfeiting 15s. to the king. It is attested by William de
Tancarvill ; at Rouen.[9] [1114–29.]

567. Grant by Stephen, count of Boulogne and Mortain, to St. Mary
of Furness of his forest of Furness and Walney with other possessions.
It is dated A.D. 1127,[10] indiction 5, epact 17. The signatories are : Henry
king of the English and duke of the Normans, Thurstan archbishop of

[1] *Ibid.* no. 626 ; Orderic, v. 206. [2] *Ante,* xxiv. 428, n. 19.
[3] Cf. *Rot. Mag. Pipae,* 31 Hen. I, p. 44.
[4] Lib. Eliensis, iii, n. 22 ; *Mon. Anglic.* ii. 617, no. 6 ; Round, *Feudal England,*
p. 269.   [5] John of Worcester, p. 25 n.
[6] *Cal. of Chart. Rolls,* iv. 434. This charter probably belongs to the period 1123–4.
[7] Round, *Calendar,* no. 378.
[8] From a *vidimus* of Philip VI in 1335, Archives Nationales, JJ. 69, no. 100 ;
Haskins, *Norman Institutions,* p. 297, where it is remarked that the date usually given
for the foundation of Aunay is 1131. Should this be maintained the date in the
vidimus, MCXXVII, must be amended to MCXXXII.
[9] Add. MS. 28024, fo. 127 d.   [10] *Furness Coucher* (Chetham Soc.), i. 123.

York, Audin bishop (of Evreux), Richard bishop of Bayeux, Robert de Sigillo, and Robert earl of Gloucester.[1]

568. Confirmation of the above by King Henry, with the same signatories.[2]

c. Dec. The king nominates Master Gilbert the Universal, a canon of Lyons and master of the schools at Nevers ('Novernis'), to the see of London.[3]

1128.

569. Confirmation, addressed generally, to the abbot and monks of St. Evroul, at the prayer of Nigel de Aubigny. It is attested by Richard bishop of Bayeux, John bishop of Lisieux, and Nigel de Aubigny ; at Caen.[4] [Before July 1129.]

570. Confirmation, addressed generally, to the monks of St. Evroul, at the prayer of William de Molines and Aubreye his wife, of various possessions. It is attested by Richard bishop of Bayeux, John bishop of Lisieux, and John bishop of Sées, Nigel de Aubigny, and William de Molines ; at Caen.[5] [Before July 1129.]

571. A plea is heard before the king and the justiciary in the castle of Caen between the abbot and monks of St. Stephen's, Caen, and Herbert the clerk. In the hearing of the king, the whole justiciary, and the barons the said Herbert makes default and, by the judgement of the king and the justiciary, St. Stephen's remains seised, to be answerable thereof henceforth to no one. The witnesses are : King Henry and the justiciary, namely John bishop of Lisieux, Robert de la Hai, and Geoffrey de Sublis ; the barons, Ralph Taisson, Roger Marmion,[6] William Patric, and Robert Carbonell.[7] [Before 1130.]

572. Notification of certain gifts made in the king's presence by William Paynel and Simon son of Geoffrey de Bosvill to St. Stephen's, Caen. It is attested by Richard bishop of Bayeux, Richard bishop of Coutances, Earl Robert the king's son, William de Aubigny, Geoffrey archdeacon of Bayeux, Ralph Taison, Simon de Bosvill, William Crassus, Robert Fitz-Bernard, Hugh Bigot, Robert de Agnis, Geoffrey Fitz-Pain, William de Bruis, Humphrey de Bohun, Robert de Sigillo, and William de Tancarvill ; (at Caen ?).[8] [Before July 1129.]

22 Mar. Godfrey abbot of Shrewsbury dies on 11 kalends of April.[9]

9 May. Nigel abbot of Eynesham dies on 7 ides of May.[10]

10 June. Geoffrey of Anjou is made a knight on Whit-Sunday.[11]

[1] *Mon. Anglic.* v. 247, no. 4.　　　　[2] *Furness Coucher,* i. 123 and 186.

[3] John of Worcester, p. 26 ; *Annals of Waverley,* p. 220.

[4] Orderic, v. 200 ; Round, *Calendar,* no. 627.

[5] *Ibid.* no. 629 ; Orderic, v. 204.

[6] Dead before 1130. Cf. *Rot. Mag. Pipae,* 31 Hen. I, p. 111.

[7] 'Emptiones Eudonis', in the Archives of the Calvados, H. 1834, no. 15 ; *ante,* xxiv. 215. Cf. Round, *Calendar,* p. 160.

[8] Round, *Cal. of Documents, France,* nos. 1411–12.

[9] 'Feria iiij' (*sic*) ; John of Worcester, p. 28. 'The ides of March (15 March) 1129' : *ibid.* p. 28 n.　　　　　　　　　　[10] *Ibid.* p. 29 n.

[11] See K. Norgate, *Angevin Kings,* i. 258–60, relying on John of Marmoutier (*Hist. Gaufridi Ducis*) against the Chronicle of Fécamp (which gives 1127) and Orderic, iv. 498 (1129).

17 June. The Empress Matilda is married to Geoffrey of Anjou at Le Mans on the octave of Whit-Sunday.[1]

During the summer Henry advances into the domain of Louis of France as far as Epernon, in Eure-et-Loire, where he remains for one week ; his object being to prevent the French king sending aid to William the newly-appointed count of Flanders.[2]

22 July. Hugh abbot of Chertsey dies on 11 kalends of August.[3]

5 Sept. Ranulf Flambard, bishop of Durham, dies on the nones of September.[4] As soon as the news of the bishop's death reaches the court in Normandy William de Pont de l'Arche hastens to the bishopric to secure the temporalities for the king's use. He is absent from the court on this business for a period of nine weeks.[5]

Henry becomes reconciled with William de Roumare,[6] to whom he gives to wife Matilda, daughter of Richard de Redvers.[7]

Oct.–Nov. The king is present at a council held at Rouen by Matthew, a monk of Cluny, bishop of Albano and papal legate, who there promulgates letters of Honorius touching the conduct of priests.[8]

573. Writ addressed to Evrard bishop of Norwich, Robert Fitz-Walter, the barons and lieges of Suffolk notifying them of the grant to the abbot of St. Edmund's of a mint in the town of (Bury) St. Edmund's, a moneyer and his exchange, as the abbot heretofore had them. It is attested by (John) bishop of Lisieux, (Bernard) bishop of St. David's, and Robert de Sigillo ; at Rouen.[9] [Before Aug. 1129.]

574. Notification, addressed to the bishop of Worcester, the sheriff, barons, and lieges of Worcestershire, of the grant to Walter de Beauchamp of the land late of Adeliz, who was the wife of Urse de Abbetot, which the same Adeliz granted to Walter. It is attested by Geoffrey the chancellor, Robert de Sigillo, William Peverel of Dover, William Fitz-Odo, William de Pont de l'Arche, Peverel de Beauchamp, Pain de Beauchamp, Robert son of William de Stoches, William Maltravers, Robert de Monteviron, Geoffrey de Abbetot, Robert son of Ralph de Hastinges, Robert de Gurnai, Robert Fitz-Fulcher, Roger son-in-law of Albert,[10] John the usher (*hostiarius*), and Henry del Broc ; at Vaudreuil (' apud Rodolium ').[11]

575. Writ, addressed to the bishops of London and Norwich, Aubrey de Ver, Robert Fitz-Walter, the barons and lieges of Essex, Norfolk, and Suffolk, and the barons and men of the honor of the abbey of St. Edmund notifying them that the king has ordered Anselm abbot of St. Edmund's to take into the demesne of his church the manor of Wrabness, (co. Essex), which Richard Fitz-Walcheline held, if it was of the demesne of the abbey

[1] See p. 546, note 11.

[2] Hen. of Huntingdon, p. 247. [3] John of Worcester, p. 29.

[4] Sym. of Durham, ii. 283 ; John of Worcester, p. 29.

[5] *Rot. Mag. Pipae*, pp. 129, 131.

[6] Cf. *ibid.* p. 105. [7] Orderic, iv. 484.

[8] *Ibid.* p. 495. A confirmation of Henry I to St. Evroul, purporting to have been issued at this council, is a forgery. See *Gallia Christ.* xi, instr., cols. 204–10.

[9] *Ante*, xxiv. 427, n. 15. [10] Dead in 1130 : *Rot. Mag. Pipae*, p. 39.

[11] Dugdale's MS. L. (no. 18), fo. 41 ; Add. MS. 28024, fo. 127. Several of the witnesses had remission of Danegeld in 1130, possibly in respect of their recent services beyond seas.

in the time of the king and his predecessors and on the day when Anselm became abbot ; because the said Richard had given the king to understand that it was not of the demesne of that church. It is attested by William de Tancarvill ; at Vaudreuil.[1]

28 Nov. Geoffrey archbishop of Rouen dies on 4 kalends of December.[2]

576. Notification to the bishop of Bath, the barons, sheriff, and lieges of Somerset, of the grant to the king's nephew, Henry abbot of Glastonbury, of a seven days' fair at Glastonbury. It is attested by Robert de Sigillo, Count Theobald, (Robert) earl of Gloucester, William (*sic*) de Tancarvill, Andrew de Baldement, William Fitz-Odo (Eudo), and Henry Fitz-Humphrey ; at Arganchy (?).[3] [Before Aug. 1129 ?]

577. Notification to the bishop of Bayeux, the barons and lieges of Normandy, of the conditional confirmation of a gift made to the church of St. Stephen of Plessis-Grimould by Richard de Rullos. It is attested by Robert de Sigillo, Roger de Fécamp, Ralph de Belfou, Robert de Ver, and Robert de Curci ; at Arganchy (' Archenci ').[4]

578. Notification to the barons of England and Wales of the confirmation to Miles (of Gloucester) of his father's land. It is attested by John bishop of Lisieux, Geoffrey the chancellor, William de Tancarvill, A(udin ?) bishop (of Evreux), William . . ., G(eoffrey) de Clinton, Robert de Oili, . . ., William de Pont (de l'Arche), and (Humphrey) de Bohun ; at . . .[5] [1127–9.]

579. Notification, addressed generally and particularly to the ministers in whose bailiwicks Robert son of Walter de Wyndesor had lands at the time of his death, that the king has rendered to William son of the said Robert the land of which his father died seised. It is attested by Robert de Hay, Drew de Moncei, William Pevrel of Dover, Pain Pevrel, Geoffrey Fitz-Pain, William Maltravers, Maurice de Windesor, Pevrel de Beauchamp, and William Fitz-John ; at Argentan (' apud Archentem ') at Christmas.[6]

During the year Hugh de Pagens, master of the knights of the Temple of Jerusalem, accompanied by two knights and two clerks, travelled through England and into Scotland, summoning the people to make the crusade. Many people took the cross during this and the ensuing year.[7]

1129.

25 Jan. William Giffard, bishop of Winchester, dies on 8 kalends of February.[8]

Henry sets Waleran count of Meulan at liberty and restores to him his possessions with the exception of his castles. Hugh de Châteauneuf is also set at liberty.[9]

---

[1] Chartul. of St. Edmund's, Camb. Univ. Lib., fo. 28 *d.* (106). Cf. *Rot. Mag. Pipae*, p. 96.

[2] Necrologies of Rouen and the priory of Sausseuse ; ' 6 kal. Decemb., indictione vii ' : Orderic, iv. 495.

[3] *Mon. Anglic.* i. 44, no. 72 (a corrupt copy). The date may be 1131. See no. 635.

[4] Initials only of witnesses : Round, *Calendar*, no. 541.

[5] Cott. Ch. xvi. 33 (much decayed).

[6] *Cal. of Chart. Rolls*, ii. 137 ; *Cal. of Pat. Rolls, 1334–8*, p. 249.

[7] *Annals of Waverley* ; Rob. of Torigny, p. 113.

[8] Chron. ; John of Worcester, p. 29.   [9] Orderic, iv. 463.

580. Notification to Walter Espec, Eustace Fitz-John, Forne (son of Sigulf), the sheriff, barons, lieges, and ministers of Yorkshire of the confirmation to St. Mary's, York, and Abbot Geoffrey, of a gift made by Turgis de Radeham.[1] It is attested by Thurstan archbishop of York; at Argentan.[2] [1123–9.]

581. Notification, addressed generally, of the grant to Hervey bishop of Ely of acquittance of shires and confirmation of his liberties. It is attested by John bishop of Lisieux, Robert de Sigillo, William de Tancarvill, William de Aubigny, Geoffrey de Clinton, and Pain Fitz-John; at Argentan.[3]

582. Writ, addressed generally for England, Normandy, and ports of the sea, directing that the demesne goods of the abbey of Vignats (Saint-André-en-Gouffern) shall be free of toll, passage, and other customs. Witnessed by J(ohn) bishop of Sées and (Stephen) count of Mortain; at Argentan.[4] [1124–35.]

583. Mandate to the sheriffs, &c., of the Cotentin, forbidding the arrest of men attending the market of Montebourg if it be possible to arrest them otherwise. Issued at Argentan, by William of Glastonbury; attested by Robert earl of Gloucester. [1123–35.][5]

584. Grant in favour of the canons of St. Stephen in the castle of the bishop of Bayeux at Plessis. The signatories include Thurstan archbishop of York, Audin bishop of Evreux, Richard bishop of Bayeux, and many canons of Bayeux; (at Bayeux ?).[6] [1123–30.]

585. Notification to the primate and bishops of Normandy of a grant in favour of the church of Evreux and Bishop Audin. It is attested by Thurstan archbishop of York, Robert de Sigillo, Nigel nephew of Bishop (Roger), and Geoffrey Fitz-Pain; at Touques (' Toucamp ').[7] [1127–31.]

586. April–June. Grant to Petronilla, the first abbess of Fontevrault, of one hundred pounds yearly in pennies of Rouen from the rent of the king's mint at Rouen, 30 marks from the farm of the city of London, and 20 marks from that of the city of Winchester. It is attested by Thurstan archbishop of York, Audin his brother bishop of Evreux, Geoffrey the chancellor, and Robert de Sigillo. ' Acta sunt hec apud Rothomagum . . . MCXXVIIII . . .,' the church of Rouen being without a shepherd.[8]

587. Another codex of this grant (without date or place of issue) has these signatories: the king; Thurstan archbishop of York; the bishops Bernard (of St. David's), Audin of Evreux, John of Sées, and John of Lisieux; Robert earl of Gloucester, William de Tancarvill, Brien (?)

---

[1] *Alias* Turgis Brundos, first feoffee of Liddel, co. Cumb. He was dead in 1130: *Rot. Mag. Pipae*, p. 30.

[2] *Cal. of Chart. Rolls*, iii. 119.

[3] Lib. Eliensis; Bentham's *Hist. of Ely*, app. no. 14. The remission to Ely of 40s. of ' Warpeni ', issued at Argentan and attested by the same persons, is preserved in the Treasury at Ely. See Bentham, app. no. 20.

[4] Chartul. of Saint-André in Archives of Calvados, fo. 19, no. 72; Haskins, *Norman Institutions*, p. 306.

[5] MS. Lat. 10087, no. 8; Haskins, *Norman Institutions*, p. 101.

[6] Round, *Calendar*, no. 539.   [7] *Ibid.* no. 283. Cf. *ibid.* no. 286.

[8] *Ibid.* no. 1459. Cf. *ibid.* no. 1053.

Fitz-Count, Geoffrey Fitz-Pain, R(obert) de la Hai, William de Aubigny, Robert de Sigillo, and William of Glaston(bury).[1]

588. Notification, addressed generally, of the remission to Roger the abbot and the convent of Fécamp of two sums of money for certain pleas 'unde iustitia mea placitaverat . . . in curia mea', in accordance with the privilege of the abbey. It is attested by John bishop of Lisieux, Robert de la Hai, Robert de Curci, William de Aubigny, Geoffrey de Clinton, and William de Glastonbury; at Rouen.[2]

589. Mandate to the justices and officials of St. Marcouf and Varreville, ordering that all the possessions of Montebourg be held freely, especially Foucarville, which was the king's alms. Witness, Robert de Hai; at Rouen.[3] [1123–35.]

590. The purchases of land, &c., made by Eudo, abbot of St. Stephen's, Caen, are confirmed by the king. The signatories are: King Henry; the bishops Richard of Bayeux, John of Lisieux, Richard of Coutances, and Turgis of Avranches; Robert de Sigillo, Robert (*recte* John) bishop of Sées, Robert earl of Gloucester, Waleran count of Meulan, Robert de Hai, Roger the sheriff, William de Aubigny, and Robert Fitz-Bernard.[4] [1129–31.]

591. Confirmation to St. Lawrence of Envremou of property in England given by Baldwin Fitz-Gilbert,[5] which late belonged to Hugh de Envremou; and grant by the king of the fishery of Arques. It is attested by Thurstan archbishop of York and William earl of Warenne; at Rouen.[6] [1123–35.]

592. Confirmation of the foundation (made in 1128) of the priory of St. Barbe-en-Auge. The signatories are the king and queen, Robert earl of Gloucester, William (earl) of Warenne, Robert earl of Leicester, John bishop of Lisieux, 'Toustain' archbishop of York, William (de Tancarvill) the 'chambellan', and Rabel his son.[7]

593. Writ, addressed to Evrard bishop of Norwich, R(obert) Fitz-Walter the sheriff, the barons and lieges of Norfolk and Suffolk, directing that Abbot Anselm and the monks of St. Edmund's shall have all their customs as in the time of King Edward and the king's father and brother. It is attested by Humphrey de Bohun;[8] at Rouen.[9] [Before Oct. 1129.]

594. Notification, addressed to the archbishop of York, the bishop of Durham, the sheriffs, barons, and lieges of the bishopric of Durham, of the restoration to the prior and monks of Durham of certain lands which had been taken from their church by Ranulf, late bishop of Durham. It is attested by Robert de Sigillo, Nigel nephew of the bishop of Salisbury, Robert earl of Gloucester, William de Tancarvill, William Fitz-Odo,

---

[1] Round, *Calendar*, no. 1052. For William of Glastonbury see Mr. Round, *ante*, xiv. 424–5, and Professor Haskins, *ante*, xxiv. 210; also *Rot. Mag. Pipae*, p. 13.

[2] Cartae Antiq. S. 3; *ante*, xxiv. 210. See the remarks in Haskins, *Norman Institutions*, p. 90.

[3] MS. Lat. 10087, no. 9; Haskins, *Norman Institutions*, p. 101.

[4] 'Emptiones Eudonis': Archives of the Calvados, H. 1834, no. 15 *bis*; *ante*, xxiv. 216.

[5] Cf. Round, *Feudal England*, pp. 159–61.

[6] Round, *Calendar*, no. 396.   [7] D'Anisy, *Archives de Calvados*, i. 93.

[8] Humphrey de Bohun II was dead in 1130: *Rot. Mag. Pipae*, p. 18.

[9] Chartul. of St. Edmund's, Camb. Univ. Libr., fo. 25, no. 51.

Robert de Brus, and William de Pont de l'Arche; at Lions-la-Forêt ('apud Sanctum Dionisium in Leonibus').[1]

2 June. The king spent Whitsuntide at Falaise, as appears by the following record:

594 A. A plea between William count of Ponthieu and Roger de Grata-panchia and Roger his son, who claimed a certain marsh from the monks of St. Martin's, (Troarn), is heard before King Henry at Falaise. The count in his notification of the judgement of the king's court states that he showed to the king how his ancestors long possessed this ground, and continues, 'Diiudicavit autem rex et eius curia per verba mea et illorum Sancto Martino et monachis remanere marescum quietum et liberum, et amplius non debere fieri inde contra eos calumniam'. The count's witnesses are: Hugh the sheriff and Robert his brother, Pain son of Hugh de Mesdavid, William de Corcella, the chaplains Ascelin and Serlo. These things were done in the year . . . 1129, in Pentecost.[2]

July? Possibly at this time Henry nominates Hugh de Amiens, abbot of Reading, to the archbishopric of Rouen.[3]

595. Notification, addressed generally for England, of the confirmation to Rainald abbot of Ramsey and his monks of their lands, churches, &c. It is attested by Hugh archbishop of Rouen, Geoffrey the chancellor, Brien Fitz-Count, Geoffrey de Clinton, Geoffrey Fitz-Pain, William de Aubigny the Breton, William de Tancarvill, William Peverel, Pain Peverel, Hamon the sewer; at Rouen.[4] [1129.]

595 A. Notification, addressed generally for England and Normandy, of the king's confirmation to St. Stephen's, Caen, of the gifts of William his father and others, in return for the crown and other ornaments demised by King William and now given up by the monks at Caen. The signatories are: Henry the king; Hugh archbishop of Rouen; the bishops Richard of Bayeux, John of Lisieux, and Roger of Salisbury; the earls Robert of Gloucester and Ranulf (of Chester); Geoffrey de Magnaville, Nigel de Aubigny, Robert de Hai, and Eustace Fitz-John.[5] [1129.]

15 July. Henry returns to England on the ides of July.[6]

1 Aug. On the kalends of August a council is held in London at which are present the two archbishops, and the bishops of Lincoln, Salisbury, London, Rochester, Chichester, Bath, Worcester, Norwich, St. David's, and Ely.[7]

595 B. Writ addressed to Walter Espec, Eustace Fitz-John, and Geoffrey Escotland,[8] directing them to do justice in any dispute with

---

[1] *Feod. Priorat. Dunelm.* (Surtees Soc.), p. 145 n.

[2] *Ante,* xxiv. 211 (3); Haskins, *Norman Institutions,* p. 91.

[3] Cf. Orderic, iv. 500. Honorius, who died 14 February 1130, approved of Hugh's election: *ibid.* note 2.

[4] Add. Ch. 33643; *Brit. Mus. Facsimiles of Charters,* no. 11; *Chartul. of Ramsey,* no. 165 (where Pain Peverel's name is omitted). See no. 631 below.

[5] Cart. Antiq. roll S, no. 22; *Mon. Anglic.* vi. 1071 (4).

[6] Sym. of Durham, ii. 283; 'Mense Iulii': John of Worcester, p. 29.

[7] Hen. of Huntingdon, p. 251. The Engl. Chron. gives the date as 30 September–4 October.

[8] *Firmarius* of the temporalities of Durham *sede vacante*: *Rot. Mag. Pipae,* pp. 130–2.

Richard, nephew of Bishop Ranulf. It is attested by the chancellor,
Robert de Sigillo, Geoffrey de Clinton, and William de Pont de l'Arche ;
at Windsor.[1] [1129–32.]

595 c. Notification to the officials and ministers of Essex of the restoration and confirmation to William de Glanvill, the king's serjeant, of the
office and land late of William De-salt-les-dames,[2] his uncle (*avunculus*).
It is attested by Ingelram de Say, William Martel, Goher de Alneto, and
Robert Avenell ; at Windsor.[3]

596. Notification, addressed generally, that Hervey bishop of Ely
shall be quit of castle-ward of Norwich. It is attested by the bishops,
Roger of Salisbury, Alexander of Lincoln, and Oine of Evreux ; Geoffrey
the chancellor, Robert earl of Gloucester, William earl of Warenne, William
de Aubigny, Brien Fitz-Count, Hugh Bigot, Miles of Gloucester, Geoffrey
de Clinton, William de Aubigny the Breton, and William de Pont de
l'Arche ; at Windsor.[4] [1123–30.]

Oct. After Michaelmas Henry proceeds to Winchester (according to
custom). He is accompanied by many of the ecclesiastics and the important
officers of his court. He gives the bishopric of Winchester to his sister's
son, Henry of Blois, a monk of Cluny and abbot of Glastonbury ;[5] and
that of Coventry and Chester to Roger, nephew of Geoffrey de Clinton.[6]

597. Writ addressed to the bishop of Norwich, Robert Fitz-Walter,
the barons and lieges of Norfolk and Suffolk, in favour of the abbot of
St. Edmund's. It is attested by John the Marshal ;[7] at Winchester.[8]
[1129–33.]

598. Writ, addressed generally, in favour of the same abbot. It is
attested by Maurice of Wyndleshor ; at Winchester.[9] [1121–33.]

598 A. Writ addressed to Archbishop Thurstan and Thurstan archdeacon (of Richmond ?) directing them to cause the bishop of Lincoln and
the church of Clayworth to have the tithes and customs which belong to
that church. It is attested by the chancellor ; at Winchester.[10] [1123–33.]

599. Notification, addressed generally, that Nicholas Basset has
surrendered to the king all the lands which he holds in chief and Henry
now grants the same to Richard Basset[11] and his heirs, to hold as Ralph
Basset his father held them at his death. It is attested by Roger bishop
of Salisbury, Alexander bishop of Lincoln, Geoffrey the chancellor, William
earl of Warenne, Brien Fitz-Count, (Robert) earl of Gloucester, Pain
Fitz-John, Aubrey de Ver, Robert de Ver, Eustace Fitz-John, Geoffrey

---

[1] *Feod. Priorat. Dunelm.* (Surtees Soc.), p. 145 n.

[2] Roger Deus-salvet-Dominas held land in Felsted, &c., in Essex in 1086 ; there
was later a Glanville manor in Felsted.

[3] *Cal. of Chart. Rolls,* i. 422.

[4] Orig. ch. in the Treasury at Ely ; Lib. Eliensis, Bentham's *Hist. of Ely,* app.
no. 18 ; *Mon. Anglic.* i. 482, no. 18.

[5] Sym. of Durham, ii. 283. Henry of Blois was elected on 11 October : Le Neve,
Fasti.

[6] Sym. of Durham, ii. 283.   [7] Cf. *Rot. Mag. Pipae,* p. 18.

[8] Chartul. of St. Edmund's, Camb. Univ. Libr., fo. 28 *d,* no. 101.

[9] *Ibid.* fo. 28 *d,* no. 102.

[10] Dean and Chap. of Lincoln, Regist. Antiquissimum, f. 4, no. 20 ; copy by the
courtesy of the Rev. Canon Foster.   [11] Cf. *Rot. Mag. Pipae,* pp. 81–2.

Fitz-Pain, Robert Harundel, and William Fitz-John ; at Waltham.[1] [1129–33.]

600. Notification, addressed generally, of the grant of the bishopric of Hereford to Robert de Betun, prior of Llanthony. It is attested by William archbishop of Canterbury ; the bishops Roger of Salisbury, Henry of Winchester, and Alexander of Lincoln ; Geoffrey the chancellor, Robert de Sigillo, Robert earl of Gloucester, Brien Fitz-Count, Hugh Bigot, Miles of Gloucester, Pain Fitz-John, Geoffrey Fitz-Pain, and Drew de Monci ; at Woodstock.[2]

601. Writ to the justices, sheriffs, reeves, and ministers of England and Wales in favour of Robert, bishop of Hereford. It is attested by John the Marshal and Pain Fitz-John ; at Woodstock.[3] [1129–33.]

602. Writ to the justices, barons, sheriffs, and ministers of England and Normandy and the seaports, and particularly to the reeves of (South-) hampton, Hastings, Dover, Barfleur, Caen, Ouistreham, and Dieppe, directing that the property and men of the abbey of Cîteaux shall be quit of toll. It is attested by the chancellor, Robert de Sigillo, and John the Marshal ; at Woodstock.[4] [1129–33.]

603. Notification, addressed generally, of the confirmation to the church of St. George, which Robert de Oillei founded in the castle of Oxford, of all the possessions given by the founder. It is attested by Geoffrey the chancellor, Robert de Sigillo, Geoffrey de Clynton, and Henry de Pomerey ; at Woodstock.[5] [1121–32.]

603 A. Writ to Restold sheriff of Oxeneford and Richard sheriff of Bucking[ham] directing that the land and men of the canons of St. George's at Oxford shall be quit of shires, hundreds, &c. It is attested by Roger bishop of Salisbury ; at Woodstock.[6]

603 B. Writ to A(lexander) bishop of Lincoln and Walter archdeacon (of Oxford) directing that Edwin son of Gedegos shall have his church of St. Giles (at Oxford) and place there what clerk he wills. It is attested by G(eoffrey) the chancellor and G(eoffrey de Clinton) the chamberlain ; at Woodstock.[7]

25 Dec. At Christmas Henry is at Winchester.[8]

William de Tancarvill, chamberlain of England and Normandy, died in this year.[9]

1130.

604. Writ addressed to Robert Arundel, William Fitz-John, G(eoffrey) de Furneaux, and the ministers of Devonshire in favour of the monks of St. Martin-des-Champs and Barnstaple. It is attested by R(obert) de Ver ; at Dilton.[10] [1129–30.]

---

[1] Rot. Sloan, xxxi. 4, no. 49.
[2] *Cal. of Pat. Rolls, 1354–8,* p. 196.   [3] *Ibid.*
[4] *Chartul. of Rievaulx* (Surtees Soc.), no. 195.
[5] Orig. charter at Christ Church, Oxford ; *Cal. of Chart. Rolls,* ii. 69.
[6] Original charter at Christ Church, Oxford, supplied by the Rev. H. E. Salter.
[7] Godstow Chartul., Excheq. K.R. Misc. Bks. no. 20, fo. 1 *d,* supplied by the Rev. H. E. Salter.
[8] Hen. of Huntingdon, p. 252. Some authorities state ' apud Wirecestriam '.
[9] Annals of St. Wandrille, *Hist. Littéraire de France,* xxxii. 204.
[10] *Cal. of Chart. Rolls,* iii. 331 ; Round, *Calendar,* no. 1270.

605. Writ addressed to the prior of St. Albans and the ministers of the abbey, directing them to permit the abbot of Ramsey to have a stream at Shitlington, co. Beds., as in the time of William I and William II, otherwise Aubrey de Ver [1] the sheriff and Richard (Basset) [1] the sheriff shall cause this to be done. It is attested by Edward of Salisbury ; [2] at Cheddar ('apud Cedreholam'). [3] [1129–30.]

606. Writ to the justices, sheriffs, and ministers of England and the seaports directing that the monks of Bath shall be quit of toll. It is attested by Robert de Ver ; [4] at Keynsham ('apud Chainesham'). [5] [1121–33.]

607. Notification, addressed generally, of the grant to the nascent monastery of Dunstable of the manor of Dunstable. It is attested by Robert bishop of Hereford, Simon bishop of Worcester, Geoffrey the chancellor, Robert de Sigillo, Nigel nephew of the bishop (of Salisbury), Miles of Gloucester, Humphrey de Bohun, Geoffrey Fitz-Pain, Pain Fitz-John, Drew de Moncei, and Maurice de Windsor ; at Combe ('apud Cumbam'). [6] [1129–33.]

29 March. Vincent abbot of Abingdon dies on 4 kalends of April, [7] and Ingulf prior of Winchester is nominated at Woodstock abbot in his stead. [8] In the Berkshire roll for 1130 a debt of 70 marks for the pleas of Geoffrey de Clinton is recorded against Vincent abbot of Abingdon, but the debt is pardoned to the said abbot ' quia mortuus est '. [9]

30 March. At Easter Henry is at Woodstock. At this time a charge of high treason is brought against Geoffrey de Clinton, the king's justice. [10] David king of Scots, who is now on a visit to the king, is deputed to inquire into the charges. [11]

There are numerous indications in the sheriffs' rolls for this year of the journey of David king of Scots to the English court. Thus Odard as sheriff of Northumberland, Anschetill de Wirecestre as *custos* or *firmarius* of the crown lands between Tyne and Tees, Bertram de Bulmer as sheriff of Yorkshire, William de Luvetot and Eustace Fitz-John as keepers of Tickhill and the honor of Blythe, Osbert Silvain as sheriff of Nottingham and Derby, and other sheriffs and wardens, charge their respective accounts for the corrody of the king of Scots coming to the king's court in England and returning from England to Scotland. [12]

608. Notification, addressed generally, of the king's confirmation of certain gifts made by Robert de Oilli to the church which he has founded in the isle of Osney. It is attested by the bishops Alexander of Lincoln and Simon of Worcester, Robert earl of Gloucester, Geoffrey Fitz-Pain, and Robert de Curci ; at Woodstock. [13] [1129–33.]

---

[1] Keepers of no less than eleven counties in 1130. Cf. *Rot. Mag. Pipae*, pp. 63, 100.

[2] He was dead at Michaelmas 1130.　　　　[3] *Chartul. of Ramsey*, no. 175.

[4] See Round, *Geoffrey de Mandeville*, p. 326.

[5] *Two Bath Chartularies* (Somerset Rec. Soc.), i, no. 47.

[6] *Mon. Anglic.* vi. 240. It appears from the Pipe Roll that the allowance of 1*d.* a day to the warden of Dunstable began at Easter 1130 : *Rot. Mag. Pipae*, p. 64.

[7] *Chron. of Abingdon*, ii. 172, 315.

[8] John of Worcester, p. 30.　　　　　　　[9] *Rot. Mag. Pipae*, p. 123.

[10] Hen. of Huntingdon, p. 252 ; *Annales Monast.* ii. 222.　　[11] Orderic, iii. 403.

[12] *Rot. Mag. Pipae*, pp. 35 ff.　　　　　　[13] *Cal. of Chart. Rolls*, iii. 417.

609. Writ addressed to Rainer de Bath, sheriff (of Lincoln), in favour of the monks of Burwell. It is attested by Geoffrey Fitz-Pain ; at Woodstock.[1] [1129–33.]

The duration of the king's visit to Woodstock and other neighbouring royal manors in Oxfordshire during the fiscal year which ended at Michaelmas 1130 may be gauged by an entry in the accounts of Robert (de Oilli ?), sheriff of Oxford.

He claims allowance against his farm of the county of 20s. by tale for the loss of farm of the multure of a certain mill, which the king's bakers kept fully employed by the space of eighty days.[2]

The four sheriffs of London claimed allowance at Michaelmas 1130 for £8 18s. 5d. expended in herrings, ointment, oil, nuts, and the carriage thereof to Woodstock ; for £45 6s. 2d. in the purchase and carriage of wine ; for £23 19s. 9d. in the purchase of pepper, cummin, ginger, towels, basins, and wine-vessels for the king's use.[3]

Anselm, sheriff of Rouen, in his account of the farm of Bosham, claimed allowance against his farm for 8s. expended in the carriage of 476 dried fish to Condover [4] and Woodstock, which the king had.[5]

The sheriff of Oxford also claimed allowance for 47s. 5½d. expended in the carriage of wine, corn, the king's and queen's robe from Woodstock to Clarendon ; and for the allowance of Roger de Causton and for conducting him to (Woodstock) Park, and from Oxford to Winchester ; [6] and for 61s. 7d. in mowing the king's meadow and for carriage of the hay to Stonesfield and Woodstock.[7]

610. Notification, addressed generally, of the confirmation to the canons of St. John the Baptist, Loddington (co. Leic.), of the alms given by Richard Basset and Matilda (Ridel) his wife. It is attested by Henry bishop of Winchester, Geoffrey de Clinton, Aubrey de Ver, and Robert de Sigillo ; at Windsor.[8] [1129–31.]

c. April. Miles of Gloucester is present at the Easter audit at the exchequer, when Ivo de Heriz, late sheriff of Nottingham and Derby, delivered 2 destriers towards the 5 which he owed. Later the same Ivo delivered the 3 remaining destriers (to the exchequer ?) in Normandy.[9]

611. Notification to Richard Basset and Aubrey de Ver and the ministers of Norfolk of the confirmation to Evrard bishop of Norwich of his customs and privileges at (Bishop's) Lynn. It is attested by Miles of Gloucester ; at Winchester.[10] [1129–33].

612. Writ addressed to Richard Basset and A(ubrey) de Ver, the sheriff, and the burgesses of Guildford ('Geldefort') directing that the men of Geoffrey Purcell,[11] the king's usher, of Catteshill ('Chatishill') and

---

[1] Round, *Cal. of Documents, France*, no. 1241.

[2] *Rot. Mag. Pipae*, p. 1.   [3] *Ibid.* p. 144.

[4] There is no other evidence of a royal visit to Condover at this time. Possibly a visit was contemplated, but was not undertaken.

[5] *Ibid.* p. 72.   [6] *Ibid.* p. 1.   [7] *Ibid.*

[8] *Mon. Anglic.* vi. 188 *b*. A second charter (*ibid.* p. 188) in somewhat similar terms, dated at Westminster, is clearly a fabrication.

[9] *Rot. Mag. Pipae*, p. 7. The presence of Miles of Gloucester at the exchequer may be explained by the circumstance that he was sheriff of the counties of Gloucester and Stafford.   [10] *Cal. of Chart. Rolls*, iv. 439.   [11] Cf. *Rot. Mag. Pipae*, p. 50.

Chiddingfold (' Chedelingefelt ') shall be as free of toll and custom as in the time of Geoffrey's father. It is attested by Miles of Gloucester ; at Winchester.[1]

613. Notification, addressed generally, of the grant to Abbot Ingulf of the abbey of Abingdon. It is attested by the bishops Roger of Salisbury and Henry of Winchester ; the chancellor, Nigel nephew of the bishop (of Salisbury), William de Pont de l'Arche, Robert de Oili, and Warin the sheriff ; at Winchester.[2]

614. Writ addressed to Richard Basset and Aubrey de Ver directing that the church of St. Edmund's and Abbot Anselm shall have the soc, &c., of their 8½ hundreds. It is attested by the chancellor and the bishop of St. David's ; at Winchester.[3]

Ansger prior of Lewes (' Laethes ') is elected abbot of Reading, at Winchester.[4]

615. Notification to the bishop of Lincoln, the sheriff, barons, and lieges of Bedfordshire that Abbot Reinald has deraigned in the king's court, to the use of his church of Ramsey, against Simon de Beauchamp, land and wood at Crawley. It is attested by the bishops Roger of Salisbury and Alexander of Lincoln, David king of Scots,[5] Geoffrey the chancellor, Robert earl of Leicester, Adam de Port, Hugh Bigot, William de Aubigny the butler, Geoffrey de Clinton, William de Aubigny the Breton, William Peverel, Pain Peverel, Walter Espec, Robert de Bruis, William de Pont de l'Arche, Henry Monk, Henry Fitz-William, and Berenger Fitz-Reiner ; at Brampton.[6]

4 May. On Rogation Sunday Henry is at Canterbury, and is present at the dedication of the new church.[7] There are also assembled there : the bishops John of Rochester, Gilbert ' the universal ' of London, Henry of Winchester, Alexander of Lincoln, Roger of Salisbury, Simon of Worcester, Roger of Coventry, Godfrey of Bath, Evrard of Norwich, Siefrid of Chichester, Bernard of St. David's, Audin of Evreux, and John of Sées,[8] also David king of Scots.[9]

At the dedication of the church of Canterbury Henry gives to the said church that of St. Martin, Dover, with its possessions.[10]

8 May. Four days later (which would be Ascension Day), the king being at Rochester, there is a serious conflagration.[11] The primate hallows the monastery of St. Andrew, being assisted by the bishops who had been present at Canterbury.[12] The king's visit is reflected in the accounts of Rualon, sheriff of Kent, for the current year, who claims allowance against

---

[1] Add. Ch. 19572 ; Chartul. of Reading, Harl. MS. 1708, fo. 18 *d.*

[2] *Chron. of Abingdon,* ii. 173. John of Worcester says Ingulf was consecrated as abbot by the bishop of Salisbury on 8 June 1130.

[3] Chartul. of St. Edmund's, Harl. MS. 743, fo. 60 *d.*

[4] John of Worcester, p. 30.

[5] He was at the English court in 1130 : Orderic, iii. 403.

[6] *Chartul. of Ramsey,* no. 167.

[7] Hen. of Huntingdon, p. 252 ; Chron.   [8] *Ibid.*

[9] Gervase of Canterbury (ed. Twysden), col. 1341.

[10] *Mon. Anglic.* i. 97 *b* ; iv. 528. See, below, a charter issued at Northampton, 8 September 1131.

[11] Chron.   [12] *Ibid.*

his farm of the lands formerly of Bishop Odo of Bayeux for 3s. 4d. expended in the repair of the drawbridge of Rochester in anticipation of the king's visit.[1]

616. Notification to Ansfrid (the sewer),[2] the sheriff and barons of Kent of the grant to the church of St. Andrew, Rochester, 'in dedicatione ipsius ecclesie ubi presens affui', of the manor of Boxley, to be held as beneficially as Geoffrey the king's chaplain had held it, and Ansfrid the clerk before him. It is attested by the primate and the bishops Gilbert of London, Alexander of Lincoln, and Siefrid of Chichester; at London.[3] [1130–1.]

18 May. Henry is at Arundel at Whitsuntide.[4]

617. Notification, addressed generally for England and the seaports, of the grant to the burgesses of Wilton that their gild merchant shall be free of toll and other imposts, as those of the burgesses of London and Winchester are. It is attested by Miles of Gloucester, Robert de Ver, and William de Pont (de l'Arche); at Clarendon.[5] [1127–33.]

William abbot of Gloucester resigns his abbey on account of old age and infirmity. Walter de Lascy, a monk of the same house, is elected in his stead, and is ordained by Simon bishop of Worcester on 3 nones of August next following; at Worcester.[6]

Serlo, a canon of Salisbury, is elected abbot of Cirencester.[7]

Aug.–Sept. Before Michaelmas[8] Henry takes passage to Normandy from Portsmouth.[9]

8 Sept. At the Nativity of St. Mary Henry is at Bec.[10]

14 Sept. Hugh, archbishop elect of Rouen, is consecrated by Richard bishop of Bayeux, on the feast of the Exaltation of the Holy Cross in the abbey church of St. Ouen, at Rouen, in the presence of (the king ? and) the Norman bishops.[11]

During the autumn Henry entertains his nephew, Theobald of Blois, count of Champagne, at Vernon-sur-Seine.[12]

618. Mandate to William de Aubigny to permit the church of Montebourg to enjoy certain land which had been given to it with the consent of the said William's father. It is attested by Robert earl of Gloucester; at Les Augerons ? ('apud Alg[eron]'), 'per W. Filiastrum'.[13] [1123–35.]

619. Writ addressed to the bishop of Salisbury and the ministers of England, Normandy, and the seaports in favour of the monks of Montebourg. It is attested by the earl of Gloucester; at Croix St. Leufroy.[14] [1123–35.]

620. Notification, addressed generally, of the settlement of a dispute before the king between the church of St. Mary, Evreux, and the monks

[1] *Rot. Mag. Pipae*, p. 64.   [2] *Ibid.* pp. 64 ff.

[3] *Mon. Anglic.* i. 178.   [4] *Annales Monast.* ii. 222.

[5] Wilton Municipal Charters, *Journ. of the Archaeolog. Assoc.* xvii. 311.

[6] John of Worcester, p. 30.   [7] *Ibid.* p. 31.

[8] ' Ad festivitatem Sancti Michaelis': Hen. of Huntingdon, p. 252; ' Mense Septembri': *Annals of Waverley.*

[9] *Rot. Mag. Pipae*, p. 125.   [10] *Annals of Waverley*, p. 222.

[11] *Ibid.*   [12] Orderic, iii. 118.

[13] MS. Lat. 10087, no. 13; *ante*, xxiv. 221, n. 13; Haskins, *Norman Institutions*, p. 102.   [14] Round, *Calendar*, no. 877.

of St. Evroul, made with the consent of Audin bishop of Evreux, Warin abbot of St. Evroul, and Peter abbot of Blois. It is attested by Hugh archbishop of Rouen, John bishop of Sées, Robert de Sigillo, Nigel nephew of the bishop (of Salisbury), John of Bayeux, Robert earl of Gloucester ' filio meo ', Geoffrey Fitz-Pain, and William Fitz-Odo ; at Vaudreuil (' apud Rodolium ').[1] [1130–1.]

621. Notification to the bishop of Salisbury, the barons of Wiltshire, and burgesses of Wilton, that the king has given Mara in Wilton to Peter the clerk of St. Martin, with all liberties. Attested by Nigel nephew of the bishop and Robert de Hai ; at Rouen.[2] [1123–35.]

621 A. Notification to the bishop of Salisbury, the sheriff, barons, &c., of Oxfordshire of the king's grant that Alexander bishop of Lincoln may give to Richard de Vernon an equitable exchange for his land required by the bishop for the enlargement of his park of Thame. It is attested by Nigel nephew of the bishop and Geoffrey Fitz-Pain ; at Rouen.[3] [1130–5.]

622. Notification, addressed generally, that the tithes of venison of the forest of Fécamp have been adjudged to Roger abbot of Fécamp and his proctors in the presence of the king and his barons. It is attested by Hugh archbishop of Rouen ; the bishops Audin of Evreux, John of Lisieux, and John of Sées ; Robert de Sigillo, Nigel nephew of the bishop (of Salisbury), Robert earl of Gloucester, William earl of Warenne, Waleran count of Meulan, Brien Fitz-Count, Robert de Hai, Hugh Bigot, William Martel, Richard Fitz-Urse, William Malcuind (' Malqd.'), William de Hastinges, Anselm de Frehelvill, Geoffrey de Culvervill, W(alter ?) de St. Martin, G. de St. Léger ; at Rouen.[4] [1130–1.]

623. Notification of a concord made between the king, (Roger) abbot of Fécamp, and Henry count of Eu concerning the claim of toll for stalls and the pontage of Winchelsea, which the count claimed against the abbot. It is attested as the last ; at Rouen.[5] [1130–1.]

624. Writ to Odo sheriff of Pembroke, ordering that the monks of Sées shall hold all their possessions in churches, lands, &c., as quietly as in the time of Arnulf and Bishop Wilfrid and Walter of Gloucester. [1128–35.][6]

625. Notification, addressed generally, that with the king's consent Roger abbot of Fécamp and his chapter have made an exchange with Nigel Fitz-William, nephew (*nepos*) of Robert earl of Gloucester, of land in Laleham (co. Midd.) for Nigel's land in Fécamp. It is attested by Roger bishop of Salisbury, Geoffrey the chancellor, Nigel nephew of the bishop of Salisbury, Roger the king's chaplain and nephew of the abbot of Fécamp, Robert earl of Gloucester ' filio meo ', Robert de Ver the constable, Brien Fitz-Count, William de Pont de l'Arche, William Martel, Richard Fitz-Urse, Robert Ghernet, Geoffrey de Maisnill, Ingram the abbot's sewer, Simon de Curci, William Palfridus, Osbert Octodenarius, and Robert Lamartra.[7] [Before June 1133.]

---

[1] Round, *Calendar*, no. 287.　　　　　　　　　[2] *Reg. S. Osmundi*, i. 349.

[3] Dean and Chapter of Lincoln, Regist. Antiquissimum, fo. 11, no. lxx, supplied by the Rev. Canon Foster.

[4] Round, *Calendar*, no. 122.　　　　　　　　　[5] *Ibid.*, no. 123.

[6] Modern copy in MS. Fr. 18953, fo. 45 ; Haskins, *Norman Institutions*, p. 305.

[7] Round, *Calendar*, no. 124, where it is dated 1134.

626. Oct.–Dec. Notification, addressed to the archbishop of Rouen and generally for Normandy, of the confirmation to the priory of St. Mary, Le Desert, of certain privileges and possessions. It is attested by the bishops John of Lisieux and Audin of Evreux, Robert earl of Gloucester, William earl of Warenne, Robert earl of Leicester, William count of Ponthieu, Robert de Ver (Wer), Robert de Vura (*sic* for Curci ?), Robert de Hay, Hugh Bigot, Hugh de Gurnai, William Fitz-Odo, and John the Marshal; at Rouen, A. incarn. D. 1130.[1]

627. Notification, addressed to the archbishop of Rouen and for Normandy generally, of the king's gift in alms of ten Rouen pounds yearly to (the leper hospital) of St. Mary Magdalen of Grand-Beaulieu at Chartres, payable by the treasurers at Michaelmas 'quando firme et pecunia mea colliguntur'. Attested by John bishop of Lisieux, Robert de Sigillo, Roger de Fécamp, Robert earl of Gloucester, Richard son of the earl, Robert de Ver, Robert de Curci, Geoffrey Fitz-Pain, Geoffrey de Mandeville, Robert de Neufbourg, and William de Roumare; at Rouen. [1123–31.] The charter having been burnt was renewed in 1135.[2]

628. Notification to the archbishop of Rouen, &c., of the grant to Odoin de Malpalet ('de Mala Palude') of the ministry of the king's pannetrie with livery in his court. It is attested by (John) bishop of Lisieux, William de H(el)ion, R(obert) de Ver, R(obert) de Curci, and John the Marshal;[3] at Montfort.[4] [1123–35.]

629. Mandate to the bishop of Coutances, the justices of Normandy, and all lords of whom the abbey of Montebourg holds land, ordering that the abbot and his church shall hold its possessions in peace like the abbey of Fécamp. Attested by Robert de Ver; at Rouen.[5] [1121–35.]

630. Notification to the archbishop of Rouen and the ministers of Normandy of the king's confirmation to Holy Trinity, Savigny, of land at Vengeons which Robert Fitz-Martin and Matilda his wife gave with the consent of Stephen count of Mortain, of whose fee it is, and of Richard earl of Chester, of whom Robert and his wife held it. It is attested by Robert earl of Gloucester, Brien Fitz-Count, and Geoffrey Fitz-Pain; at Quillebeuf ('Wellebeof').[6] [1123–8, 1130–1, or 1133–5.]

631. Notification, addressed generally, of the confirmation to Rainald abbot of Ramsey of the lands acquired by him during his abbacy. It is attested by Geoffrey the chancellor, Brien Fitz-Count, Geoffrey de Clinton, and Geoffrey Fitz-Pain; at Bonneville.[7] [1127–30.]

632. Writ addressed to John bishop of Lisieux, (Robert) earl of Gloucester, Ranulf earl of Chester, Robert de la Hai, and the ministers in whose bailiwicks the canons of Bayeux have lands, in favour of the said canons. It is attested by Robert de Sigillo and G(eoffrey) de Clinton; at Argentan.[8] [1127–32.]

---

[1] *Ibid.*, no. 411.

[2] *Cartulaire de la Léproserie du Grand-Beaulieu*, no. 1, from a *vidimus* of 1469; Haskins, *Norman Institutions*, p. 106.   [3] 'Martel': MS.

[4] Round, *Calendar*, no. 1280; Round, *The King's Serjeants*, pp. 199 ff.

[5] MS. Lat. 10087, no. 15; Haskins, *Norman Institutions*, p. 102.

[6] Round, *Calendar*, no. 797.

[7] *Chartul. of Ramsey*, no. 166. See no. 595 above.

[8] Round, *Calendar*, no. 1436.

633. Notification, addressed to the sheriffs, &c., of Normandy and to the provost, officers, and burgesses of Argentan, of the king's grant of a house-plot (*unam mansuram terre*) in Argentan, in the ditch between the burgh and the causeway, to Robert and Hamelin his *loricarii*. Attested by R(obert) de Curci, the marshals John and Wigan, and Rainald Fitz-Count ; at Argentan.[1] [*c.* 1130–5.]

20 Dec. Rainald abbot of Ramsey dies on 13 kalends of January.[2]

1131.

13 Jan. Henry has an interview with Pope Innocent II at Chartres on the ides of January.[3] This is said to have been due to the influence of St. Bernard.[4]

635. 13 Jan. Notification to the archbishops of Canterbury and York, the bishops of London and Winchester, &c., of the grant to the abbey of Fontevrault of 60 marks yearly from the farm of London, and 40 marks yearly from that of Winchester. It is attested by Hugh archbishop of Rouen ; the bishops John of Lisieux, John of Sées, Audin of Evreux, and Richard of Bayeux ; Robert de Sigillo, Count Theobald, Robert earl of Gloucester, William earl of Warenne, Rabel de Tancarvill, Hugh Bigot, Brien Fitz-Count, Geoffrey de Clinton, and Andrew de Baldimento ; at Chartres on the octave of the Epiphany.[5]

636. Writ, addressed generally, in favour of the monks of Troarn. It is attested by Robert de Ver and John the Marshal ; at Caen.[6] [1127–35.]

638. Writ, addressed to R(abel) de Tancarvill and the barons and lieges of Caux, concerning the recent removal of the market of the abbot of St. Wandrille from that place to Caudebec. It is attested by Robert de Ver and William Fitz-Odo ; at St. Wandrille.[7] [1130–5.]

5 Feb. At Rouen on the feast of St. Agatha the king confirms to Bernard the abbey of St. Michel. Richard, the preceding abbot, had died on 12 January.[8]

639. Notification, addressed to the archbishop of Rouen and the bishops, barons, &c., of Normandy, that the king has granted in alms to the martyrs Gervase and Protase and the bishop of Sées the whole fief of William Goth at Laleu as he held it in the days of the king's father. This fee Henry had bought from Aveline niece of William and from Richard de Lucy her son and the heirs, they having rendered it to Robert son of the earl of Gloucester and afterwards quit-claimed the same in the king's presence. Confirmed in the sight and hearing of Hugh archbishop of Rouen ; the bishops John of Lisieux, Audin of Evreux, Richard of Bayeux, and John of Sées ; and Robert de Sigillo, Nigel nephew of the bishop of Salisbury, Robert earl of Gloucester the king's son, William earl of Warenne, Waleran count of Meulan, Robert earl of Leicester; Robert de Hay and Hugh Bigot, sewers,

---

[1] From the original, MS. Lat. 10083, no. 4 ; Haskins, *Norman Institutions*, p. 306.

[2] John of Worcester, p. 31 n. ' Post Pascha ' (1131) : Hen. of Huntingdon, p. 252.

[3] Hen. of Huntingdon, p. 252 ; Orderic, v. 25.

[4] See his Lives in *Opera* (ed. Migne), ff. 1094, 1156. Bernard attested a charter cited below, no. 640.

[5] Round, *Calendar*, no. 1460.

[6] *Ibid.* no. 479.   [7] *Ibid.* no. 169.

[8] *Neustria Pia*, p. 387, citing Codex S. Mich., fo. 79.

Rabel [de Tancarvill] the chamberlain, Brien Fitz-Count the constable, and Geoffrey de Clinton ; at Rouen, February, 1131.[1]

May. Henry meets Pope Innocent at Rouen.[2]

640. Notification, addressed generally, of the grant to St. Peter's, Cluny, of 60 marks yearly out of the farm of the city of London and 40 marks yearly out of the farm of the city of Lincoln. Pope Innocent, at the king's request, has confirmed this gift. The signatories are : King Henry and Matilda the empress, his daughter.[3] Done at Rouen, A. incarnat. D. 1131, indiction 9, in the month of May, on Sunday, in the presence of Pope Innocent II ; the archbishops Oldegar of Tarragona and Hugh of Rouen ; the bishops Geoffrey of Chartres, John of Lisieux, and John of Sées ; the abbots Bernard of Clairvaux, Suger of St. Denis, and Bozon of St. Bachus (Angers) ; William earl of Warenne, Robert earl of Gloucester the king's son, Robert de Sigillo, Robert de la Hai, Rabel the chamberlain of Tancarvill, Nigel (' Nahelis ') the treasurer, and Halo prior of St. Oswald's (Gloucester).[4]

641. Writ to the archbishop of Rouen and the bishops and barons of Normandy directing that the monks of St. Peter (Saint-Père) of Chartres shall hold their churches, lands, &c., as beneficially as in the days of the king's father. Witness, the bishop of Lisieux ; at Rouen.[5] [1107–35.]

642. Confirmation of gifts made by Robert de Brus to the canons of Guisborough, co. York. The signatories are : the king, Archbishop Thurstan, Geoffrey Fitz-Pain, the count of Ou (*sic*), William de Vernun, W. (*sic*) the chamberlain of Tancarvill, Robert de Novo Burgo, Roger de Toeni, Rabel, and William the butler.[6] [1129–35.]

643. Notification, addressed to R(ichard) bishop of Coutances and the sheriffs, &c., of the Cotentin, of the king's confirmation to the abbey of Montebourg of the church of Montfarville (Manche) with its fair and tithes, given by Samson de Montfarville with the consent of his lord Robert de Neubourg. Attested by the said Robert and William de Aubigny ; at Rouen.[7] [1124–31.]

644. Confirmation of various grants of alms made to the monastery of St. Ouen, Conches, by Roger de Toesni the elder, and others. The signatories are : the king and Queen Adelaide, Hugh archbishop of Rouen, Audin bishop of Evreux, William earl of Warenne, Amaury count of Evreux, Hugh ' cognominatus Hugoh ' the king's sewer, Roger de Toesni (' de Totteneio '), the prior of St. Oswald's (Gloucester), Robert de Neubourg, and Geoffrey Fitz-Pain.[8]

645. Notification to Hugh archbishop of Rouen, John bishop of Lisieux, the bishops and barons of Normandy, of the confirmation of various grants

---

[1] Copy made from the *Livre rouge* of Sées, fo. 77 (MS. Lat. 11058, fo. 3) ; Haskins, *Norman Institutions*, p. 299.

[2] Continuator of William of Jumièges ; William of Malmesbury, *Hist. Novella*, lib. i. 454.

[3] Round, *Calendar*, no. 1387.   [4] *Ibid.* no. 1388.

[5] Original in MS. Lat. 9221, no. 7 ; Haskins, *Norman Institutions*, p. 304.

[6] Original in the library of Hornby Chapel, co. Lancs. (the seal sewn up in a bag) : *Early Yorkshire Charters*, no. 671. Dubious.

[7] MS. Lat. 10087, no. 10 ; Haskins, *Norman Institutions*, p. 101.

[8] *Gallia Christ.* xi, instr., col. 128.

made to St. Martin's, Ecajeul, by William the chamberlain of Tancarvill and Rabel his son and others. The signatories are : the king and queen, John bishop of Lisieux, Rabel (de Tancarvill) the chamberlain, Thurstan archbishop of York, (Robert) earl of Gloucester, William earl of Warenne, Robert earl of Leicester, and Pain Peverel.[1] [1129–35.]

646. Writ, addressed generally for England and Normandy, in favour of the prior and convent of Bruton. It is attested by Robert de Ver and John the Marshal ; at Rouen.[2] [1127–35.]

2 July. Geoffrey abbot of Tavistock dies on 6 nones of July.[3]

13 July. William abbot of St. Peter's, Gloucester, dies on 3 ides of July.[4]

647. Notification, addressed to the archbishop of Rouen and the sheriffs and lieges of Normandy, of the king's confirmation to St. Mary's of Bec of the lands and goods which William Pevr(el) had given in alms in Touffreville (Turfreivilla), saving the right (if any) of William's kinsfolk therein. Attested by R(obert) de Sigillo, G(eoffrey) Fitz-Pain, and A(nselm) the sheriff ; at Rouen.[5] [1120–35.]

648. July–Aug. Confirmation to the abbey of Bec, made in the presence of Hugh archbishop of Rouen ; the bishops John of Lisieux, Audin of Evreux, and John of Sées ; Robert de Sigillo, Nigel nephew of Roger bishop of Salisbury, Robert earl of Gloucester, William earl of Warenne, Waleran count of Meulan, patron of the abbey, Robert earl of Leicester, Walter Gifard, Rabel de Tancarvill, Brien Fitz-Count, Hugh Bigot the sewer, Robert de la Hai the sewer, Humphrey de Bohun the sewer, William Fitz-Odo the constable, William de Roumare, Henry de Pomerey, and Geoffrey Fitz-Pain. ' Peracta feliciter apud Archas in transitu meo in Angliam, anno ab incarnatione Iesu Christi M.C.XXXI et regni mei XXXI.' [6]

649. Confirmation of various gifts made to St. Georges, Bocherville. It is attested by John bishop of Lisieux, Robert de la Hai, and Geoffrey Fitz-Pain ; at Arques, ' in transitu meo '.[7]

650. Notification to the justices of Normandy, the sheriff, barons, and burgesses of Rouen, of the confirmation to the cordwainers and shoe-makers of Rouen of their gild. It is attested by Robert de la Hay and William Mauduit ; at Arques, ' in transitu meo '.[8]

651. Notification to the archbishop of Rouen, the justiciary and sheriff of Arques, and the barons of Normandy of a grant to the monks of St. Lawrence of Envermeu. It is attested by Robert de la Hai, Brien Fitz-Count, William Martel, William Fitz-Odo, Humphrey de Buthun, Robert sheriff of Arques, and Walkeline Maminoth ; at Arques.[9]

652. Aug. Notification to the archbishop of Rouen and his ministers of Normandy of the grant to St. Wandrille and Abbot Alan of a market on Saturday at St. Wandrille and on Sunday at Caudebec. It is attested

---

[1] Round, *Calendar*, no. 569.

[2] *Cal. of Chart. Rolls*, iii. 270.　　　　　　　　[3] *Mon. Anglic.* ii. 490 *b*.

[4] *Chartul. of St. Peter's, Gloucester*, i. 15.

[5] Bec Chartulary (fragment) in Archives of the Eure, H. 91, fo. 35 ; Haskins, *Norman Institutions*, p. 306.　　　　　　　[6] Round, *Calendar*, no. 373.

[7] *Ibid.* no. 197.　　　　[8] *Ibid.* no. 107.　　　　[9] *Ibid.* no. 398.

by John bishop of Lisieux, Audin bishop of Evreux, Robert de Sigillo, Henry count of Eu, Robert de la Hai, Geoffrey Fitz-Pain, and Anselm the sheriff ; at Dieppe, ' in transitu meo '.[1]

653. Confirmation to the church of Sées, made at Dieppe, A. incarnat. D. 1131, ' me Henrico in Anglia regnante et Normannorum ducatum tenente, Innocentio papa secundo Ausonie cathedre presidente'. The signatories are : Hugh archbishop of Rouen, Audin bishop of Evreux, John bishop of Lisieux, Robert de Hai the sewer, Humphrey de Bohun the sewer, Rabel the chamberlain, William Fitz-Odo the constable, and William Mauduit the chamberlain.[2]

After 1 Aug. After the feast of St. Peter *ad Vincula* Henry returns to England [3] accompanied by his daughter, the Empress Matilda,[4] who has quarrelled with her husband, Geoffrey of Anjou.

654. Notification, addressed generally, that on the occasion of the dedication of the church of the martyrs Gervase and Protase of Sées the king has granted, for the use of the canons, 10 librates of land at Bristelmetonam (Brighthampton), a member of the manor of Benton (Bampton), free of hidage, gelds, &c., with soc and sac and other liberties. Attested by the archbishops William of Canterbury and Thurstan of York ; the bishops Alexander of Lincoln, Henry of Winchester, Gilbert of London, and Roger of Salisbury ; Geoffrey the chancellor, Robert de Sigillo, Robert earl of Gloucester, Waleran count of Meulan, Hugh Bigot and Humphrey de Bohun sewers, Miles of Gloucester, Robert de Ollei, Payn Fitz-John, Eustace Fitz-John, Henry de Ferrers, Geoffrey Fitz-Pain, and Richard Basset ; at Waltham, 1131.[5]

30 Aug. Hervey bishop of Ely dies on 3 kalends of September.[6]

8 Sept. On the Nativity of St. Mary a great court of pleas is held at Northampton before the king, at which the magnates of the kingdom are assembled. It is here decided that the king's daughter shall return to the count of Anjou, who is requesting her to return.[7]

655. Notification, addressed generally, that the church of Malmesbury, formerly the see of the bishop of Wiltshire, shall be rendered to the bishop of Salisbury. This is done in the council at Northampton, on the feast of the Nativity of St. Mary, in the presence and hearing of Peter Ruffus, cardinal priest of the holy Roman church, and of these under-written, who approve of the same, namely : the archbishops William of Canterbury and Thurstan of York ; the bishops Gilbert of London, Henry of Winchester, Alexander of Lincoln, John of Rochester, Siefrid of Chichester, William of Exeter, Robert of Hereford, Simon of Worcester, Roger of Chester, and Evrard of Norwich ; the abbots Ancher (*recte* Ansger) of Reading, Ingulf of Abingdon, Walter of Gloucester, Geoffrey of St. Albans,

---

[1] Round, *Calendar*, no. 168 ; *Neustria Pia*, p. 173.

[2] Library of Alençon, MS. 177, fo. 99 ; Haskins, *Norman Institutions*, pp. 300-2.

[3] Chron.   [4] Hen. of Huntingdon, p. 252.

[5] Copy in *Livre rouge* of Sées, fo. 71 ; Haskins, *Norman Institutions*, p. 302.

[6] John of Worcester, p. 31 n. ; ' at the beginning of winter ' : Hen. of Huntingdon, p. 252.

[7] Hen. of Huntingdon, p. 252. William of Malmesbury records a renewal of fealty to the Empress Matilda at this council : *Hist. Novella*, lib. i. 455.

Herbert of Westminster, Warner of Battle, and Hugh of St. Augustine's, Canterbury ; Geoffrey the chancellor, Robert de Sigillo, Nigel nephew of the bishop of Salisbury ; the earls Robert of Gloucester, William of Warenne, Ranulf of Chester, Robert of Leicester, and Roger of Warwick ; Brien Fitz-Count, Miles of Gloucester, Hugh Bigod, Humphrey de Bohun, Pain Fitz-John, Geoffrey de Clinton, William de Pont de l'Arche, Richard Basset, Aubrey de Ver, Richard Fitz-Gilbert, Roger Fitz-Richard, Walter Fitz-Richard, Walter de Gant, Robert de Ferrers, William Peverel of Nottingham, Baldwin de Redvers, Walter of Salisbury, William de Moion, and Robert de Arundel.[1]

656. Confirmation of the grant by Queen Matilda to the church of St. Mary, Salisbury, of her right in the toll of the market at Salisbury ; [2] and of property in Salisbury given by Agnes the wife of Hubert de Ria, Henry her son, and Croc the huntsman. It is attested by William archbishop of Canterbury; the bishops Gilbert of London and Alexander of Lincoln ; the abbots Anscher of Reading and Ingulf of Abingdon ; Geoffrey the chancellor, Geoffrey de Clinton, William de Pont de l'Arche, and Richard Basset ; at Northampton.[3]

657. Notification, addressed generally, of the grant to the abbey of Cluny of 50 marks yearly from the farm of the city of London and the like sum from the farm of the city of Lincoln. It is attested by the archbishops William and Thurstan ; the bishops Roger of Salisbury, Henry of Winchester, Alexander of Lincoln, and Gilbert of London ; Geoffrey the chancellor, Robert de Sigillo, Robert earl of Gloucester, Brien (Fitz-Count), Hugh Bigot the sewer, Miles of Gloucester, and Pain Fitz-John ; at Northampton.[4]

658. Writ to the sheriff of Norfolk to render to A(nselm ?) abbot of St. Bennet's, Holme, the land late of Adam the sewer, which had been quit-claimed before the justices, Aubrey de Ver and Robert Fitz-Walter, in Norfolk. It is attested by Robert Avenel; at Northampton.[5] [1131–3.]

659. Notification to Alexander bishop of Lincoln, R(ichard) Basset and Aubrey de Ver, and the lieges of Huntingdonshire of the confirmation to St. Mary's, Thorney, of the grant of a market at Yaxley. It is attested by Geoffrey the chancellor, William de Aubigny the Breton, R(ichard) Basset, and Baldwin Fitz-Gilbert ; at Brampton.[6] [1129–33.]

660. Grant to William archbishop of Canterbury and Christ's Church, Canterbury, of the (priory and) church of St. Martin, Dover. It is attested by the archbishops Thurstan of York and Hugh of Rouen ; the bishops Roger of Salisbury, Henry of Winchester, Gilbert of London, William of Exeter, Robert of Hereford, Alexander of Lincoln, Simon of Worcester, Evrard of Norwich, and Godfrey of Bath ; Geoffrey the chancellor,

---

[1] *Sarum Charters and Documents* (Rolls Ser.), p. 6.

[2] Cf. *Rot. Mag. Pipae*, p. 13.   [3] *Reg. of St. Osmund*, i. 202.

[4] Round, *Calendar*, no. 1389 ; *Chartul. of Montacute* (Somerset Rec. Soc.), no. 192. Cf. *ibid.* no. 193.

[5] Chartul. of St. Bennet's, Holme, Cott. MS., Galba E. ii, fo. 33 *d*.

[6] *Cal. of Chart. Rolls*, i. 65 ; Cott. MS., Aug. ii, fo. 12. Henry I and Queen Matilda wore their crowns on three several occasions in the timber-built chapel at Brampton, co. Hunt. : *Abbrev. Placit.* (Rec. Comm.), p. 95. Possible dates for these visits are Whitsuntide in 1103, 1111, and 1114.

Robert de Sigillo, Nigel nephew of the bishop (of Salisbury), Robert earl of Gloucester, William earl of Warenne, Ranulf earl of Chester, Robert earl of Leicester, Brien Fitz-Count, Hugh Bigot, Humphrey de Bohun, Miles of Gloucester, Pain Fitz-John, Richard Fitz-Gilbert, Robert de Ver, Robert de Essex, Richard Basset, and Aubrey de Ver. 'Apud Northamptonam data et concessa, sed apud Westmonasterium confirmata, communi celebrato consilio, anno ab incarnatione Domini millesimo C. tricesimo primo feliciter in Christo Iesu, domino nostro, Amen.' [1]

661. Notification, addressed generally, of the grant to William Maledoce (i.e. Mauduit), the king's chamberlain, of the land of Michael de Hamslape, which the said Michael held at his death, and of which he made the king his heir, with Matilda his daughter, whom the king gives to William to wife. It is attested by the archbishops William of Canterbury and Thurstan of York ; the bishops Evrard of Norwich, Roger of Salisbury, and Alexander of Lincoln ; Geoffrey the chancellor, Robert de Sigillo, Robert earl of Gloucester, William earl of Warenne, Ranulf earl of Chester, Roger earl of Warwick, Robert earl of Leicester, Brien Fitz-Count, Rabel de Tancarvill, Robert de Ver, Hugh Bigot, Humphrey de Bohun, Aubrey de Ver, Richard Basset, Geoffrey Fitz-Pain, Robert de Essex ; William de Montefichet, Hamon de St. Clare, R(oger) de Valoignes, Drew de Monci, William Fitz-Odo, Robert de (*sic*) Avenel, and R(obert) de Curci ; at London.[2]

662. Notification, addressed generally, of the confirmation to St. Mary's, Evreux, of the gift made by Audin bishop of Evreux of the land of Bramford in Suffolk. It is attested by the archbishops Thurstan of York and Hugh of Rouen ; Bernard bishop of St. David's and Henry bishop of Winchester ; William earl of Warenne, Stephen count of Mortain, Miles of Gloucester, Pain Fitz-John, and Geoffrey Fitz-Pain.[3] [1131–3.]

663. Writ in favour of the monks of Ramsey directing that they and their men shall be quit of toll on goods for their own use. It is attested by William de Rumare ; at Buckingham.[4] [1121–33.]

664. Notification, addressed generally, of the confirmation to the abbey of Cluny of certain manors in England which had been given by Ernulf de Hesdin.[5] It is attested by Hugh archbishop of Rouen, Thurstan archbishop of York ; the bishops Henry of Winchester, Roger of Salisbury, Alexander of Lincoln, and Bernard of St. David's ; Geoffrey the chancellor, Robert earl of Gloucester, and Brien Fitz-Count ; at Woodstock.[6] [1131–3.]

664 A. Confirmation to the monks of Tirun of land in Nately and Mapledurwell (co. Hants) granted to them by Adam de Port, which grant has been confirmed by Adam's wife and sons. It is attested by Bernard bishop of St. David's, John of Bayeux, Robert earl of Gloucester, and Robert Fitz-Martin ; at Woodstock.[7] [1131–3.]

665. Writ to Richard Basset and Aubrey de Ver, the sheriff and barons

[1] *Mon. Anglic.* iv. 538, no. 7.   [2] Add. MS. 28024, fo. 21.
[3] Round, *Calendar*, no. 288.
[4] Chartul. of Ramsey, Vesp. E. ii, fo. 14.
[5] Cf. *Rot. Mag. Pipae*, p. 18.   [6] Round, *Calendar*, no. 1386.
[7] Original charter at Winchester College, supplied by the Rev. H. E. Salter.

of Nottinghamshire, to authorize a diversion of the king's highway in Newark by the bishop of Lincoln. It is attested by Geoffrey the chancellor and William de Aubigny the Breton ; at Woodstock.[1] [1129–33.]

666. Notification to the barons and lieges of Sussex and Middlesex that Herbert abbot of Westminster, before the barons of the exchequer, has by their judgement deraigned the land of Parham and Mapleford (co. Suffolk) against Herbert Fitz-Herbert, that Herbert shall no longer be able to claim anything therein, and that the abbot can hold it in his demesne if he so wills and do his will thereof. ' Et precipio,' &c. It is attested by the bishop of Salisbury ; at Woodstock.[2] [1121–33.]

25 Dec. At Christmas Henry is at Dunstable.[3]

1132.

667. Writ to Rualon sheriff (of Kent) and the reeve of Canterbury in favour of the canons of Colchester. It is attested by Geoffrey the chancellor ; at Colchester.[4] [1129–33.]

668. Writ to Hugh de Watervill and all barons, sheriffs, &c., through whose lands the ships of St. Edmund's carry his stone, notifying them that these ships and men have the king's peace. It is attested by Aubrey de Ver ; at St. Edmund's.[5] [c. 1129–33.]

669. Notification to Roger bishop of Salisbury and generally for Berkshire of the grant of liberty to Pain Peverel to give his daughter Matilda in marriage to Hugh son of Fulbert de Dover [6] with his manor of Shifford after his death. It is attested by William de Montefichet, Robert de Ferrers, William Fitz-Odo, Rotrou de Doli, William Le Sor(ell), Robert Pevrel brother of Matilda, William Pevrel, Hamon Pevrel, Hameline de Asnevill, Walter de Beauchamp, Pevrel de Beauchamp, William de Lusoriis, and Pain de Beauchamp ; at Waltham.[7] [1131–3.]

670. Notification to the bishop of London, Aubrey de Ver, and the barons of Essex of the grant to Eustace de Barenton, the king's serjeant, of the land late of Geoffrey the forester in Hatfield (Broad Oak), for the custody of the king's forest. It is attested by Robert de Sigillo, William de Montefichet, Aubrey de Ver, Robert de Ver, and Robert de Essex ; at London.[8] [1131–3.]

671. Notification, addressed to the archbishop of Canterbury and generally, of the grant to the king's citizens of London of (the *comitatus* of London and) Middlesex at farm for £300 per annum. It is attested by (Henry ?) bishop of Winchester, Robert Fitz-Richard (?), Hugh Bigot, Alfred de Toteneis, William (de) Aubigny, Herbert the king's chamberlain, William de Montfichet, Hasculf de Tani, John Belet, and Robert Fitz-Siward ; at Westminster.[9] [1131–3.]

---

[1] *Mon. Anglic.* vi. 1273, nos. 24 and 41.

[2] *Abbrev. Placit.* p. 84 *b* ; Robinson, *Gilbert Crispin*, p. 46.

[3] Hen. of Huntingdon, p. 253. [4] *Mon. Anglic.* vi. 106.

[5] Chartul. of St. Edmund's, Camb. Univ. Libr., fo. 24, no. 42.

[6] Cf. *Rot. Mag. Pipae*, p. 158. [7] *Cal. of Chart. Rolls*, iv. 266.

[8] Brit. Mus., Add. Ch. no. 28313 ; *Brit. Mus. Facsimiles of Charters*, no. 8.

[9] *Foedera* (Record Comm.), i. 11 ; Stubbs, *Select Charters*, p. 103. The date is after Michaelmas 1130. Cf. *Rot. Mag. Pipae*, pp. 143–4, 148.

10 April. At Easter Henry is at Woodstock.[1]

672. Writ addressed to the sheriffs of Norfolk and Suffolk in favour of the abbot of St. Edmund's. It is attested by Maurice of Windsor ; at Woodstock.[2] [1121–33.]

29 April. After Easter, namely on 3 kalends of May,[3] a great court of pleas is held at London at which numerous matters are considered, particularly a dispute between the bishops of St. David's and Llandaff concerning the boundaries of their respective dioceses.[4]

673. Notification to the justices, R(ichard) Basset and Aubrey de Ver, the burgesses of Norwich and ministers of Norfolk, of the grant of three-pence per diem from the farm of the county of Norfolk to the hospital of the poor of St. Paul, Norwich,[5] which Odlent used to have ; and mandate to the sheriff of Norfolk to pay the allowance out of his farm. It is attested by William de Warenne (*sic*), Hugh Bigot, Roger de Fécamp, R(obert) de Ver, and A(ubrey) de Ver ; at Westminster.[6] [1131–3.]

674. Notification to the bishop of Ely, the barons, justices, sheriffs, and lieges of Cambridgeshire that Bernard abbot of Ramsey [sometime] deraigned in the king's court at St. Ives, before the justiciary whom the king sent there,[7] against Pain Peverel the land of Stow and Girton ; this the king confirms and warrants.[8] It is attested by Roger bishop of Salisbury, Pain Fitz-John, and William de Houcton ; at Westminster.[9] [1121–33.]

27 July. On 6 kalends of August Robert earl of Gloucester is at Cardiff. He confirms to the monks of Montacute the gifts which Robert de la Hai gave to them.[10]

675. Notification to the bishop of Chester, N(icholas) de Staford, the barons, sheriffs, ministers, and lieges of Staffordshire, of the confirmation of a final concord made between the prior of Kenilworth and Hugh, the king's watchman (*vigilis*), concerning land in Walton (co. Staff.). It is attested by R(oger) bishop of Chester, Miles of Gloucester, Pain Fitz-John, Aubrey de Ver, William de Aubigny the Breton, and W(illiam) de Clinton ; at Beckenham (' Beccheham ').[11]

676. Notification to the justices, sheriffs, barons, foresters, and ministers of Surrey of the grant to the monks of Bermondsey of warren in their lands in Surrey. It is attested by Robert de Ver and Aubrey de Ver ; at Beckenham.[12]

---

[1] Hen. of Huntingdon, p. 253.

[2] Chartul. of St. Edmund's, Camb. Univ. Libr., fo. 25, no. 53.

[3] Chartul. of Kenilworth, Harl. MS. 3650, fo. 75 ? ; *Staffs. Collections* (Salt Soc.), ii. 206.

[4] Hen. of Huntingdon, p. 253.

[5] Not recorded in the Pipe Roll of 1130 ; but recorded in that of 1156 and in subsequent years.

[6] Cott. Roll, ii. 19 ; *Mon. Anglic.* vi. 700 *b* ; *Cal. of Chart. Rolls*, iii. 71.

[7] The plea mentioned belongs to the period 1102–7.

[8] Presumably after the death of Pain Peverel.

[9] *Chartul. of Ramsey*, no. 161.

[10] *Chartul. of Montacute* (Somerset Rec. Soc.), no. 165.

[11] Chartul. of Kenilworth, Harl. MS. 3650, fo. 75 ; *Staffs. Collections* (Salt. Soc.), ii. 207. See also Rot. Cott. (Brit. Mus.), xiii. 6, no. 5. The above document contains evidence that Geoffrey de Clinton, the elder, was dead : *Staffs. Collections*, ii. 195–209.

[12] *Cal. of Chart. Rolls*, iv. 182.

677. Notification to the archbishop of Rouen, the ministers and lieges of England and Normandy of a grant to the hospital of Falaise. It is attested by the bishops Roger of Salisbury, Henry of Winchester, and Alexander of Lincoln ; Geoffrey the chancellor, Robert de Sigillo, Robert earl of Gloucester, William earl of Warenne ; the sewers Hugh Bigot, Humphrey de Buhun, and R(obert) de Curci ; Geoffrey Fitz-Pain, Miles of Gloucester, Pain Fitz-John, R(ichard) Basset, and Aubrey de Ver ; at Marden ('apud Marendonam '), A. ab incarn. D. 1132.[1]

678. Notification, addressed generally, of the grant to Alexander, bishop of Lincoln, of the manor of Biggleswade. It is attested by Roger bishop of Salisbury, Geoffrey the chancellor, Nigel nephew of the bishop (of Salisbury), Robert de Sigillo, Robert de Ver the constable, Humphrey de Bohun the sewer, and William de Pont de l'Arche the chamberlain ; at Gillingham, A. ab incarn. D. 1132.[2]

25 Dec. At Christmas Henry is at Windsor. He is suffering from a disorder.[3]

1133.

679. Confirmation to the nascent monastery of Rievaulx of the gifts made by Walter Espec. It is attested by William archbishop of Canterbury ; the bishops Roger of Salisbury, Alexander of Lincoln, Henry of Winchester, Robert of Hereford, Bernard of St. David's, John of Rochester, Algar of Coutances, and John of Sées ; Geoffrey abbot of St. Albans, Robert de Sigillo, Nigel nephew of the bishop (of Salisbury), Robert earl of Gloucester, William earl of Warenne, Stephen count of Mortain, Ranulf earl of Chester, Robert earl of Leicester, Miles of Gloucester, Humphrey de Bohun, Robert de Curci, Eustace Fitz-John and Pain his brother, William Maltravers, Geoffrey Fitz-Pain, Jordan Painel, and Aubrey de Ver ; at Windsor near the house of Gundewin the tent-keeper (*cortinarius*[4]) at the edge of the wood, A. incarnat. D. 1133.[5]

680. Writ addressed to William de Pont de l'Arche and the collectors of Winchester, directing that the land of Hyde and of the exchange of the abbey of Winchester shall be quit of geld, as the land of the abbey was quit where it used to stand, and especially of the geld of 400 marks. It is attested by Roger bishop of Salisbury ; at Windsor ; also by William the abbot [of Chertsey ?].[6] [1127–33.]

681. Notification to the bishop of Salisbury, the chancellor and the barons of the exchequer, of the release to the Cistercian monks of Rievaulx of 2*s.* of Danegeld, 'id est Themanetale', upon 9 carucates of land given by Walter Espec from his demesne. It is attested by the archbishop of Canterbury and the bishops of Coutances and Sées ; at Windsor.[7] [1131–3.]

---

[1] Round, *Calendar*, no. 609.

[2] *Mon. Anglic.* vi. 1271, no. 7 ; *ante*, xxxiii. 726.

[3] Hen. of Huntingdon, p. 253.

[4] See the ' constitutio domus Regis ' in *Red Book of the Exchequer* (Rolls Ser.), iii. 813.

[5] *Chartul. of Rievaulx* (Surtees Soc.), no. 194.

[6] *Mon. Anglic.* ii. 445, no. 14.

[7] *Chartul. of Rievaulx* (Surtees Soc.), no. 196. This writ (*breve regis*) was necessary to the sheriff of York when discharging his account of the Danegeld at the exchequer.

8 Feb. 'Ad caput ieiunii' a court is held in London for the further hearing of the dispute between the bishops of St. David's and Llandaff ; and that between the archbishop (of Canterbury) and the bishop of Lincoln.[1]

682. Notification, addressed to William archbishop of Canterbury, Gilbert bishop of London, the citizens of London, and generally, of the king's grant to the church of St. Bartholomew, London, and Prior Rahere of various privileges and immunities. It is attested by the bishops Henry of Winchester, Roger of Salisbury, and Bernard of St. David's ; Geoffrey the chancellor, Stephen count of Mortain, William de Aubigny the Breton, Aubrey de Ver, Richard Basset, Miles of Gloucester, Pain Fitz-John, Robert de Curci, Hugh Bigot, ' and many other barons of my kingdom ' ; at Westminster, A. incarnat. D. 1133, and the thirty-third year of the king's reign.[2]

683. Notification, addressed to the citizens of London and generally, of the king's grant that the church which Prior Rahere, his clerk, has founded is to be free, as one of the king's demesne chapels. It is attested by Henry bishop of Winchester, Geoffrey the chancellor, Stephen count of Mortain, Aubrey de Ver, Richard Basset, and Miles of Gloucester ; at Westminster.[3] [1129–33.]

684. Notification to Richard Basset, Aubrey de Ver, and the sheriffs, &c., of Norfolk, of the grant of 100*s.* yearly from the hundreds of Walsham and Blofield to Evrard bishop of Norwich, in exchange for the church of Stinton. It is attested by the chancellor, Robert de Sigillo, Richard Basset, and Aubrey de Ver ; at Westminster.[4] [1129–33.]

685. Notification, addressed generally, of the confirmation to the nuns of St. Mary's, Wikes, of gifts made by Walter Mascherel and Alexander his brother, at the prayer of Edith their sister. It is attested by Bernard bishop of St. David's, G(eoffrey) the chancellor, R(obert) de Sigillo, ... and William Maltravers ; at Westminster.[5] [1123–33.]

25 Mar. The Empress Matilda gives birth to a son at Le Mans.[6] He is named Henry.

26 Mar. At Easter Henry is at the New Hall in Oxford.[7]

686. Writ, addressed to Eustace Fitz-John and Walter Espec, in favour of the canons of St. Peter's, York. It is attested by Geoffrey the chancellor ; at Oxford.[8] [1129–33.]

Richard Fitz-Samson, bishop of Bayeux, dies during Easter week.[9]

30 April–3 May. At Rogationtide a council is held at Winchester to continue the consideration of the matters heard at the London court.[10]

687. Notification, addressed generally for Yorkshire, of the grant to Eustace Fitz-John of soc and other liberties in the manor of Brompton, near Pickering, which he holds of the fee of Roger de Mowbray, Robert

---

[1] Hen. of Huntington, p. 253.
[2] Cart. Antiq. roll L, no. 11 (1) ; *Mon. Anglic.* vi. 298.
[3] Add. MS. 34768, fo. 18.   [4] Cott. ch. ii. 4.
[5] *Facsimiles of National MSS.*, pt. i. no. 5 (of doubtful character).
[6] Robt. of Torigny, p. 123 ; Orderic, v. 46 n.
[7] Hen. of Huntingdon, p. 253.
[8] *Mon. Anglic.* vi. 1179, no. 18; Lansd. MS. 193.
[9] Orderic, iv. 18 n   [10] Hen. of Huntingdon, p. 253.

de l'Isle, and Roger de Clere. It is attested by Miles of Gloucester,
R(obert) de Curci, Pain Fitz-John, William de Aubigny the Breton, and
W(illiam) Fitz-John ; at Winchester.[1] [1129–33.]

688. Notification to the archbishop of Canterbury and generally that,
with the assent of William archbishop and legate and Alexander bishop
of Lincoln, an abbey for canons has been founded at Messenden in the fee
of William de Messenden. The king confirms this. It is attested by
William archbishop of Canterbury ; the bishops Henry of Winchester,
Alexander of Lincoln, Bernard of St. David's, and Robert of Hereford ;
Robert de Sigillo, Robert earl of Gloucester, William earl of Warenne,
Robert earl of Leicester, Miles of Gloucester, R(obert) de Curci, Aubrey
de Ver, R(ichard) Basset, and R(obert) de Ferrers ; at Winchester, A. ab
incarnat. D. 1133.[2]

689. Notification, addressed generally, of the confirmation to the canons
of Breamore of gifts made by Baldwin de Rivers and Hugh his uncle.
It is attested by Miles of Gloucester the constable, Pain Fitz-John, Richard
Basset, and William de Pont de l'Arche ; at Winchester.[3] [1127–33.]

690. Writ to Pain Fitz-John and the barons of Herefordshire in favour
of Robert bishop of Hereford as against Roger de Candos. It is attested
by Geoffrey the chancellor, Geoffrey Fitz-Pain, and William de Pont de
l'Arche ; at Winchester.[4] [1127–33.]

691. Notification to the bishop of Winchester, the justices, &c., of
Hampshire, of the grant to St. Peter's monastery, Bath, of the land of
Dogmersfield (co. Hants) with the church, as it was formerly held by
Ranulf bishop of Durham and afterwards by the king. It is attested by
Geoffrey the chancellor, Robert de Sigillo, R(obert) de Curci, R(obert)
de Ver, R(ichard) Basset, A(ubrey) de Ver, and W(illiam) de Aubigny the
Breton ; at Winchester.[5] [1129–33.]

692. Notification to the bishop of Lincoln, the justices, sheriffs, barons,
and lieges of Huntingdonshire, of the confirmation to the abbot and monks
of Ramsey of the manor of Walton, as it was given by Albreda, who was
the wife of Eustace de Scellea, of whose inheritance it was, and confirmed
by Walter de Bolebech, lord of that fee. It is attested by Brien Fitz-
Count, Miles of Gloucester, R(obert) de Curci, A(ubrey) de Ver, and
Eustace Fitz-John ; at Winchester.[6] [1129–33.]

693. Confirmation, addressed generally, in favour of the nuns of
Elstow. It is attested by the king (*sic*), T(hurstan) archbishop of York,
R(oger) bishop of Salisbury, John Fitz-John, and R(obert ?) de Brus ;
at Winchester.[7] [1120–33.]

28 May. After Whitsuntide, namely on 5 kalends of June,[8] Henry
gives the bishopric of Ely to Nigel, nephew of Roger bishop of Salisbury,[9]

---

[1] *Cal. of Close Rolls*, 1313–8, p. 287.

[2] *Chartul. of Missenden*, Harl. MS. 3688, fo. 188

[3] *Cal. of Chart. Rolls*, iv. 261.

[4] *Charters of Hereford Cathedral* (ed. Capes), p. 5.

[5] *Two Bath Chartularies* (Somerset Rec. Soc.), i, no. 55 ; *Dep. Keeper's Rep.* xxx.
app., p. 206.   [6] *Chartul. of Ramsey*, i. 157.

[7] *Mon. Anglic.* iii. 413, nos. 3 and 6 (of doubtful character).

[8] ' Apud Burnam ' (*sic*) : Hist. Eliensis, Vesp. A. xix, fo. 38.

[9] *Angl. Sacra*, i. 619 ; Hen. of Huntingdon, p. 253.

and that of Durham to Geoffrey Rufus, his chancellor.[1] He also creates a new bishopric at Carlisle[2] and nominates Adelwold, or Ailulf, prior of St. Oswald's, Nostel, as the first bishop.[3]

694. Notification to the archbishop of York, bishop of Durham, and the barons of Yorkshire and Northumberland of the restoration to William Fitz-Udard of Bamborough of the land which his father had held. It is attested by Eustace Fitz-John, Walter Espec, William de Pont de l'Arche, William Maled(octus), and W(alter ?) de Bolebec ; at Westminster.[4] [1131–3.]

695. June–July. Notification to the archbishop of York, bishop of Winchester, the justices, sheriffs, barons, and lieges of York and Hampshire, of the confirmation of a prebend in the church of St. Peter, York, for the benefit of William (Fitz-Herbert) the treasurer. It is attested by Thurstan archbishop of York, the bishops Roger of Salisbury and Nigel (elect) of Ely, Walter Espec, Eustace Fitz-John, and Geoffrey Fitz-Pain ; at Westminster.[5]

696. Notification, addressed generally, of the grant to Alexander bishop of Lincoln that he may assign a third part of the service of knights of the bishopric to perform castle-ward at Wark (i.e. Newark). It is attested by Roger bishop of Salisbury, Geoffrey the chancellor, and William de Pont de l'Arche ; at Blackmoor.[6] [1123–33.]

696 A. Notification to the barons, &c., of Lincolnshire, Rutland, and Northamptonshire, of the king's pardon to Alexander bishop of Lincoln of 300 marks for the pledging of Holme (' pro vadio de Holma '). It is attested by (Roger) bishop of Salisbury and Geoffrey the chancellor ; at Blackmoor (' Blachemora ').[7] [1123–33.]

697. June–July. Notification, addressed to the archbishop of Rouen and generally (for Normandy), of the grant to the church of St. John the Baptist and the hospital of Falaise of the gifts of Goinfrid and Robert his son. It is attested by the bishops Roger of Salisbury, Henry of Winchester, Alexander of Lincoln, John of Sées, Adelwold of Carlisle, Algar of Coutances, and Siefrid of Chichester ; Eudes abbot of Caen, Geoffrey the chancellor, Robert de Sigillo, Robert earl of Gloucester, William earl of Warenne, Robert earl of Leicester, Henry count of Eu, Hugh Bigot, Robert de Curci, Humphrey de Buhun, Robert de Ver, Miles of Gloucester, Geoffrey Fitz-Pain, Pain Fitz-John, Aubrey de Ver, Richard Basset, Hamon de Falaise, Henry de Pomerey, and William of Glastonbury ; at Winchester, A. ab incarnat. D. 1133.[8] [28 May–31 July 1133.]

698. July. Notification, addressed generally for England, of the grant to Aubrey de Ver and his heirs of the office of great chamberlain of all England (' magistram camerariam meam totius Anglie '), to hold by hereditary right, as beneficially as Robert Malet held it, ' with the liveries

---

[1] *Ibid.* [2] *Ibid.*

[3] John of Hexham, ii. 285.

[4] *Ancient Charters* (Pipe Roll Soc.), no. 19.

[5] Farrer, *Early Yorkshire Charters*, no. 132 ; *Mon. Anglic.* vi. 1179, no. 24.

[6] *Mon. Anglic.* vi. 1274, no. 44.

[7] Dean and Chapter of Lincoln, Reg. Antiquiss., fo. 11, no. lxix ; copy from the Rev. Canon Foster.

[8] Round, *Calendar*, no. 610.

and lodgings of my court which belong to the office of the chamberlain '. It is attested by Roger bishop of Salisbury, Geoffrey the chancellor (and) bishop of Durham, Nigel bishop of Ely, Robert de Sigillo, Robert earl of Gloucester, Brien Fitz-Count, Robert de Ver the constable, Humphrey de Bohun, Hugh Bigot, William de Aubigny the Breton, Richard Basset, and William de Pont de l'Arche ; at Fareham, 'in transfretatione regis '.[1] [Date as last.]

699. Notification to Henry bishop of Winchester, the sheriff, barons, and lieges of Surrey of the grant to William abbot of Chertsey of a fair at Chertsey. It is attested by Robert Avenel and W(illiam) Maltravers ; at Fareham.[2] [1129–33.]

700. Notification, addressed generally, of the grant to the bishop of London and the dean and canons of St. Paul's that, whereas the chief barons and citizens of London have a customary right to be buried in such church as they please and to have their own parish priest to accompany the corpse to the place of burial, this is to be observed, and particularly with regard to ' Cristeschirche '. It is attested by (Roger) bishop of Salisbury ; at Fareham.[3] [1130–3.]

701. Notification, addressed generally, of the grant to Alexander bishop of Lincoln that he may make a bridge over the Trent at his castle of Newark. It is attested by (Roger) bishop of Salisbury, (Geoffrey) the chancellor, and Eustace Fitz-John ; at Fareham.[4] [1130–3.]

702. Writ, addressed to the barons, vavasours, and lords of lands in Well wapentake, co. Lincoln, in favour of (Alexander ?) bishop of Lincoln. It is attested by (Roger ?) bishop of Salisbury and Geoffrey the chancellor ; at Fareham.[5] [1123–33.]

703. Writ, addressed generally, in favour of Siefrid bishop of Chichester. It is attested by Miles of Gloucester and Humphrey de Bohun ; at Fareham.[6] [1125–33.]

704. July–2 Aug. Notification, addressed generally, of the grant to St. Mary of Cirencester and Serlo the first abbot, made with the consent of Pope Innocent, of the land and churches of Reimbald the priest, saving the tenures of Roger bishop of Salisbury, William son of Warine the sheriff, and Nigel nephew of the bishop of Winchester (*sic*) for their respective lives. It is attested by the archbishops William of Canterbury and Thurstan of York ; the bishops Roger of Salisbury, Henry of Winchester, Alexander of Lincoln, Geoffrey of Durham, Nigel of Ely, Robert of Hereford, and John of Rochester ; Robert de Sigillo, Robert de Ver, Miles of Gloucester, Robert de Oilli, Hugh Bigot, Robert de Curci, Pain Fitz-John, Eustace and William his brothers, and William de Aubigny the Breton ; at Westbourne (' apud Burnam '), 'in transfretatione mea ', A. incarnat. D. 1133 and the thirty-third year of the king's reign.[7]

---

[1] Madox, *Baronia Angl.*, p. 158 ; *Hist. of Exchequer*, i. 56 n.

[2] Harl. Ch. 58, H. 37 ; *Mon. Anglic.* i. 432, no. 14.

[3] Cart. Antiq. roll N, no. 13 (19).

[4] *Mon. Anglic.* vi. 1274, nos. 42 and 47.   [5] *Ibid.* 1272, no. 19.

[6] Hist. MSS. Comm., *Various Coll.* i. 181 ; *Cal. of Chart. Rolls,* iv. 439 ; also a writ attested by Eustace Fitz-John, at Fareham   *ibid.*

[7] *Mon. Anglic.* vi. 177.

705. Notification, addressed generally, of the grant to William son of Walter de Beauchamp, the king's despenser, of the land which was his father's. It is attested by the archbishops William of Canterbury and Thurstan of York; the bishops Roger of Salisbury, Henry of Winchester, Alexander of Lincoln, Bernard of St. David's, Robert of Hereford, Siefrid of Chichester; Geoffrey the chancellor, Nigel nephew of the bishop (of Salisbury), Robert earl of Leicester, Robert de Ver, Miles of Gloucester, R(obert) de Curci, Hugh Bigot, Humphrey de Buhun, Pain Fitz-John, Eustace Fitz-John, Geoffrey Fitz-Pain, W(illiam) Maltravers, William de Aubigny the Breton, William de Pont de l'Arche, and W(illiam) Maled(octus); at Westbourne.[1]

706. Notification, addressed generally, of the confirmation of the gift made by Robert earl of Leicester of 5¾ carucates of land in Garendon ('Gerold.') to the monks of St. Mary's, Garendon. It is attested by the archbishops William of Canterbury and Thurstan of York; the bishops Roger of Salisbury, Henry of Winchester, and Alexander of Lincoln; and Geoffrey the chancellor.[2] [1129–33.]

707. Confirmation, addressed generally, in favour of the church of St. Mary, Porchester. It is attested by the bishops Henry of Winchester, Roger of Salisbury, Bernard of St. David's, Nigel elect of Ely, and Geoffrey elect of Durham; Brien Fitz-Count, Robert de Veer (*sic*), Hugh Bigot, Humphrey de Bohun, Aubrey de Ver, and Richard Basset; at Westbourne, ' in transfretatione mea '.[3]

708. Writ, addressed to William de Aubigny, William Fitz-Hacon the sheriff, the barons and lieges of Lincolnshire, in favour of Alexander bishop of Lincoln. It is attested by the bishops Roger of Salisbury and Nigel of Ely, Richard Basset, and Aubrey de Ver; at Westbourne.[4] [1130 or 1133.]

709. Writ addressed to the bishop of Norwich, Richard the archdeacon, Richard Basset, and Aubrey de Ver and their ministers directing that the canons of the king's alms of Gipeswich shall be impleaded touching the property of their church only before the bishop of Norwich, Richard Basset, and Aubrey de Ver. It is attested by Richard Basset; at Westbourne.[5] [1130 or 1133.]

710. Writ, addressed to Gilbert bishop of London, in favour of Holy Trinity priory, London. It is attested by the bishop of St. David's; at Westbourne.[6] [1129–33.]

711. Notification to the archbishop of Canterbury and Helewise the archdeacon of the confirmation to St. Augustine's, Canterbury, of certain churches and parishes which were held by Abbot Hugh I in the time of the archbishops Anselm and Ralph. It is attested by Robert de Veer (*sic*); at Westbourne.[7] [1130 or 1133.]

---

[1] Add. MS. 28024, fo. 127 *d*.

[2] Lansd. MS. 415, ff. 22 *d*, 23 *d*. The date assigned to the foundation of Garendon—28 October 1133—appears to be some months too late.

[3] *Mon. Anglic.* vi. 244.   [4] *Ibid.* 1274, no. 43.

[5] *Cal. of Pat. Rolls, 1334–8*, p. 476.

[6] *Ancient Charters* (Pipe Roll Soc.), no. 16.

[7] *Dep. Keeper's Rep.* xxx, app., p. 198, no. 12; *Hist. Monast. S. Augustini Cantuar.* p. 365.

712. Writ, addressed to W(illiam) de Pont de l'Arche[1] and his ministers of Westbourne ('Burn.'), directing them that Gilbert Chaylot shall hold the land in Chichester, late his father's, in as beneficial a manner as his said father held it. It is attested by Geoffrey Fitz-Pain; at Westbourne.[2] [1130 or 1133.]

713. Confirmation to the abbot and monks of Reading of the manor of Rowington ('Rokinton in Warwicsyre'), which Adelicia de Everei (or Iveri) gave them with the king's consent. A.D. 1133, 'peracta feliciter in Domino'.[3]

714. Writs, addressed (*a*) to Baldwin de Rivers and Pain the reeve of 'Hamton', and (*b*) to William de Pont de l'Arche and Pain the reeve of 'Hamton', directing them that the abbot and monks of Reading shall have the land which Robert the priest gave them, to hold as beneficially as the same Robert and Ketel his ancestor held it by another writ.[4] [1129–33.]

2 Aug. On Wednesday, 4 nones of August, being the day after Lammas, as Henry lay in the ship which was to carry him overseas to Normandy, there was an eclipse of the sun.[5]

715. Notification, addressed generally, of the confirmation to St. Mary's, Bec, of a gift made by Brien Fitz-Count and Matilda his wife, of the manor of Little Ogbourne (co. Wilts.). It is attested by Hugh archbishop of Rouen, Audin bishop of Evreux, Robert de Sigillo, Robert earl of Gloucester, Hugh Bigot, Humphrey de Buhun, Robert de Ver, Robert de Curci, and Geoffrey Fitz-Pain; at Rouen, A. incarnat. D. 1133.[6]

1134.

3 Feb. Robert 'Curtehose', late duke of the Normans, dies at Cardiff castle on 3 nones of February.[7]

716. Henry directs an inquiry to be made touching the fees of barons, &c., who hold fees of the church of St. Mary, Bayeux. This is done by Robert earl of Gloucester, the king's son, at Bayeux, after the death of Richard, late bishop of Bayeux.[8]

717. Writs to the respective sheriffs, barons, and ministers of Lincolnshire and Nottinghamshire in favour of Alexander, bishop of Lincoln. Both are attested by Geoffrey Fitz-Pain; at Arganchy ('Archenc.').[9] [1123–33.]

718. Notification, addressed to Hugh archbishop of Rouen and generally for Normandy, of the king's confirmation of a grant made by Enguerran Oison and William his son to the church of Sées, of three house-plots (*mansuras terre*) held of the bishop for building the houses of the canons

---

[1] *Firmarius* in 1129–30 of the honor of Arundel, of which Westbourne was a member, as also certain lands in Chichester: *Testa*, p. 227.

[2] Hist. MSS. Comm., *Various Coll.* i. 181.

[3] Chartul. of Reading, Harl. MS. 1708, fo. 18.   [4] *Ibid.* fo. 18 *d.*

[5] Chron.; John of Worcester, p. 37.   [6] Round, *Calendar*, no. 374.

[7] *Chartul. of St. Peter's, Gloucester*, i. 15.

[8] D'Anisy, *Archives de Calvados*, ii. 426.

[9] *Mon. Anglic.* vi. 1275, nos. 51–2; Vesp. E. xvi, fo. 10 *d.*

regular. The grant had been made when Enguerran the grantor's son had
been made a canon there, and confirmed before the king and his barons
at Sées. In return the bishop had given six oxen and a horse worth
100 shillings of Le Mans. It is attested by John bishop of Lisieux,
Geoffrey ('Galtero', MS.) Fitz-Pain, Jocelin de Bailleul, and Robert de
Sigillo ; at Sées.[1] [1133–5.]

719. Notification to Hugh archbishop of Rouen, &c., of the grant to
the abbey of St. Père-de-Chartres of certain tithes from Moulins. It is
attested by Hugh archbishop of Rouen, the bishops John of Lisieux and
Audin of Evreux, Stephen count of Mortain, and Robert earl of Gloucester ;
at Sées.[2] [1130–5.]

William archbishop of Canterbury and Alexander bishop of Lincoln
cross to Normandy to interview the king touching the dispute which
existed between them.[3]

720. Notification to the archbishop of Rouen and the ministers of
Normandy of the restoration to the church of Coutances and Bishop Algar
of the church of St. Mary of Alderney. It is attested by Matilda the
empress ; Hugh archbishop of Rouen ; the bishops Alexander of Lincoln,
Nigel of Ely, John of Sées, John of Lisieux, Adelwold of Carlisle, and
Audin of Evreux ; Robert earl of Leicester, Brien Fitz-Count, Robert de
Ver, Robert de Curci, Humphrey de Bohun, Hugh Bigot, R(obert ?)
Bertram, W(illiam) de Vernun, W(illiam) son of the earl (of Gloucester),
John (of Bayeux ?) 'Viariz' (*sic*) ; at Rouen, A. ab incarnat. D. 1134.[4]

After 15 April. On Low Sunday the monks of Belmont removed
to Mortemer in the forest of Lyons, and soon afterwards King Henry
visited them, and gave them land for a grange and various liberties.[5]

721. The king sends letters to the clergy and laity of the bishopric of
Lincoln touching the settlement of a dispute made before the king, the
bishops, barons, and all the court between the abbot of Peterborough and
the bishop of Lincoln concerning the parish church of Peterborough.
They are attested by Adelwold bishop of Carlisle, Robert de Sigillo,
Robert earl of Gloucester, William earl of Warenne, and Brien Fitz-
Count ; at Rouen.[6]

722. Notification to the ministers of Normandy and Rouen of the grant
to Audin ('Oyno') bishop of Evreux of property at Rouen. It is attested
by Adelwold bishop of Carlisle, (Robert) earl of Leicester, Roger de Fécamp,
William de Ely, and Ralph de Hastinges ; at Rouen.[7]

May. Geoffrey, second son of Matilda and Geoffrey of Anjou, was born
at Rouen at Pentecost.[8]

723. Publication of an enactment, addressed to the archbishop of
Rouen and his ministers in Normandy, in favour of the abbey of Bec.
It is attested by the bishops Audin of Evreux, Adelwold of Carlisle,
and Siefrid of Chichester ; Robert de Ver, Robert de Curci, Hugh Bigot,

---

[1] Copies in MS. Alençon 177, fo. 104, and *Livre rouge*, fo. 71 *d* ; Haskins, *Norman
Institutions*, p. 307.

[2] Round, *Calendar*, no. 1258.   [3] *Annals of Waverley*, p. 224.
[4] Round, *Calendar*, no. 959.   [5] *Gallia Christ.* xi. 308.
[6] *Mon. Anglic.* vi. 1275, no. 50 ; *ante*, xxiii. 726 ; Vesp. E. xvi, fo. 9 *d*, no. 33.
[7] Round, *Calendar*, no. 289.   [8] Rob. of Torigny, *s. a.*

Robert de la Hai, Brien Fitz-Count, Geoffrey Fitz-Pain, Drew de Moncei, and Baldwin Fitz-Gilbert ; at Rouen, A. incarnat. D. 1134.[1]

724. Mandate to the justices of the Cotentin, to William de Bruis and the foresters, to permit the monks of Montebourg to take trees for firewood and building, also pannage, quit of all custom. The foresters shall be free of liability for the trees so taken, as far as warranted by the monks' tallies. Attested by Robert earl of Gloucester ; at Rouen. Issued by Robert de Hai. [1123–35.][2]

725. Notification, addressed to the archbishop of Rouen and the barons and justices of Normandy, of the king's confirmation to St. Mary's, Rouen, of liberties in the forest of Aliermont for the dean of that church and the canon of Angerville. Attested by John bishop of Lisieux and Robert the sheriff ; at Rouen. [1107–35.][3]

8 or 10 Aug. Gilbert bishop of London dies on his way to Rome ; as also does Urban bishop of Llandaff,[4] who has gone to Rome in connexion with his dispute with Bernard bishop of St. David's.

1–7 Sept. Verneuil is burned during the first week of September.[5]

726. Notification, addressed generally for Lincolnshire, of the grant to Ives the monk of Bardney of the abbey of Bardney with confirmation of the possessions which Walter de Gant has given. It is attested by Alexander bishop of Lincoln, John bishop of Lisieux, and Robert de la Hai ; at Verneuil, ' in expeditione '.[6]

727. Notification, addressed generally for Huntingdonshire, of the surrender made before the king by William de Houctone, his chamberlain, to the monastery of Ramsey and Abbot Walter of the manor of Bradenache. It is attested by the bishops John of Lisieux and (Adelwold) of Carlisle ; Robert de Sigillo, Roger de Fécamp, Robert earl of Gloucester, Aubrey de Ver, Robert de Ver, Robert de Curci, Hugh Bigot, Geoffrey Fitz-Pain, Geoffrey de Magnevill, William de Glastonbury, Robert Arundel, and G(eoffrey) de Fourneaux ; at Falaise.[7] [1133–5.]

728. Precept addressed to the justices, &c., of Normandy and the ports of the sea, directing that the nuns of St. Mary of Vilers (-Canivet) shall have freedom from toll, passage, and other customs for all their demesne goods. Attested by A(delwold) bishop of Carlisle, R(obert) earl of Gloucester, and R(obert) de Ver ; at Falaise. [1133–5.][8]

729. Notification to the justices of Normandy, the sheriff of Rouen, the barons and burgesses of Rouen, and the lieges of Normandy of the gift to Anselm, abbot of St. Edmund's, of one ' plectura ' of land at Rouen for a lodging, next that which the king gave to G(eoffrey) Fitz-Pain. It is attested by Adelwold bishop of Carlisle, Richard de Belfou, R(obert) de Curci, and A(ubrey) de Ver ; at Falaise.[9]

---

[1] Round, *Calendar*, no. 375.

[2] MS. Lat. 10087, no. 11 ; Haskins, *Norman Institutions*, p. 102

[3] Cartulaire de Philippe d'Alençon in the Archives of the Seine-Inférieure, G. 7, p. 792 ; Haskins, *Norman Institutions*, p. 305. See Round, *Calendar*, no. 8.

[4] Hen. of Huntingdon, p. 253 ; Le Neve, *Fasti*.   [5] Orderic, v. 41.

[6] *Cal. of Pat. Rolls, 1377–81*, p. 399.   [7] *Chartul. of Ramsey*, no. 182.

[8] Original in the Archives of Calvados, nos. 47–66 ; *vidimus* of the bishop of Sées, *ibid.* no. 48 ; Haskins, *Norman Institutions*, p. 308.

[9] Chartul. of St. Edmund's, Camb. Univ. Libr., fo. 25 d, no. 55 ; Add. MS. 14847, fo. 34 d.

730. Notification to the bishop of Norwich, the barons, &c., of Suffolk, of the render and confirmation to Aubrey de Danmartin of his father's land. It is attested by Robert earl of Gloucester, Stephen count of Mortain, Brien Fitz-Count, R(obert) de Ver, and Humphrey de Bohun; at Argentan ('apud Arg.').[1] [1123–35.]

731. Writ, addressed to the barons, &c., of Normandy, directing that the monks of Troarn shall not be impleaded concerning the church of Vire, which the king had given them in alms, by reason of the claim by the monks of La Couture, because these had made default before the king at Argentan. Witnessed by Hamon of Falaise; at Argentan.[2] [1107–35.]

1135.

732. Writ to the justices and keepers of the bishopric of Bayeux directing that Reginald son of Robert Nep (*sic*) shall have the tithe which Ralph de Rais detains of the fee of Hugh de Crepacor (and ?) Robert de Ver,[3] as he deraigned the same in the king's court. It is attested by (Robert) earl of Gloucester; at Arganchy ('apud Arch . . .').[4] [1123–35.]

733. Notification to the archbishop of Rouen and his ministers of Normandy of the gift made by William Tanetin and Robert de Bretevill his lord to St. Mary of Vignaz of certain lands. It is attested by Nigel bishop of Ely, Robert de Sigillo, Roger the treasurer, Richard de Belfou, Richard son of the earl of Gloucester, and Robert archdeacon of Exeter, the king's chaplains; Robert de Curci, Hugh Bigot, and Geoffrey Fitz-Pain; at Caen, A. incarnat. D. 1135.[5]

734. Notification, addressed generally, of an enactment, concerning those who break the truce and peace of the church, made in the presence of Hugh archbishop of Rouen; the bishops John of Lisieux, Audin of Evreux, John of Sées, Algar of Coutances, Nigel of Ely, and 'Aelolf' of Carlisle; and Robert de Sigillo. It is attested by (Robert) earl of Gloucester, Stephen count of Mortain, Robert earl of Leicester, Walter ('William' in MS.) Giffart, Brien Fitz-Count, R(obert) de Curci, Hugh Bigot, William Fitz-Odo, and William Fitz-John; at Rouen, A. Gratie 1135.[6]

1 Aug. to 1 Nov. Henry visits Sées, Alençon and district, and Argentan.[7]

16 Aug. Godfrey bishop of Bath dies on 17 kalends of September.[8]

735. Notification to the bishop of Exeter, the sheriff, Alfred (son of Johel) de Totnes, and the barons and lieges of Devonshire of the confirmation to the abbey of St. Martin-des-Champs, Paris, of the church of Barnstaple and other possessions which Johel (de Totnes) gave. It is attested by John bishop of Lisieux, Robert de Sigillo, Robert earl of Gloucester, (Henry) count of Eu, Baldwin de Redvers, William Fitz-Odo, William de Vernun, Ilbert de Lacy, and Robert de Curcy; at Perriers-sur-Andelle ('apud Pirarios ').[9]

---

1 Add. Ch. 11233.

2 Copy in *Chartrier rouge*, MS. Lat. 10086, fo. 40 *d*; Haskins, *Norman Institutions*, p. 304.

3 ' detinet de feodo Hugonis de Crepacor, Roberti de Ver, sicut illam dirationavit.'

4 *Livre Noir de Bayeux*, no. 37.   5 Round, *Calendar*, no. 590.

6 Round, *Cal. of Docs., France*, no. 290.   7 Orderic, v. 47.

8 John of Worcester, p. 38.   9 *Mon. Anglic.* v. 198, no. 3.

Henry, disturbed by the news from Wales, makes three attempts to cross the Channel,[1] but is detained in Normandy owing largely to the constant quarrels which arise between the Empress Matilda and her husband.[2]

25 Nov. He is at Lions-la-Forêt.[3] Returning from a day devoted to the chase he partakes too freely of a dish of lampreys, contrary to the advice of his physician (Grimbald), who had forbidden him to eat this dish because it always disagreed with him. The heavy meal, taken into a body which had been much weakened by strenuous labours and family anxieties, brings on a seizure which in the course of a week proves fatal.[4]

1 Dec. Hugh archbishop of Rouen and Robert earl of Gloucester were present during the last days of the king's illness.[5]

ADDITIONS AND CORRECTIONS

23 c. Notification to Robert bishop of Lincoln of the confirmation of the alms, namely the land of Asgarby, which Roger Fitz-Gerold gave to St. Mary's, Lincoln, and put *in prebendam* to the use of Robert de Grainvill, canon of Lincoln, by Bishop Robert's consent. It is witnessed by Robert Fitz-Hamon and Gilbert Fitz-Richard ; at Winchester.[6] [1100–7.]

42 A. Notification to Earl Simon and William de Cahaines that the king has restored to St. Mary's, Lincoln, and Bishop Robert Kilsby (co. Northampton), to hold as beneficially as in the time of Kings Edward and William I. It is attested by Roger Bigod and Hamon the sewer ; at Westminster.[7] [1100–5.]

100. 31 July. This entry should be renumbered **24 A** and the reference added : Dean and Chap. of Lincoln, Regist. Antiquiss. (13th C.), fo. 8 *d*, no. 61.

101. This should be renumbered **24 B** and dated shortly after 31 July, 1101 ; with additional reference : *ibid.* fo. 8 *d*, n. 62.

105 A. Writ to Osbert the sheriff (of Lincoln) directing him to permit Robert de Grainvill to have his prebend of Lincoln, as the king granted it to him by his writ (*breve*). It is attested by Hugh de Evermou ; before Arques.[8] [1104–6.]

256 A. Writ to the barons of the exchequer directing that the land of St. Mary's, Lincoln, shall be in custom on account of the aid which the king has to the use of his daughter, namely that it shall be quit, as the king's father directed. It is witnessed by Roger bishop of Salisbury and Ranulf the chancellor ; at Westminster.[9] [1110.]

259 A. Writ to Osbert sheriff of Lincoln directing him to justly cause Hugh the canon to have the land of Hundon (' Hauendon ', in Caistor, co. Linc.), which the men of Roger the Poitevin hold, if it belongs to the

---

[1] Orderic, v. 45.

[2] Hen. of Huntingdon, p. 254 ; Roger of Howden, i. 187.

[3] 'Apud Sanctum Dionysium in silva Leonum' : Hen. of Huntingdon, p. 254. Le Prevost states that this is Lyons-la-Forêt (Eure). Sir J. H. Ramsey says that it is St. Denis-le-Ferment.

[4] William of Malmesbury, *Hist. Novella*, ii. 536.

[5] *Ibid.*   [6] Dean and Chap. of Lincoln, *Reg. Antiquiss.*, fo. 8 *d*, no. 58.

[7] *Ibid.* fo. 6 *d*, no. 43.   [8] *Ibid.* fo. 8, no. 57.   [9] *Ibid.* fo. 5, no. 32.

alms of the king's father, namely to the church of Caistor (' Castra '). It is attested by Ranulf the chancellor ; at Perry Court (' Peri ').[1]

322 A. Writ to Geoffrey the sewer of Count Stephen (of Brittany) and his ministers commanding them to restore to Robert bishop of Lincoln seisin of the church of Hough-on-the-Hill (' Hac '), as Count Stephen gave it to the bishop, to hold until the count returns. They are promptly to restore anything taken, otherwise Osbert sheriff of Lincoln shall promptly do so. It is attested by Nigel de Oilli ; at Windsor.[2] [1100–15.]

[1] *Ibid.* fo. 7 *d*, n. 50.

[2] *Ibid.* fo. 11, no. 71. The above abstracts are derived from transcripts recently made by the Rev. Canon Foster, and generously forwarded to me for inclusion in this itinerary.—W. F.

INDEX

Place names are printed in italics

The author is indebted to Mr. John Brownbill, M.A., for compiling the index.

CORRIGENDA

P. 10, no. 26. In the witnesses, William Maleth should be added after Robert Maleth and Roger the chaplain after Everard. Peschal should be Pecche and Winfrid Unfrid. See the facsimile in Add. MS. 5846 (Cole, xlv), p 387.

P. 50, no. 226 A. *For* to Justice *read* to do justice to.

Lightning Source UK Ltd.
Milton Keynes UK
UKOW042213030712

195431UK00006B/37/P